AF608304

FAIR COPIES

Reproducing the English Lyric from Tottel to Shakespeare

Fair Copies

Reproducing the English Lyric from Tottel to Shakespeare

MATTHEW ZARNOWIECKI

UNIVERSITY OF TORONTO PRESS
Toronto Buffalo London

Toronto Buffalo London
www.utppublishing.com

ISBN 978-1-4426-4718-3

Library and Archives Canada Cataloguing in Publication

Zarnowiecki, Matthew, 1975–, author
Fair copies : reproducing the English lyric from Tottel to Shakespeare / Matthew Zarnowiecki.

Includes bibliographical references and index.
ISBN 978-1-4426-4718-3 (bound)

1. English poetry – Early modern, 1500–1700 – Criticism, Textual. 2. English poetry – Early modern, 1500–1700 – Manuscripts. 3. Lyric Poetry – History and criticism. 4. Transmission of texts – England – History – 16th century. 5. Printing – England – History – 16th century. 6. Early printed books – England – 16th century. 7. England – Intellectual life – 16th century. I. Title.

PR535.T47Z37 2013 821'.040903 C2013-902882-X

University of Toronto Press acknowledges the financial assistance to its publishing program of the Canada Council for the Arts and the Ontario Arts Council.

University of Toronto Press acknowledges the financial support of the Government of Canada through the Canada Book Fund for its publishing activities.

For my parents,
Susan and Jim Zarnowiecki

Contents

Illustrations

Acknowledgments

Fair Copies was begun and completed at Columbia University, and several other institutions provided crucial support. These include the Shakespeare Birthplace Trust, which provided funding for writing at the earliest stages of the project; the Folger Shakespeare Library and the Huntington Library, both of which have provided grants for archival research; the New York Public Library, whose Wertheim Fellowship provided space for writing and research; and Auburn University, which provided a semester's leave as the project neared completion. I thank them all for making this work possible.

Even more, I owe this book to people. First to my mentors at Columbia: Anne Lake Prescott and David Kastan, for guiding and presiding; Alan Stewart and Molly Murray, who have read nearly every line of the project over many iterations; and Jean E. Howard and Julie Crawford, for advice and guidance. At Auburn, I benefited from career and writing advice from Paula Backscheider and Constance Relihan. I hope to emulate their scholarship, and, if it were possible, their generosity. The pages in manuscript have benefited from many careful readers, including András Kiséry, Tiffany Werth, Allison Deutermann, Karen Emmerich, Bill Blake, Gavin Hollis, Vimala Pasupathi, Marie Rutkoski, Andrea Walkden, Joanna Cheetham, Patricia Akhimie, Brynhildur Heiðardóttir Ómarsdóttir, and Miriam Skey and Barb Porter at University of Toronto Press. They have saved me many times from the errors of my ways.

A version of part of chapter 2 appeared in *Early Modern Literary Studies*, and a version of part of chapter 4 appeared in *The Sidney Journal*. I thank them for permitting this reprinting.

Finally, my family and my loved ones and my friends have sustained me throughout the process, even when I was far away, or nearby but locked away in one library or another. To them all, especially Elizabeth, my love and thanks.

A Note on the Text

Fair Copies treats the reproduction of poetry through time, and asks how different mediums and formats affect the meaning of lyric poems. These questions inform how I modernize spellings and punctuation in early modern texts, and how I represent letter forms which are no longer in use in English. In more than a few cases (see the list of figures above), I have decided to present the text in facsimile, in order to show the poem or poems as they appeared in an early modern printed edition. In other cases, I have settled on the following, necessarily somewhat haphazard, set of guidelines:

- I retain early modern spellings in most cases. Two exceptions are: first, the "Old" *Arcadia* of Philip Sidney (chapter 4), where I quote Katherine Duncan-Jones's modernized edition because it is the most readily available edition of the poems and prose drawn from its earliest, manuscript sources; and, second, some quotations of *Shake-speares Sonnets* (chapter 5), which I am quoting from Stephen Booth's edition both because he presents side-by-side modernized and 1609 texts, and because many facsimiles of the 1609 quarto are available in print and on the internet.
- I retain some early modern letter forms of the early printed editions; that is, I do not substitute *i / j* and *u / v* for their modern equivalents. However, I do substitute modern "s" for early modern "ſ." Also, I do not attempt to reproduce early modern ligature forms. This may be an inconsistency, but I have decided that ligatures and "ſ" do not usually carry sufficient information to warrant the distraction caused by their reproduction here (see chapter 2 for one exception), but that *i / j* and *u / v* differences often do provide phonetic, or semantic, or historical typographic information that is worth retaining.
- I retain the early modern punctuation of early printed editions, but I standardize spacing between characters. In bibliographical citations, I do

> not attempt to represent the capitalization or italics of the originals. Any publication information not available on title pages, but known from colophons, dedicatory material, the *Short Title Catalogue*, or other sources, is provided in the Works Cited section in brackets. In chapter 3, I attempt to reproduce or refer to the use of multiple fonts in the poems and prose of Gascoigne's *A Hundreth Sundrie Flowres*. Finally, I silently expand abbreviated words, with the abbreviated letters in italics.

In other words, my copies of poems within this book are designed to reproduce the poems with purposeful differences, and thus to adhere faithfully to the unfaithfulness of early modern copying practices.

FAIR COPIES

Introduction

Faire, kinde, and true, is all my argument,
Faire, kinde and true, varrying to other words,

Shakespeare, sonnet 105.9–10

Chidiock Tichborne is known for a single, eighteen-line poem. It was composed as he awaited execution for his part in the Babington Plot of 1586, an attempt to assassinate Queen Elizabeth. In explaining his actions, Tichborne claimed to have been a pawn, or a "silly housedove," who fell in with the wrong crowd. His assessment was probably not far off, since the plot went to the highest levels, with encrypted messages passed between Anthony Babington and Mary, Queen of Scots, messages which were surreptitiously intercepted by Francis Walsingham, through the use of a double agent. Three poems and a letter survive from Tichborne's time in prison. Now called "Tichborne's Lament," the best known of these poems renders Tichborne's liminal state thus:

The springe is paste, and yet it hath not sprung
The frute is deade, and yet the leaues are greene
My youth is gone, and yet I am but yonge
I sawe the woorld and yet I was not seene
My threed is cutt, and yet it was not spunn –
And nowe I liue, and nowe my life is donn.[1]

Each stanza ends with the same last line, so that Tichborne's poetic thread is drawn out even as he cuts it off. The poem is almost entirely in the present tense, even as every conclusion Tichborne reaches is about how his life has ended, and how everything in his life has suddenly come to naught. His speaker is living, feeling, and writing "nowe," and at the same time he is a dead man.

"Tichborne's Lament" is a lyric poem; it dwells in the moment. This feature is perhaps the defining quality of lyric poetry. Amatory lyrics expostulate the pleasures of love anticipated and fulfilled, or they express the pangs of despised or impossible love. Shepherds sing pastoral lyrics in concert or competition, while elegies lament the one who is no longer present, who has passed, and is now the past. Tichborne's lament is poignant largely because he is stretched between present and past, and speaks both in and beyond his moment.

The text of the poem has been widely copied, and there are two different, even opposing, impulses for making copies of this poem. The first is to save, preserve, and extend the text's life. This mode of copying claims to sustain the identity of the original, and commemorate, or even resuscitate, its original occasion. The earliest extant manuscript of Tichborne's poem contains such a claim. In a smaller, less elaborate hand than the rest of the text are two addenda, one before the poem and one after, both of which bear witness to the original: "I haue theise verses written by him selfe" at the top of the page, and "Written by him sealfe • 3 • dayes before his exequution: I haue the originall written with his owne hande" at the left of his name below the poem. As Tichborne's editor Richard Hirsch notes, that original is lost.[2] But the drive to return to the original poem, or to preserve the first, authorial copy, is a strong one.

The other impulse is not to preserve, but to alter and re-purpose the original. Some copying impulse drove dozens of early modern English hands to copy "Tichborne's Lament." To borrow a phrase from internet culture, the poem "went viral." But these manuscript copies are in substantially different forms, sometimes rehearsing only the refrain line.[3] The earliest printed version appropriates Tichborne's personal lyric into a wider context celebrating the survival of the queen and the defeat of her would-be assassins.[4] There are also early musical adaptations of the poem (John Mundy in 1588 and Richard Allyson in 1606). The preservational impulse can be found today in printed anthologies of English lyric poetry, and in copies of the poem on internet sites. But people continue to reproduce the poem with their own mutations added. They record lounge-style rock song versions of the poem, or versions of their own voice reciting it, with new stanzas added.[5] These copies, if that is what they are, both reproduce Tichborne's poem and change it, adapting it to a new context, purpose, message, and form. They both are, and are not, "Tichborne's Lament."

Lyric poetry lives in the present. But poems on paper (and in other media) extend through time, and proliferate in number, and are changed in the process. They are, in other words, reproduced. *Fair Copies* traces the development of a new poetic form during a crucial moment of English literary history, 1557–1609. During these years, English printers and poets developed a range of responses to the new possibilities which printed collections of lyric poetry afforded. What we find, examining the seminal printed poetry collections of this period, is that printers and poets fully engage the conflicts sketched above, in which textual reproduction serves to preserve a lyric present, but also to adapt and change lyric poems in later iterations. One way they do so is technological; the printed book of poetry is in some ways an unprecedented form, and experimentation with it abounds. But poetic producers also demonstrate a new set of thematic preoccupations, centred around both textual and sexual reproduction. Poets exhibit a metacritical awareness of their new medium, writing reproduction into metaphors of poetic production, elaborating fictive representations of poetic copying, and making reproduction a central, defining feature of the process of producing poetry. The works that come out of this period of English literature thus meditate on, poeticize, and *enact* a new, reproductively centred poetry.

The authors represented in this study – George Gascoigne, Edmund Spenser, Philip Sidney, and William Shakespeare – are those who engage most deeply with the reproduction of lyric poems in larger printed objects. The point of origin for my study is 1557, the year in which Richard Tottel's *Songes and Sonettes*, the most influential printed verse miscellany in English, was printed. It is also the year that the Stationers' Company was incorporated and the penultimate year of Mary Tudor's reign; this moment thus condenses political, religious, social, artistic, and technological change. Certainly there were printed English verse collections before 1557, such as *The Court of Venus* (also known as *A Boke of Balettes*), printed in the late 1530s.[6] But Tottel's collection was the first to be widely copied and dispersed. It reached nine editions by 1587, and three editions were printed in just two months in the summer of 1557.[7] It also spawned a generation's worth of poetic collections, so that not only were its poems copied and recopied, but its methodology, its mode of copying, was itself copied. One might argue that *Songes and Sonettes* did not found, but rather merely participated in, a wider cultural phenomenon encompassing all sorts of large-scale collections, including compendiums, breviaries, dictionaries, commonplace books and quotation books, legal compilations, books of martyrs, rhetorical instruction-books, and others.[8] Nevertheless, Tottel's anthology not only showed other compilers and printers and poets how poetry could be reprinted and reproduced; it also copied the Henrician-era verse of Wyatt, Surrey, and a host of other poets whose works had existed in scattered manuscripts before that. Tottel's collection explicitly discusses preserving these authors' poems, but it also transforms these poems in a variety of ways.

The transformations that accompany the collection, arrangement, and representation of English lyric in printed verse miscellanies are the subject of the first two chapters of *Fair Copies*. By 1573 Gascoigne is already reacting to, and somewhat satirizing, printed collections of poetry like Tottel's. His collection slyly purports to be the work of various authors, and contains a range of metatextual commentary on how textual reproduction quickly escapes the control of the poetic producers and compilers. As the recent increase in studies on manuscript miscellanies shows, handwritten poetic and miscellaneous compilations are an extraordinarily rich and diverse archive; they can help to reveal what early modern reader-writers copied, and how individual copiers work both to preserve and transform texts.[9] Collection, arrangement, copying, and dissemination are textual actions that all writers engaged in during this period, so that printed verse miscellanies point the way for the later collections in my study, which are not nearly so miscellaneous. The last three chapters, examining works produced in the 1580s and 1590s, show how Spenser, Sidney, and Shakespeare are deeply considering the issues raised by textual reproduction, particularly by the spectre of poetic works being subject to the kinds of collection, arrangement, and reappropriation which are readily available in the models of both manuscript and verse miscellanies.

My study ends in 1609, with the first complete edition of Shakespeare's sonnets. Or rather, it ends in 1599, when two of Shakespeare's sonnets are first printed. Or rather, it ends in 1640, when a new version of Shakespeare's sonnets is printed, substantially different from the 1609 collection, and likely the most readily available edition for nearly seventy years. These days, we know what the book of Shakespeare's sonnets is: 154 sonnets, with an enigmatic dedication, followed by the narrative poem *A Lover's Complaint*. But the fact that this book is so fungible in the late sixteenth and early seventeenth centuries, that it can take so many forms and so many people can have a say in its production and form, represents the culmination of my arguments and observations in *Fair Copies*. This book exists in reproductions with mutations, and Shakespeare relentlessly worries the theme of mutation through time throughout his sonnets. In his sonnets, as in the books of poetry by Gascoigne, Spenser, and Sidney, the fairer copy is the more mutated one. Shakespeare's collection of lyric poems therefore realizes fifty years' worth of textual and artistic experimentation with the practice and concept of fair copying.

I Medium-close Reading

The New Criticism's advocacy of what has come to be called "close reading" is well known. Although no one would claim to be a New Critic now, more than a half-century after the heyday of Cleanth Brooks's *The Well-Wrought Urn*, and W.K. Wimsatt's *The Verbal Icon*, it is difficult to escape the influence of close reading, which remains central to practical criticism. It is often what we ask undergraduates to do when they write about not only poetic, but literary texts of all sorts. To "do a close reading" has come to mean any examination of the text's minute details, usually without emphasizing its cultural, historical, and religious underpinnings. Cleanth Brooks recognizes that rather than emphasizing "historical backgrounds" or "literary history," he is seeking "what residuum, if any, is left after we have referred the poem to its cultural matrix."[10] The text (for Brooks, short or medium-length lyric poems) can thus be treated as an isolated hermeneutic object, separable from any consideration of the condition of its production. Its complexities, such as irony and paradox, render it a complete object whose coherence is to be pursued and apprehended. But discontent with close reading's critical blindness to what Brooks calls the "cultural matrix" has propelled a variety of responses, including Marxist and feminist reading practices, New Historicist readings, as well as a renewed attention to material culture and the history of the book. Recently, there has also been a critical move to "distant reading," which departs radically from close reading, examining wide social and literary trends by aggregating individual literary works into much larger pictures and patterns.[11] The literary work as data-point is, it seems, the opposite of close reading.

In *Fair Copies*, I propose a reading method that I call "medium-close reading." I acknowledge that my reading method owes much to New Criticism, and I do read poetry closely in this study. But rather than relying only on the text, or primarily on context, I wish to read early modern English lyrics at a middle distance, both temporally and spatially. I wish to recognize that lyrics exist through time, and that rather than being single, static instantiations, they vary and mutate when reproduced. My reading method is medium-close in this sense because I most often examine two or three such mutations, early in the print history (and sometimes, manuscript history) of a given poem. I thus eschew the critical editor's long view, in which every variation of a text must be noted and accounted for, and the timeless view, in which a single version of a poem is treated as its only possible form. Medium-close reading also operates at a spatial level, by emphasizing that in their material instantiations, early modern English lyric poems hardly ever occur alone. They are instead surrounded by other poems; incorporated into prose stories; preceded by descriptions of their original occasions; followed by explanations and related materials; written as duos or runs of three or four or five poems; or formed into playful dialogues, in which answers or rejoinders are proffered.[12] In other words, medium-close reading requires an adjusted reading method since there is not a single textual object, The Poem, which can be neatly excised from its context. Reading at a medium-close level means accenting, at times, the radical dependency of a poem's meaning on those poems adjacent to it. It also serves as a way constantly to remind us that there may be many different units of textual analysis in a single literary work.

A second, related emphasis of medium-close reading is attentive reading and interpretation of the media in which early modern lyric poetry is written and reproduced, and the forms and genres which lyric poets choose and create. Certainly the New Critics paid close attention to poetic form. Yet as my first two chapters will demonstrate, Elizabethan English verse miscellanies encompass all three major poetic media available at the time: the voice, the pen, and the press. Medium-close reading requires attention not only to how poems change across these media, but how poets adjust their formal and generic choices to both canonical and emergent lyric forms. Spenser's *Shepheardes Calender* and Sidney's *Arcadia* demonstrate how crucially the poetic medium affects our reading practice. It is difficult to imagine a close reading of any poem in Spenser's *Calender* which does not account for this work's woodcuts and elaborate textual apparatus. Likewise, discussions of the *Arcadia* must begin with the question of whether the manuscript or printed version is being examined, since the change in medium, in this case, means a radical alteration in the text. Close readings of these works must, therefore, be medium-close; they must read the poems and their media as mutually constitutive.

Medium-close reading arises directly out of the poetic objects I have chosen to study: complex lyrical collections, most of which have intricate early histories of manuscript and print reproduction. But it is also the methodology of early modern English poets themselves, particularly Gascoigne, Spenser, Sidney, and Shakespeare, as well as their printers, and compilers such as Tottel. These agents are doing their own medium-close reading in that they are scrutinizing the media available to them, and are conscious of the new medium of print and the new poetic objects being created in this medium. They are also cognizant that the new poetic forms being invented are heavily invested in, and dependent on, textual reproduction. So we ought to pay special attention to those metaliterary moments when these authors accent their medium within their poems. What we find is that these authors are coming to terms with the idea that their works will be rewritten, recopied, modified, and changed. They meditate on this process. They create poetic speakers who struggle for control over their poetic utterances and scribal productions. They even sometimes address the textual reproductive process directly in paratextual material. In other words, my own interest in medium-close reading is founded on a pattern in which English poets write about their media in the poetic works themselves.

Shakespeare's sonnets represent the depth of potential metapoetical meditation about reproduction and medium. Shakespeare takes up the subject of the reproduction of beauty in a huge range of media: beauty in flower form, perfume form, human form, and especially in the form of paper and ink and copies, and copies of copies. But poets such as Samuel Daniel and Michael Drayton are also considering reproduction in their poetry. The titles of Daniel's *Delia* (1592), and Drayton's *Ideas Mirrour* (1594) play upon a deep-seated intellectual heritage regarding imitation, mimesis, and Neoplatonic thought. The foundation of this heritage is the "idea" itself, the disembodied and dematerialized essence that can exist irrespective of material. But as Wendy Wall and others have noted, these books were recopied multiple times within their authors' lifetimes, and the mutating material form changes the meanings within.[13] Copying and reproduction insinuate themselves into the language of these poets because copying and reproduction, always a part of the art of poetry making, are now being written into books of poetry as both the immediate and ultimate fate of each poem or collection. Shakespeare's sonnets end my project because they take on these issues of textual reproduction, but also because their complicated textual history reveals that they too are caught up in a web of mutation and appropriated copying. Shakespeare's speaker bears a much more complicated relationship to time than just the desire to make copies, and by doing so, win out over Time, the *edax rerum.* Instead, the past and present and future are much more fluid than stone monuments, and copying – whether it is reproducing a person, a poem, or a person in a poem – turns out to involve a host of mutations. Appropriately, the book of Shakespeare's sonnets has also undergone many mutations. The reproductions of this book, with their attendant ideas of fidelity and mutation, can instruct our understanding of the poems in the book. This lesson is at the heart of medium-close reading, which discovers authors considering problems of textual and human reproduction in their poems, and which finds these problems borne out in later reproductions of those poems.

In all the cases I examine, the new conditions of textual reproducibility spur authors to consider, simultaneously, the traditional eternal fame mentioned by Ovid and Horace and other poets, as well as the very first intimations of poetic immortality – the first reproductions, the first time a poem is re-uttered, or written by hand anew in a manuscript, or printed in a book of poems. These firstlings are often radically different from the originals; they are mutated in the process of copying. Moreover, Gascoigne and Spenser and Sidney and Shakespeare all actively depict copying as a process in which the original is mutated, or adopted by foster parents, or reconceived, or reappropriated and disseminated. In each case, the loss of the original is at stake, but so is the gain of the copy. *Fair Copies* considers both the losses and gains of these poetic reproductions.

II Fair Copies

My use of "fair" springs from many sources, most conspicuously Shakespeare, for whom fairness and foulness provide no end of linguistic and thematic fodder. As recent critics have shown, Shakespeare's most pervasive dichotomy is not a transcendent one: we ignore the racial, dynastic, and colonial overtones of Shakespeare's use of "fair" at our peril.[14] Fairness can no longer stand innocently for beauty, but it continues to be used in the arena of justice. Textual copying and reproduction are connected linguistically and conceptually to this usage in the copyright doctrine of "fair use." It is in this sense, involving the ethical dimensions of beauty and its preservation, that Elaine Scarry claims that "beauty prompts a copy of itself."[15]

In what follows, "fair copies" are those that resist identical, faithful reproduction in favour of mutation. This usage modifies my most immediate source for the term "fair copies," textual criticism, especially that of early modern drama. For textual critics, a fair copy is to be distinguished from "foul papers." The former is a text which is intended to be presentable to others, for example to the Master of the Revels or to a theatrical impresario like Philip Henslowe. The latter is the rough copy of the author, perhaps full of scribblings and cross-outs and interlineations and mistakes – the garbage of the author's original. The foulness of foul papers is noted in contemporary documents such as those of Robert Daborne, a playwright and scribe, who uses phrases like "fayr written" and "to write this fayr" in describing copies he was making for Henslowe. Examining this and other evidence, Grace Ioppolo concludes that "'Foul' therefore seems to have been the contemporary descriptive term for authors' own papers, sheets or copies of the working draft of a play and was most probably a term, like 'fair' copy or sheets, that Jonson, Shakespeare, Heywood and Middleton also knew and used."[16] But if we read Fredson Bowers's commentary on the same evidence of Daborne's scribal copies for Henslowe, the result is that "foul sheets" do not seem quite so foul. Bowers instead claims that foul papers can be understood as "the author's last complete draft" and thus "satisfactory to him to be transferred to a fair copy."[17]

Bowers, as a critical editor, uses "fair copy" as part of the search for copy-text, which has been defined, in a classic essay by W.W. Greg, as "whatever extant text may be supposed to represent most nearly what the author wrote."[18] The task of critical editors, as conceived by its exponents in the early twentieth century, is to examine all extant versions of a work, establish the relationships between them, decide which is to be the copy-text, and then make any emendations according to the standards he or she has adopted.[19] The all-important decision of which edition or version to adopt as copy-text thus has at its heart the posited ideal of the fair copy, which is linked directly to the author's intentions. For example, summarizing Greg's contributions to the field, Thomas Tanselle claims that Greg's prescribed methodology "sought to reconstruct, insofar as the printed texts would allow, the text of the author's fair copy manuscript."[20] Elsewhere, both Greg and Bowers refer to the "archetype," the always-lost originary point in a genealogical line of descent from copy to copy. The language of authorial intention, copy-text, and fair copies has thus dominated the theory and practice of critical editing for many years. But more recent challenges and modifications to the centrality of copy-text have accented the social forces at work in textual production, so that not only an author's intentions, but those of a larger set of publishing agents compete for attention when deciding how to reproduce a text.[21] The desire to replicate the intentions of a certain printing house at a certain time comes to its logical end in the recent explosion of so-called unedited texts, made possible by photographic facsimiles on paper, microfilm, or in electronic form.[22]

Each of these modifications in its way attests to both the durability and the fictionality of the imaginary fair copy, always lost, always a desideratum. As David Kastan puts it, editorial theory "posits as its object of desire a work that never was, an ideal text of an author's intentions that no materialization does (or can) bear witness to."[23] For Kastan, the Platonic archetype of an author's work is an unapproachable impossibility, not because the original is lost, but because works always exist in physical forms whose production involves not only authors but printers, compositors, and editors, as well as publication of the play through performance.[24] At the same time, as David Greetham has argued, striving towards the ideal text can be seen throughout the history of the word; Greetham mentions the first efforts to standardize Homer's works alongside the efforts of The Center for the Editing of American Authors.[25]

Greg, Bowers, Kastan, and Ioppolo are all primarily concerned with the production and reproduction of play-texts. Greg recognizes that he is primarily concerned with copies in the form of printed books, and that "the extant manuscripts of a work have usually only a collateral relationship, each being derived from the original independently, or more or less independently, of the others."[26] Given the possibility of this independent, "collateral" relationship, which resists backward tracing to the first printed instance, we might ask how, or even whether, to continue to search for the fair copy posited by the copy-text model, in the case of early modern English lyric poems. That is to say, we might ask where the "fair copy" of a given poem or set of poems resides.

In objecting to the positing of a singular "fair copy" of a work, Jerome McGann and other proponents of social textuality provide instances in which a single edition representing multiple, significantly different versions would be impossible, including Wordsworth's *Prelude*, Rossetti's *House of Life*, and many others.[27] Early modern poems, with a few notable exceptions, often are extant only in a few early copies, whether printed or manuscript. Yet if "fair" means definitive, then the number of fair copies is vanishingly small.[28] One desideratum of early modern English lyric poetry is the "presentation copy," an elaborate and preferably flawless version of the given work, often created in order to be humbly presented as a gift to a powerful patron. George Gascoigne, one of the authors in my study, is pictured in just such a position: on bended knee, presenting the queen with a collection of papers. Meanwhile, his motto, *Tam Marti quam Mercurio*, appears thrust from the ceiling by a disembodied hand. If ever there were a fair copy, this must be it: not only readable, but beautifully copied and assembled, and then humbly presented by the author himself to the highest authorizing patron in the realm.[29] Richard McCoy and Wendy Wall, however, have noted how Gascoigne's posture complicates this picture; they see the depiction as both humble and aggressive.[30] Even more basically, however, the work in question, a masque at Kenilworth entitled *The Tale of Hemetes the Heremyte*, was almost certainly not written by Gascoigne, but rather translated by him, and elaborated with emblems and other devices in this copy.[31] Not only is the presentation copy a complex collaborative text, but Gascoigne would also go on to authorize an anonymous printed version after the New Year's gift in 1576; *The Princely Pleasures at Kenelworth Castle* was printed as an octavo volume in 1576, and included in George Gascoigne's posthumous *VVhole woorkes*, 1587.[32] In this case at least, it would be difficult to link the presentation copy closely to the ideal copy-text sought by the New Bibliography. This manuscript book, though it is certainly in one sense a fair copy, should not be seen as the text's single, originary, and authorizing moment. Nor, in this case, is it the version in which the author's final intentions are realized, before what Bowers calls the "veil of print" drops permanently, and obscuringly, over subsequent copies.[33]

Rather, as I argue in the chapter on Gascoigne's poetry, fair copies are often those in which the collateral relationship between copies is openly acknowledged, even embellished. That collateral relationship is one in which both copying and mutation occur at the moment of reproduction. Fair copies in this sense are neither the best copy out of many (as in copy-text) nor the single copy in the author's hand presented to all eternity (as in the presentation copy). Instead, they are "fair" precisely because they are, in the other language of the New Bibliography, so foul.

This sort of fair copying is not rooted in twentieth-century editorial theory but in sixteenth-century writing practices, which encouraged creative copying. As Ann Moss and others have shown, the practice of commonplacing was an ingrained habit of textual reproduction, with its early history in medieval *florilegia*. Reading *was* writing, since the act of reading so often involved copying *sententiae*, aphorisms, and the wisdom of authorities. Compilations of rhetorical theory and practice in the *ars dictaminis* tradition provided for the enactment of rhetorical strategies via reproduction: they reproduce by compiling exemplars, but they also promote reproduction by implying that the trajectory of copied material goes from authorities to compendiums, and from compendiums back out into the larger textual network of letters, treatises, speeches, conversations, and so forth. Commonplace books thus are copies that themselves promote copying. As Moss shows, the poetical commonplace books of late sixteenth-century England lie along a common arc of collection and reproduction of sources that includes John Foxe's commonplace book, Erasmus's *De copia*, and a host of Latin collections and treatises from prior centuries.[34] The textual action of commonplacing is most often compared to the behaviour of bees, which, as Seneca puts it, "blend those several flowers into one delicious compound that, even though it betrays its origin, yet it nevertheless is clearly a different thing from that whence it came."[35] The different thing, the copy that is no longer a copy, is what Puttenham says sets poets apart from mere slavish copiers: "The very poet makes and contrives out of his own brain both the verse and matter of his poem, and not by any foreign copy or example, as doth the translator, who therefore may well be said a versifier, but not a poet." Crucially, however, Puttenham goes on to say that poets *do* imitate those things which they decide to describe, so that the poet "in that respect is both a maker and a counterfeiter, and poesy an art not only of making, but also of imitation."[36]

This tension, between copying and making, might well be seen in every textual production of the period. Printed commonplace books from the sixteenth century, as well as letter-writing breviaries and other compendiums, do in fact encourage slavish imitation and exact copying at the same time that they extol new textual productions. *Copia*, as the structuring principle for Erasmus's collection, provides copy. This way of thinking of the word highlights a central etymological, and practical, tension: "a 'copy' was something from which copies were produced."[37] Whatever we may think of Erasmus's long list of epistolary salutations and valedictions, having them at hand would mean that a letter could be comprised almost entirely of pieces gleaned from breviaries like this one, or even from other letters. No doubt many were. Alan Stewart and others have shown just how pervasive letter-writing breviaries were, and how the copying of letter models shapes familiar discourse, transactions of affect, and the representation of letter-writing on stage and in prose fiction.[38] The copying of letter formulae, subjects, or individual subscriptions, like the copying of *sententiae*, would seem on the surface to be directly opposed to the notions of poetic originality evident in the writing of George Puttenham, and to the notions of rhetorical originality debated by Cicero, Politian, and others.[39] But practically, in a textual world suffused with copy-making, where anything to be noted, saved, preserved, and redeployed had to be copied, at least into a personal manuscript commonplace book, or even a printed compendium – in this world, the line between copying and poetic "making" becomes difficult to discern, if not altogether illegible.

This has been one of the main insights of recent studies of early modern reading practices, which include studies of the reading and reception of Shakespeare's poetry; of Sidney's poetry and manuscript circulation; of the material practices of reading; and of the work done by compilers, scribes, and annotators of manuscripts.[40] For example, the reading practices which Sasha Roberts traces show us not simply the reception history of Shakespeare's poetry, but the ways in which poetic creation, reading, and copying are interrelated, often inseparable actions rather than a sequence starting with the author's pen and ending with the printed book. My study benefits enormously from the work of these studies, which painstakingly track readerly practices: marginalia and other annotations, commonplacing, and the compilation of both printed and manuscript miscellanies out of prior sources. In the case of Tottel's *Songes and Sonettes,* it seems obvious that the creation of this miscellaneous collection of poetry constitutes an act of reading as well as reproduction. Tottel adds titles, and he makes adjustments to both metre and diction, much to the chagrin of many later critics. Tottel's editorial actions thus are in the same category as many of the textual actions examined so closely by Roberts and others. But Tottel's actions should be set within a larger system of poetic reproduction, a system that includes the poetic collections of Gascoigne, Spenser, Sidney, and Shakespeare. Their poetry is collected, transformed, and mutated even in its supposed originary form and at its supposed originary moment, so that reading and writing and reproduction all coalesce into a new, and hybrid, object that cannot be reduced to the sum of its individual lyric parts. In this sense, I am inclined to reassess Stephen Orgel's assertion, counter to the traditional view of print culture as a regularizing force, that "not only was the Renaissance book never concerned with replication, but the culture as a whole had no interest in books as exact copies."[41] The books of poetry I am examining certainly *are* concerned with replication, but they also acknowledge that they are not producing exact copies. Moreover, there are plenty of poets, such as Samuel Daniel, who at least express a concern with the idea of their books being exact copies, and the potential danger or regret of an inexact copy being released prematurely into the world.[42] "Fair copies," as I am using the term, are concerned more with the creative imitation of prior authorities – with invention, novelty, and change – than with textual fidelity.

III Human Copies

The bee's mysterious amalgamation of flowers into honey provides a classic metaphor for creative copying. But just as common, and far more important, are the metaphors – rife throughout classical, medieval, and early modern literature – that equate textual reproduction and human reproduction. Human reproduction involves the creation of copies in both biblical and Neoplatonic interpretations. The key text for English Protestant poets is Genesis 1–3, which sanctions and sanctifies reproduction in two ways. First, it pronounces humans to be the images of God, copied by resemblance. Second, while the Fall may have ensured that human births are painful, God's injunction to be fruitful and multiply (Genesis 1:28) requires people to copy themselves and thus to fulfil God's mandate of dominion and lordship on earth. Genesis 1–3 thus makes human reproduction an orthodox action not simply as a result of the imperfections resulting from the Fall, but in spite of them.

Just as relevant to early modern English as these biblical injunctions are Neoplatonic versions of reproductions, with their accent on interactions between matter and form. The poets in my study (especially Sidney and Spenser) see desire, beauty, and reproduction on a continuum which involves not only the reproduction and growth of bodily matter, but also the pursuit of beauty, wisdom, and virtue. For Diotima, in *The Symposium*, artists and poets are the ones who engage in this aspect of reproduction, which inevitably involves the prior work of previous souls, texts, and artists. For Plato, in *Symposium*, *Theaetetus*, and elsewhere, physical human copying is much inferior to a de-sexualized reproduction of ideas. Nevertheless, Plato figures himself as a dialogic midwife in the birth of ideas, a metaphor that acknowledges the central importance of human reproduction even while eschewing it in favour of discursive idealism.[43]

Marsilio Ficino's influential commentary on Plato's *Symposium* ingests and elaborates on these ideas. Ficino too moves from physical human examples to the realm of ideas. For him, "venereal madness" leads to a kind of ugliness (intemperance), so that "the desire for coitus (that is, for copulation) and love are shown to be not only not the same motions but opposite." Proper human love is quite different: "[w]hen we say 'love,' understand 'the desire for beauty,'" which is itself harmony, that can exist in souls, bodies, colors, sounds, and other entities.[44] Desire thus is not just to create or reproduce bodily matter in the natural world, but also to create, or re-create, wisdom and virtue. As Harry Berger summarizes it, "the soul internalizes these forms, makes them personal, makes them new."[45] In these Platonic and Neoplatonic formulations, we again find the tension with which I began, between reproduction as preservation and reproduction as creation. Yet Berger's formulation of Ficino, in which the soul internalizes forms and then "makes them new," sounds very much like Ezra Pound's famous modernist directive. The poets in my study, particularly Gascoigne, Sidney, and Shakespeare, demonstrate exactly this tension, between bodily and idealized forms, and between preservation and novelty.

The biblical directive demands that humans copy themselves as matter to fill the void and achieve dominion over God's other self-replicating beings. The Neoplatonic directive demands that people copy not only the beauty that resides in their material forms, but also in their intellects and souls. Both directives structure how poets of the time period see their poetic tasks. Rather than poets simply applying *imitatio*, the long-standing rhetorical practice of textual copying, to poetry, I argue that "be fruitful and multiply" and "beauty prompts a copy of itself" encourage lyric poets to see human copying and textual copying as parts of a larger system in which all components engage in reproduction by copying.

When Shakespeare begins with "From fairest creatures we desire increase," therefore, he combines both biblical and Platonic idealistic discourses into an intensely human version of fair copying.

Like Plato, Aristotle connects human reproduction directly to textual production, but differs on a key question: whether form and matter are distinct or inseparable. The Platonic view is that form is not inherent in matter, and so poetry presents something like the copy of a copy, while the Aristotelian view is that form is inherent in matter, so that poets are instead "actualizing the potential of matter itself."[46] The distinction helps to answer a key question: exactly how is writing like reproduction? It depends. Sometimes writing is like being pregnant and giving birth; sometimes writing is like ejaculating; sometimes writing is like being impregnated, or being full of thoughts is like being pregnant. For Montaigne, whose use of the metaphor is typically widely inclusive, writing can be like both mothering and fathering. And very often in the early modern period, not only is writing like reproduction, but the written text is like an infant or a child, especially an orphan, a foster child, or a deformed monstrous child.

This last example is perhaps the most common of all in early modern English printed paratextual materials. Poets, striking a posture of facetious self-denigration,[47] claim to be willing to abandon their club-footed Oedipal creations to the wilds. But they also celebrate textual pregnancy. Sidney famously depicts a poet who is "great with child to speak" while "biting my truant pen" in the opening poem of *Astrophel and Stella*. For Sidney, the pangs of childbirth are an available conceptualization of the struggle to read other authors' poetry and yet emerge to write his own.[48] Rather than referring to the bee-flower-honey analogy, which would be appropriate here, Sidney combines poetic making with human reproduction. His poetic work is not that of a bee gathering flowers of language, but that of a woman struggling to bring forth her child. His muse not only speaks to him, or through him, but gestates within him.

Human reproduction itself was undergoing significant conceptual changes in the early modern era. While these changes are not the main focus of my study, nevertheless the recent burgeoning of critical analyses of midwives' manuals and early modern physiological treatises helps to reveal the assumptions about bodies and their copies which underlie Sidney's and other writers' metaphors of pregnant authors and infant texts. Most crucially, as Elaine Hobby and others have argued, the technical aspects of childbirthing were shifting in the early modern period; where midwifery had once been a mysterious realm of women's work, new intellectual developments rendered reproduction a matter of science. Perhaps the most important early modern text in this process was Eucharius Rösslin's *Rosengarten*, which was reprinted fourteen times between 1513 and 1541, ten more between 1562 and 1608, and was translated into Dutch, French, Spanish, Danish, Czech, and English.[49] As Wendy Arons and others have argued, this text attempted to codify and disseminate knowledge about childbirth, but did so in such a way as to discount, and often discard, the practical, experience-based knowledge of midwiving that had accumulated during the 1400 years between the writing of Soranus's *Gynecology* and Rösslin's *Rosengarten*.[50] The publication of Thomas Raynalde's version beginning in 1540 marks the *Rosengarten*'s entry into the English vernacular; it was available in this form throughout the sixteenth and seventeenth centuries.[51] Jane Sharp's *The Midwives Book* (1671), according to Elaine Hobby, in part comprises an ironic reaction to the discounting of midwives' experience, to the privileging of ancient male medical authorities, and to "the misogyny that underpinned accepted ideas about the female reproductive body."[52]

These texts made known and distributed technical points about human sexuality and reproduction, in contrast to the more abstracted, philosophical treatments of Plato's *Theaetetus*, Aristotle's *De Generatione Animalium*, and Ficino's commentaries. For my purposes, the most important of these new ideas is that female orgasm was necessary to conception, and that both male and female seed combined to form the new human copy. This idea of the bisexuality of reproduction has significant implications for the analogy between the conception of people and the conception of ideas. So, Montaigne considers himself both father and mother to his texts; Sidney's poems are the offspring not only of his mind but of a process involving his sister's, and other female agents' active participation; and Shakespeare's uneasy portrayal of human reproduction seems anxious to omit or deny the woman's role in the procreation poems, even as it problematizes physical copulation in ways reminiscent of Ficino's commentary. I am not arguing that early modern English poets needed books like *The Birth of Mankind* to tell them where babies come from. Rather, I am accenting the increasing importance of reproduction: we can see the overt presence of technical theories of reproduction in both midwives' manuals and poetry collections. At stake in both of these is conceptual control over popular understanding of how new people, and new texts, are made.

The explanatory power of human reproduction was thus being applied to textual reproduction, and vice versa. If the reproduction of human bodies would be better understood through the composition and dissemination of textual compendiums of knowledge (the premise of *Rosengarten*), it was nevertheless also true that the practices of textual reproduction, both in print and manuscript culture, were also continually being defined in human bodily terms. In other words, the methods and terms of manuscript and print copies, as well as of human copies, were interpenetrating and mutually informing discourses.[53]

Nowhere is this discursive interpenetration more clearly demonstrated than in the state of recent critical texts that examine early modern textual and sexual reproduction together, especially *Printing and Parenting*, a set of essays edited by Douglas Brooks; Tom MacFaul's *Poetry and Paternity in Renaissance England*, Jeffrey Masten's *Textual Intercourse*, Stephen Guy-Bray's *Against Reproduction*, and David's Glimp's *Increase and Multiply*. These critiques demonstrate just how widely the two reproductive discourses engage each other, both now and in early modern Europe. *Printing and Parenting*, for example, includes examinations of the terminology of printing technology, Ben Jonson's ideas of fatherhood, maternal copying in *The Mirror for Magistrates*, and metaphors of paternity suffusing both royal printing and censorship.[54] Brooks traces the merging of discourses of "kin and ink ... of parenting and printing" to a moment of emergence in the 1450s, and stresses the potential exactness of printed copies, and their importance to both sovereign lines of succession and mirroring activities of artistic production.[55]

This model of identical copying, however, is precisely what the authors and printers in *Fair Copies* seem to struggle with, engage, and ultimately resist. For these authors, the poetic process always already involves reproduction, but reproduction does not produce identical copies perfected for posterity. Instead, it produces changed, mutated, imperfect copies which sometimes resemble their parents, but often do not. Concerning Rabelais and the common analogy of artistic production to mirroring, Brooks claims that "the desired outcome of both reproductive activities is the same: the production of identical copies."[56] Fixity, standardization, and copying fidelity are the hallmarks of printed works, according to the traditional view of print culture's impact.[57] But the authors in this study confront both the desirability and the possibility of identical copies.

The Platonic and Aristotelian models of reproduction render literary works into conceptions. Either a single parent (Platonic model) or two parents (Aristotelian model) bring forth the work, the offspring, analogous to the whole book of poetry. But in order to examine poetic media closely, at the level of individual poems and groups of poems related in time and space, we might also introduce an anachronistic entity: the gene. That is, instead of human bodies, books of poetry can be understood as collections of reproducible units that are constantly and inevitably being reconfigured and mutated even as they are being recopied and printed. The philosophical and anatomical discourses I refer to above contain no inkling of genetics, of course, but they do contain concepts related to genetics, such as resemblance of offspring to progenitors (but not identicality, except in asexual reproduction), necessity or drive to reproduce, and the positing of a species or form or idealized version of an entity, which is realized in individuals who are different by definition, because they are instantiated in different matter.

The genetic metaphor for textual reproduction allows us to consider whether a seemingly individual corporate body is in fact divisible. With regard to human bodies, this insight is a twentieth-century phenomenon, perhaps best explained by

Richard Dawkins. In *The Selfish Gene*, Dawkins (building on the work of Watson and Crick as well as later sociobiologists including E.O. Wilson) argues that we should see sexual reproduction as a constant reshuffling of genetic material, so that each individual organism's particular genetic arrangement is extremely short-lived, while individual genes in the arrangement can be long-lived, even tending potentially towards immortality. Dawkins stresses that the immortality of DNA molecules resides in their ability to be replicated faithfully through both temporal and material changes.[58] The so-called individual corporate body is thus entirely divisible because it is simply a mish-mash of the chromosomes of the mother and the father, whereas individual genes within those chromosomes can be replicated through time and matter, in different iterations (cousins, sisters, brothers, great-grandchildren) who cannot be said to be identical to their progenitors.

For textual reproduction, the explanatory power of this insight is considerable. Dawkins himself makes the connection by introducing what he calls "memes," which are his units of cultural reproduction. Dawkins is vague about what memes actually are: they could be tunes, or catch-phrases, or fashions, but they could also be the idea of God (which he takes up in a different book), or cultural entities that become encoded as patterns of neurons in brains.[59] But they do so with imperfect fidelity, and so they are part of a larger class of "slightly inaccurate self-replicating entities."[60] For early modern lyric, this idea is particularly powerful because it allows us to see reproduction as a process that occurs on the level of a set of poems, or a single poem, or even a single line or couplet. It also helps us to envision these poetic units as entities which are surviving by replicating themselves in human brains, and perhaps doing so irrespective of the owners of those brains. In other words, the operant metaphor is not a scribe copying, or a printer printing, or people having a child, but a virus reproducing itself in multiple hosts.

Rösslin's text and other treatises on human reproduction tell us much about how Sidney and other poets understood their actions of authorship and the continued lives of their works. But genetics and its commentators help us to analyse the cultural reproduction of bits of text, and to suggest the possibility of a different replicating organism than just the Author. The marginalia in the early manuscript of "Tichborne's Lament" show a desire to reproduce the Author, even though the copier could be seen as blindly following the dictates of a viral entity, a copying automaton serving an invisible master. The poem is instructive not only bibliographically, but aesthetically, because its subject is brevity, and the capability of the speaking, poetic subject of both being and not being present. A reader of this poem may or may not call it "Tichborne's Lament" and may or may not call to mind Chidiock Tichborne in the moments of reading. A copier of the poem extends it in time, changes its place, reinscribes it in a different context, and thus makes a fair copy of the poem, which is at once partially the same and partially different. The authorial model of reproduction falls short here, while the genetic model may have greater explanatory power.

In each chapter of *Fair Copies*, then, multiple reproducing agents are discernible, including the author, the printer, the collector or compiler, the poem's later appropriators, and even the self-interested poem (or bit of the poem) itself. In chapter 1, I examine Richard Tottel's strategies for negotiating opposing impulses: to represent Surrey's and Wyatt's works as poetic history, but also to render them into a more current form. This textual action shares crucial qualities with texts printed by legal printers, documenting laws that were in force one year, and repealed, or "annihilated," the next. Tottel's primary output was legal texts, and both kinds of collection engage the representation of annihilation, a paradoxical textual action that both requires and eschews exact reproduction.

Chapter 2 explores the multiplicity that is a central principle of Gascoigne's negotiation of authorship as a non-nobleman and in a changing poetic field. Sexuality, textual exchange, and multiplicity are intertwined for Gascoigne. His characters struggle to preserve pleasure, and the elusive, ephemeral nature of delight leads to strategies of both physical and lyrical preservation. But the author himself, and the originary version of the text, are often the cost of reproduction, so that Gascoigne preserves his delight by relinquishing it to future versions of his poems.

In chapter 3, I shift from printed verse miscellanies to Spenser's *Shepheardes Calender*, particularly the travails of Colin Clout's poetic output. I argue that Spenser deliberately creates many moments in which the poet's refusal to sing is a problematic but necessary part of a larger process. That process involves the judgments and participation of a wider poetic community, who ultimately reproduce his songs and poems. The final appearance of Colin Clout shows him at last both reproducing the work of others, and allowing his own work to be reproduced.

Chapter 4 continues the exploration of how poems are reproduced in both pastoral and print, with Philip Sidney's *Arcadia*. My term "lyric surrogacy" addresses a pattern in Sidney's Old *Arcadia* (circulated in manuscript in the 1580s and not printed until the early twentieth century) in which poems are discarded by their author, but taken up and cared for, even owned, by a different agent. Sidney, I argue, presents in his fictional Arcadian world a strikingly similar process to that which his works would undergo in the decades following his death. This process is one that can be revealed only by looking at Sidney's fictive representations of poetic reproduction, alongside actual reproductions and adaptations of Sidney's work.

Finally, in chapter 5, I reevaluate the earliest reproductions of Shakespeare's lyric poetry by focusing on the three earliest printed versions of his sonnets, *The Passionate Pilgrime* (1599), the first quarto of the sonnets (1609), and John Benson's 1640 *Poems: By Wil. Shakespeare. Gent.* These texts have all been judged to be fault-ridden and error-filled; my examination traces these textual faults alongside the pattern of fault and error in Shakespeare's sonnets. What we find is that the sonnets are faulty by design. Their essential faultiness reverberates through each reproduced version. For Shakespeare, the "fair copy" is one that reproduces with mutations, so that faultiness is constitutive of human reproduction, both sexual and textual.

Shakespeare's collection of sonnets ends my study because Shakespeare most deeply considers the connection between poetics and reproduction. But his collection also represents, and grapples with, the same poetic conundrums faced by Tottel, Gascoigne, Spenser, and Sidney. The poetic product, in each case, is not one that tends towards perfection, but one that instead adapts and mutates, that is preserved by change, and that retains its identity by taking on the identities of its new, reproducing poetic agents. Just as Richard Tottel copies his Wyatt and Surrey with a difference, John Benson reproduces Shakespeare's poetry by introducing mutation. In doing so, I argue that he creates not a bastardized version of an original text, but in fact a fair copy.

1

The "vnquiet state" of the Lover: Richard Tottel's Lyric and Legal Reproductions

In an article on fact-checkers in prominent newspapers and magazines, a dire warning appears: "Any error is everlasting … Once an error gets into print it will 'live on and on in libraries carefully catalogued, scrupulously indexed … silicon-chipped, deceiving researcher after researcher down through the ages, all of whom will make new errors on the strength of the original errors, and so on and on into an exponential explosion of errata.'"[1] To anyone but fact-checkers and editors, this kind of claim may seem self-important and overblown. But editors traffic in error, and as David McKitterick has argued, the advent of print did not bring complete standardization, but instead an argument over how much variation was acceptable.[2]

Proliferation of error, at least at the scale threatened above, was only just becoming possible in mid-Tudor England. The purpose of this chapter is to explore how practitioners of lyric were coming to redefine their artistic productions in the face of such possibilities. Although I begin in 1557, the year of the incorporation of the Stationers' Company and the year of the first edition of Richard Tottel's *Songes and Sonettes*, the printed publications on which I am focusing all have an aspect of untimeliness and multiple chronologies because they encompass long stretches of time.[3] Tottel was primarily a legal printer, and his publications reference laws and proclamations backward in time sometimes as far as Magna Carta, but always have a relentless push to the present as their defining feature. Tottel is best known, however, for *Songes and Sonettes*, which reproduces verse of an earlier time. His compilation shares with the legal publications the push to the present, which must always be a key component to lyric. Tottel's collection has been admired for its influence even as his editorial changes to the poetry of Sir Thomas Wyatt and Henry Howard, Earl of Surrey, have been vilified as editorial meddling. Less critical attention has been paid to a key feature *Songes and Sonettes* shares with his legal printings. Both his lyric and legal compilations share a new condition of reproduction, in which the palimpsestic printed object simultaneously refers to, and annihilates or supersedes, other versions. In his legal printings this mode of discourse is assumed: referencing changes to the laws on a year-by-year or reign-by-reign basis is one of the main purposes of the printed compilation. Although Tottel never directly comments on his editorial methods, his lyric collection often proceeds in an analogous way, where the present state of the poem assumes and sometimes directly references other textual states of the same material. This new mode of poetic production therefore assumes reproduction at the outset, and it assumes multiplicity and dissemination as well. The changing conditions of lyric production lead Tottel to a number of reproductive strategies in his collection, not least of which is the creation of "The Lover," a kind of printed Everyman of lyric. This figure, who coexists with epitaphs written both by and about Wyatt and Surrey, demonstrates the palimpsestic quality of Tottel's compilation. As legal compilations enshrine the annihilation and replacement of defunct laws, the lyrics in Tottel's collection both refer to and replace their previous versions. In both cases, there is a crucial referential quality to the versions of poems and laws – the compilation is never a fully realized object. Rather it exists in a constantly updating and organic textual process, one which necessarily points outside of itself, to other texts, for its full realization. As will become clear in my analysis of these legal and lyric examples, the newness of Tottel's collections is as vexed an issue for lyric poetry as it is for law. Both seek the authority of precedents even as they stress the overriding importance of presentness.

Given its importance to the history of English poetry, it is worth noting that the anthology which Tottel printed in 1557 has two distinct titles. It is often referred to as "Tottel's Miscellany," a name which seems to have been given to it in 1870 by Edward Arber.[4] This is the first printed edition to carry this title; Arber also includes, below this, a modified version of the original 1557 title: *Songes and Sonettes, written by the right honorable Lorde Henry Haward late Earle of Surrey, and other*. He thus recognizes that the book probably known in its own time as "Songs and Sonnets" had also come to be known as "Tottel's Miscellany." There are other, earlier references to the work as a miscellany, or as "Tottel's Miscellany," before Arber's title page. These include John Payne Collier, who uses "Tottel's Miscellany" in the table of contents of his five-volume collection of English poetry (1866–70); Sir Egerton Brydges, who refers to "Tottel's Miscellany" in his 1814 reprint of Francis Davison's poetry; and a 1780 reference to "this valuable miscellany" by Thomas Warton in his history of English poetry.[5] The word "miscellany" as an English word is first credited to Ben Jonson by the *OED*, in a 1601 usage. The *OED* cites the first usage of "miscellany" as part of a book title in 1615, but a 1609 collection of songs uses the word. The first collection of English poems to be labelled a miscellany seems to be in 1643.[6]

What is apparent from these scattered usages is that there was no word for what Tottel was doing when he printed English lyric poetry as *Songes and Sonettes*; the word "miscellany" was not yet common parlance. Instead, the heyday of English printed verse miscellanies, 1557–1602, saw a whole range of imaginative titles, including *A handefull of pleasant delites* (probably 1566), *A smale handfull of fragrant flowers* (1575), *The paradyse of daynty devises* (1576), *A gorgious gallery, of gallant inventions* (1578), *A banquet of daintie conceits* (1588), *The phoenix nest* (1593), *The passionate pilgrime* (1599), *Englands Parnassus* (1600), and *A poetical rapsody* (1602). Before Tottel there were probably several poetic miscellanies printed in the reign of Henry VIII, including *A Boke of Balettes*, also known as *The Court of Venus*. As these titles reveal, and their longer versions explicate, these collections are only loosely generically connected, perhaps because there was no one activity that all these printers and poets were pursuing. They may have been collecting elegant lyrics for posterity, or codifying English ballads, but they also may have been reproducing verse that had, until the moment of printing, only been privately circulated in manuscript. Patronage or profit may have been at stake, and compilers may have been praising the memories of poets who had passed. Some or all of these motives may have operated to some degree within a single collection. However, it is important to note the difference between the alternative titles to this collection. When the thing is called *Songes and Sonettes, written by the right honorable Lorde Henry Haward late Earle of Surrey, and other*, we are accenting the products of the poet. When the thing is called *Tottel's Miscellany*, the accent instead is on the publishing house: Tottel as collector, compiler, printer, and perhaps manager or colleague of the compositors, the bookseller, and other agents involved in material production.[7]

Both titles should be brought to bear on our understanding of this collection and its influence. Moreover, as Arthur Marotti, Wendy Wall, and other critics have argued, this and other early printed English verse miscellanies demonstrate a readerly and editorial freedom to reproduce lyrics in various ways, to both preserve and alter simultaneously.[8] This double action is freeing, but it also produces vexed relationships to time and to identity. Our critical reading practices need to account for these vexed relationships, and to uncover evidence that poets were also considering the alteration and reproduction of their own verse. In what follows, I attempt to extend the traditional methods of close reading to "medium-close read" some of the poems in *Songes and Sonettes / Tottel's Miscellany*. In this case, medium-close reading helps us to account for the more expansive textual environment of these poems, an environment that includes not only the first 1557 printing (which is itself several printings), but also the manuscript contexts of the poems, and in at least one case, a later printing that attempts to correct and expunge the record which Tottel's edition creates. In later chapters, the poets

I examine begin self-consciously to refer to the processes by which their poetry is reproduced, including vocal performances, manuscript copying, and printing. Tottel seems to be far from unconscious about *what* he is doing, but he remains virtually silent about *how* he is doing it. His reproductive methodology is apparent in the collection itself, and in critics' negative reactions to his editorial changes. But it is also written into Tottel's legal printings, which went on simultaneously in his printing house. In both legal and lyric printings, there is a double emphasis on both the present and the past of the poem or law, so that reproduction occurs simultaneously with both the production of the law, and the production of the lyric. Tottel's legal printings have not been examined in connection with his poetic works, but the legal texts can inform our understanding of Tottel's reproductive strategies, his ways of keeping the law and the lyric in the present.

I The Law and the Lover: Marking Effacement

Richard Tottel's printed output in the year 1557 shows a combination of both large-scale literary and legal productions, sometimes at a seemingly breakneck pace. In that year he published or copublished five separate non-legal texts, in addition to three titles of legal interest. By April he had collaborated with John Cawod and John Waley to print a comprehensive collection of Thomas More's works. In June and July came the first and second printings of *Songes and Sonettes* and Surrey's *Certain Bokes of Virgiles Aeneis*; Tottel thus printed three books of poetry in the space of two months. An edition of *Litletons Tenures*, the definitive compendium on property law, was printed by the end of October. At some point in the year, perhaps after October, Tottel also reprinted a collection of pleas of the crown, compiled by William Staunford. By the end of the year (i.e., March), Tottel was printing William Baldwin's *A treatyce of morall philosophy containing the sayinges of the wise* ("the xxix. daie of Januarye" according to its colophon) and the first edition of Thomas Tusser's *A hundreth good pointes of husbandrie* ("the third day of February").[9]

Most important, on 16 October 1557 Tottel printed a collection of statute laws which had been edited by William Rastell, who fled to Louvain in 1549, returned to England during the reign of Mary Tudor, and fled again in the reign of Elizabeth I. I will refer to it simply as *A colleccion*, but its title reveals the scope of its ambitions: *A colleccion of all the statutes (from the begynning of Magna Carta vnto the yere of our Lorde, 1557) which were before that yere imprinted.*[10] This title exemplifies one of the most important tensions in Tottel's printing career, which spanned some of the most tumultuous moments of sixteenth-century English politics. That tension is between currency and venerability, between the new and the classic, between the ancient authorities and modern practitioners, and between the institutions of the Catholic church and the innovations of the Reformation. *A collecion* joins with philosophical, religious, and literary productions in exemplifying these peculiarly Renaissance tensions. In 1553, Tottel was granted a rare privilege to print "all and almaner bokes of oure Temp[or]all lawe called the com[m]on lawe whatsoeuer they be" for seven years.[11] The privilege was renewed in 1559 soon after Elizabeth had become queen. Tottel's survival and prosperity depended, therefore, on projects that compiled large amounts of material for the use of students and practitioners of law. Currency, in the form of the most recent changes to the law, and ancient authority, in the form of the oldest and most venerable precedents, were both valuable properties of these compilations.

William Rastell, not Tottel, was the editor of *A colleccion*, though there is evidence that he and Tottel worked together closely during Mary Tudor's reign.[12] Rastell in turn was processing the work of editors of statutes before him, and bringing those collections up to date by including the most recent statutes. One of Rastell's most important innovations was that he edited his collection of statutes by subject, rather than by the year of reign. *A colleccion* encourages readers to see the story of each corner of the law as it unfolds through the years. Sometimes great gaps of time exist, when laws have been applicable with little or no change for long periods. At other times, the laws change rapidly. A few key examples will suffice. Here are the second and third sections of "bokes and images," detailing statutes from Henry VIII's and Edward VI's reigns, after a long section on "highe and vnreasonable prices" of books:

> 2 ¶An.34.H.8.ca.I was an act against reading of *th*e Byble in english, and other englishe bokes of doctrine, and against plaies, so*n*ges and rimes, and against preaching & teaching of doctrine, but *th*e statute was repelled by .I.E.6.ca.12.
>
> 3 ¶An.3.E.6.ca.10 it was enacted that all bookes of the seruice of *th*e churche in latin, and all images of saintes that were or had bene in any churche or chappell, should bee abolished and destroyed, and the bookes burned. But this acte was after in Anno.I.M.I.parliamento.cap.2. repelled.
>
> Se Aliens .2. Newes .1. (*A colleccion*, 1557, fol. 38v–9r)

The "treason" section of *A colleccion* is also of interest; the following brief section appears after several pages detailing treasonable offences as described and defined in various reigns:

> 16 ¶An.33.H.8.cap.21. it is enacted that yf the kyng dyd mary a woman thynkyng her to be the*n* a maide where she was not, if she dyd not declare her vnchast lyfe to the kyng before the mariage, it is treason. And that if *th*e Quene or the princes wyfe

> do p*ro*cure any parson to haue carnal knowledge with her, or any dooe p*ro*cure any of them to the lyke, that the*n* the Quene & the princes wife & the other so p*ro*curing .&c. is treso*n*, but these treaso*ns* be repelled by I.E.6.ca.12. & by I.M.I. cessione as appereth here folowing .18.&.20. (*A colleccion*, 1557, fol. 446r)

Here are legal records of two of the most contentious religious and political issues of Henry VIII's reign. But I am primarily interested in the formal qualities of these passages. They demonstrate their double duty, both to the past of the law and to its present state. They both enshrine laws in a printed form, and desanctify any given law by showing that many laws have been repealed, changed, and nullified.

The passage above seems lurid, but it is just one of many in a closely printed text, recording as well the most quotidian of statutes and regulations. Moreover, *A colleccion* was only one of several methods of recording and reproducing the law. The statutes themselves were constantly being churned out by successive parliaments, and sometimes required distribution in the form of a proclamation by the sovereign. Alongside these were manuscript records of the courts and of all the writs which a working lawyer might need.[13] Yearly digests of new court cases, usually called "year books," were another form of legal writing.[14] These are collections of a smaller scale insofar as they aim to record and compile court proceedings within a finite time period. Finally, compilations such as *A colleccion* have a more comprehensive goal. Others, such as Fitzherbert's *La Graunde Abridgement* (first published 1514–17), Littleton's *Tenures* (c. 1480), and Fortescue's *De laudibus legum Angliae* (c. 1470) gather together massive data-sets and thus could serve as reference works for both legal theory and practice.[15] Commentators such as Howard Jay Graham and Alan Cromartie argue that these legal collections actually make practice into theory; by collecting and codifying, they serve to release both common law and statute law from the inaccessibility of existing only in particular cases, situations, practices, and decisions. Rather than being a reason-based activity which could be known only by specialists and through practice, these texts show that "The evident presupposition … was that the law was something which could be written down."[16]

However, against this monumentalizing, theorizing, and generalizing view of the legal collections, we must also set Rastell's concern with the present, with legal currency. In a prefatory address to his readers, Rastell states that "All the printed statutes expired or repelled, or concernyng priuate parsons or some priuate places, I haue left out of this worke" (sig. ¶iir). Instead, he reproduces in full only the laws that "be now in force and of effect." Far from codifying laws into general principals, his collection amplifies the conflict between rejected law and current law by professing a strict faithfulness to the sources that document earlier, but still current, statutes. His faithfulness to original sources forbids him from producing a collection that would completely digest the laws for any common English reader; instead he declares "I haue put euery statute in the tonge that it was first written in. For those that were first written in latin or in frenche, dare I not presume to translate into English, for feare of misse interpretacion" (sig. ¶iiir). If one were interested only in all current laws, then no other statute books would be necessary. But he underscores the importance of consulting "the great boke of statutes" should the reader seek to understand a particular statute in depth, or to examine the prefatory material that Rastell usually skips.

"Great boke of statutes" refers to the precursor to Rastell's collection, a book that had been published by Tottel in 1553–4, by William Middleton (to whom Tottel had been apprenticed) in 1542, and in a different format by Robert Redman in 1533. These books reproduce full texts of statutes enacted in each year of a ruler's reign. The 1533 edition, for example, proceeds from the 25th year of Henry VIII's reign (its year of publication) backward to the first year of the reign of Edward III. It is clear that out of books such as these, compilations such as Rastell's were drawn. However, Rastell's crucial decision to represent laws by subject rather than by reign emphasizes the chronological progress of individual laws themselves, including origin, modification, repeal, and sometimes, reintroduction.

A colleccion thus seeks a comprehensive reproduction of individual statutes. Its textual methodology is therefore both palimpsestic and genealogical. It represents the progression through time of statutes, but also only alludes to non-current stages of those statutes. Not surprisingly, genetic criticism is the contemporary critical practice most closely allied to *A colleccion*'s methodology. Genetic critics delve into both the *avante-texte* and the changes texts undergo during printed iterations. The successive generations and mutations of the text, as it is reproduced across media, are the primary focus of genetic critics.[17] The product of genetic criticism is closely linked to both works like *A colleccion* and, as I argue below, to a more expansive, medium-close reading of some of the most important poems in *Songes and Sonettes*. This product is an analytical and textual story, in which individual changes are seen as part of a larger process of textual mutation. In the case of both *A colleccion* and many of the lyrics in *Songes and Sonettes*, the representation of annihilation is a key component. It is a new kind of textual reproduction, which pursues both textual conservation and textual mutation.

The passages quoted above enact these opposing goals. The "treason" example is the most lurid of many that are reproduced in *A colleccion*, only to receive the final note that the law has been repealed, usually in the first year of Edward VI's reign, but sometimes in Mary's reign. Rastell's text is itself a reproduction; it paraphrases the original Henrician statute, printed in *The Great Boke of Statutes* in 1542.[18] In this earlier version, neither the people nor the legal principals are as generalized as in *A colleccion*. Instead, the statute is titled "An acte concernyng the atteynder of the late quene Katharine and her complices," and it primarily provides an account of the accusations against her, repeatedly emphasizing "the peryll of your most royall person, the danger and trouble of this your hole realme."[19] The specific names and charges are noted, including the principals (the queen, Jane Rochford, and Thomas Culpepper) as well as a list of those who were already accused and convicted of misprision of treason, allegedly for knowing of the queen's affairs but concealing that knowledge. Moreover, Rochford and the queen had not yet been executed for their treasons, while Culpepper had. Simultaneously occurring in one document, then, are the descriptions of alleged treasons whose suspects had already been executed, descriptions of alleged treasons whose suspects soon would be executed, and the generalizing of those cases into a new definition of treason.[20]

Fifteen years later, in Rastell's summary version, the specifics of the case are surrendered, and law itself is effaced at the end of the section. But this effacement paradoxically calls attention to the thing effaced: it declares the law to be null even as it records and reproduces that law, if only in a summarized form. Of Henry VIII's treason laws, J.H. Baker writes, "This series of statutes has been condemned, with justice, as the most repressive body of penal legislation ever passed in England."[21] A good deal of the total "treason" section of *A colleccion* is dedicated to undoing these laws: again and again, Henry VIII's treason laws are declared null, while those written in the reign of Edward III are declared current and in effect. The "treason" section thus attends to the present treason laws by effacing the recent present and by returning to the distant past. What *A colleccion* pointedly does not do, however, is to destroy the record of the Henrician laws. Instead, it reproduces those laws, even as it marks their repeal.

This textual mode, simultaneous reproduction and effacement, is all the more striking given passages such as that in the "bokes and images" section, quoted above. The law that is reproduced in this section calls for the extirpations for which the English Reformation is known: books and images should be "abolished and destroyed" and "burned." Even as its text mandates the destruction of books and images, *A colleccion*'s stance on former texts undermines this activity, since it does not fully extirpate the textual traces of laws which Rastell (not to mention Tottel) is in fact preserving and reproducing.

The clash between the two goals of preservation and currency is all the more extreme in *A colleccion*'s sections on "Rome," "heresy," "Monasteries, Abbeys, &c," and "crowne." These sections encompass more of the greatest religio-political upheavals of mid-Tudor England, especially the Marian reign, and *A colleccion* reflects these convolutions. For example, the "Rome" section begins with a declaration that since the twentieth year of Henry VIII's reign, "much false & erronious doctrine hath bene taught preached, & writte*n*." These erroneous doctrines and parliamentary acts are then listed in a kind of litany of misguided religious legislation. After each listing, the consistent response is effacement. The exact phrasing varies slightly, but usually includes the declaration that the statute just referred to "shall from hencefoorth be repeled, adnulled, reuoked, adniehilated, and vtterly made voyde for euer" (sig. BBbviiiv). The paradoxical textual action of preserving effacement is clear even from the phrasing here, which depends on the alternation between motion toward a goal, occurring in the "ad-" prefixes, and motion away from an evil, occurring in the words "repeled" and "reuoked." The impossibility of the stated goal, annihilation, is demonstrable in a paradoxical phrase that combines creation with nullity: the law is to be "made voyde." At the same time, the text stretches from the present moment to eternity: "from hencefoorth" to "for euer."

But even without this heady verbal mix of purposes and directions, the paradox of reproduction and effacement is clear from sections such as "Rome," which documents religious upheavals, and "Crowne," which documents adjustments to the English succession. A reader proceeding down one of these pages can see a succession of phrases such as "wherin is declared the kinges marriage wyth Queene Katherine to be voyde," "*th*e deuorce betwene the king and Anne Bolleyn is confirmed and her issue made illegittimate," and "the issue betwene the kyng & Queene Jane bee made heyres to the crown," among others (sig. Mivv). Of course, the succession was of paramount importance to both of Henry VIII's daughters, and in the 1559 reprinting of *A colleccion*, there is a much augmented "Crowne" section. Once again there is a notable tension between the law's evanescence and sovereign protestations of permanence. The statutes in the 1559 *Colleccion*'s "crowne" section renew the Oath of Supremacy, revive statutes such as those placing the English sovereign at the head of the church, and repeal all of the relevant statutes made in Philip and Mary's reign, which had in turn repealed those of Henry VIII. The language of these changes is by now familiar: the new version of the succession "shall stande, remayne, & be *th*e law of this realme for euer," while the previous version "shal be vtterly frustrate, voide & of none effect." The statute then clarifies the extent of this replacement: "And also shall and maye be cancelled, defaced, & put in perpetuall obliuion at your hignes will & pleasure, as if *th*e same had neuer ben had, made, declared, set forth published, or promulged."[22]

Parliament polemically pushes to the extreme edges of the law's reach in this passage, and those edges are temporal: its will extends forever, and previous wills might as well never have existed. But "forever" and "never" must have seemed quite implausible in light of the recent changes from Henry VIII's statutes (mostly extended in Edward VI's time, with a few notable exceptions) to Mary I's, and back to Henry VIII's during the first year of Elizabeth I. Protestations of eternal textual life, usually the province of lyric love poetry, are here made by individual statutes, but directly contradicted by the form of *A colleccion*. Its attention to the law's distant origins in the *Magna Carta*, its thematic organization with an intrinsic chronology for each item, and its close attention to the original language in which each law was couched all accent the iterations of the law over a long period of time. Although it retains a careful faithfulness to the original versions of those laws, it also accents the mutations and annihilations that have occurred along the way. Rastell's collection seeks a comprehensive, and we might say genetic view of each law, one which accounts for multiple moments of reproduction, and the change that accompanies each of these moments. To focus only on legal currency, on only those laws "whiche be nowe in force and of effect," ignores Rastell's referring readers to the earlier *Great Boke of Statutes*; his constant reminders to readers that he is passing over nullified statutes, even while referring to the exact year and chapter of those statutes; and his inclusion, in both the 1557 and 1559 *Colleccions*, of material that is contrary to the laws of the reigning queen.

Tottel's Miscellany prints the poetry of both living and deceased authors. Surrey and Wyatt and a few others were among the dead by 1557, while Nicholas Grimald and other authors were alive at the time of the first printing, and were labelled "uncertain" and "other" in the text. Both titles – *Songes and Sonettes, written by the right honorable Lorde Henry Haward late Earle of Surrey, and other*, and *Tottel's Miscellany* – contain dubious possessives. It is not known whether Tottel actually edited the book, and various contenders have been posited as the editor, none with any surety.[23] In the original title, only the Earl of Surrey is named, while everyone else is covered under the phrase "and other."[24] The brief address to the reader, by Tottel or by whoever edited the collection, famously declares that he is publishing "those workes which the vnge*n*tle horders vp of such tresure haue heretofore enuied the."[25] It does not purport to be a systematic treatment of, or repository of, English lyric poetry. However, it has been called the foundational book of printed English poetry, and Elizabeth Pomeroy, the only author of a full monograph on English verse miscellanies, calls it a "sourcebook for eloquence."[26] Pomeroy justifies this label primarily by showing the abiding influence of the collection, both in resuscitating interest in vernacular English poetic production, and as an exemplar of what a collection of poetry could consist of, and do: "The subsequent miscellanies varied greatly, but Tottel's book was the model for them all."[27] Although the category of "miscellany" refuses systematicity, nevertheless *Songes and Sonettes* shares with *A colleccion* a sense that the subject at hand can be known comprehensively through the compendious printed book. Both concern themselves with the utmost currency of their subjects, by bringing into the present the laws and the lyrics that have been in circulation and in use.

Songes and Sonettes also shares with *A colleccion* the paradox of reproducing annihilation, and it is for this reason that the legal collection is so informative to our understanding of how mid-Tudor poetry begins to incorporate reproduction directly into production. Chiefly, and most obviously, it does so by reprinting and repackaging elegiac poetry, laments for those who have passed. However, the editorial interventions in this collection also complicate the assumption that it is simply reproducing poems which would otherwise have lain dormant and unread. Tottel's collection is instead an agent of change: in the act of reproducing and representing otherwise lost poetry, the collection also begins to enshrine reproduction with a difference as one of the primary modes of poetic production in sixteenth-century England. This reproduction with a difference – copying and changing text – is at once consonant and at odds with some of the most basic goals, modes, and tendencies of lyric poetry. To return for a moment to the example of Chidiock Tichborne's lament, we see that the manuscript witnesses of this poem often evince a desire to preserve the evanescent, ephemeral moment, the passing of which Tichborne laments: "My glass is full, and now my glass is run, / And now I live, and now my life is done." As mentioned in the introduction, one manuscript includes marginalia purporting to have the original copy in Tichborne's own hand. But an answer poem, printed in a short pamphlet collection in 1586, and perhaps written by Thomas Kyd, provides a very different view of Tichborne. The poem ends:

> Thou trodst the earth, and now on earth thou art,
> as men may wish thou neuer hadst beene made.
> Thy glorie and thy glasse are timeles runne,
> And this, O *Tychborne*, hath thy treason done.[28]

The point here is not that Tichborne's death was celebrated as the just deserts of a traitor, though those sentiments are clearly conveyed in this heavy-handed answer poem. Rather, it is that Tichborne's poem is undergoing a reproductive mutation simply by virtue of the context in which it is copied. This version, and the other manuscript and printed versions of the poem, all concatenate to form a multi-varying poetic object, one which resides in an intertextual condition rather than as a single entity that is endlessly and invariably reproduced. The conditions of reproducibility extend what was Tichborne's lament into a whole range of others' laments and answers. In this collection, the poem is steered towards an entirely other purpose, even as its original text is (supposedly) copied verbatim. Reproduction and annihilation occur visibly and simultaneously.

Tottel's collection achieves this sort of complex, mutating poetic reproduction on a much larger scale. Below, I concentrate on two key elegies for Sir Thomas

Wyatt, before turning towards Tottel's use of "the lover" and his use of titles as a way of marking both reproduction and loss. In all cases, I maintain that the reproductive conditions we have seen above in *A colleccion*, especially the competing claims of currency and veneration, are amply evident in Tottel's verse miscellany. These opposing impulses, to preserve and to maintain currency, are at the heart of lyric praises and laments. One of the great achievements of the collection is therefore to both encourage and disrupt the sense that what we are reading belongs to a former time, the time of the Earl of Surrey or of Sir Thomas Wyatt, a time that has passed. Instead, Tottel's editorial interventions, like those of Rastell's *Colleccion*, carry us through to the present even as the collections purport to reproduce the past of these texts. The lyric, like the legal, must be current, but that currency is always haunted by an accumulation of annihilations, the little deaths of monarchs, poets, pleasures, laws, and poems. Medium-close reading helps to demonstrate how the new conditions of reproducibility combine with lyric's concern with the present.

There is no question that *Songes and Sonettes* is concerned partly with preserving past lyrics: it does in fact preserve some poetry that is otherwise lost or that remains only in a few manuscripts. As Ruth Hughey and Hyder Rollins showed in the early twentieth century, the sources for *Songes and Sonettes* include the Arundel Harington manuscript, a family manuscript compiled partly by Sir John Harington of Stepney, and the Egerton manuscript, which is a key source for poetry by Sir Thomas Wyatt. Both the Arundel Harington and Egerton manuscripts span large periods of time, and are in several hands, making their relationship to *Songes and Sonettes* more difficult to discern; Hughey hypothesizes a lost manuscript that served as copy for the printing of *Songes and Sonettes*. She conjectures that the Wyatt poems in the Arundel Harington manuscript may represent a "median stage" of the Wyatt poems between the Egerton states and the states in *Songes and Sonettes*.[29]

Moreover, as Hyder Rollins and Paul Marquis have shown, *Songes and Sonettes* itself went through substantial changes in its first, 1557, printings, the first on 5 June and the second on 31 July (called "A" and "B" by Rollins, and "Q1" and "Q2" by Marquis). A third edition, also dated 31 July 1557, is closely related to Q2 but might have been printed at any time between Q2 and the 1559 edition.[30] One of many significant changes is that the poems of Nicholas Grimald are significantly reduced, and his full name becomes "N.G."[31] The "uncertain authors" section is also augmented in the 1557 Q2 text. In the rest of the sixteenth-century editions (Q–Q10), there are fewer substantive changes, most of which are in Q3, and an accumulation of errors like those warned against at the beginning of this chapter.[32] However, we have already seen above that the title and the contents were again made fluid in the eighteenth- and nineteenth-century reprints; these have their own peculiar stories, including two printing house fires that destroyed, totally or partially, the reprints in progress.[33]

Such reproductive variations in *Songes and Sonettes* continue into the present. For example, *Early English Books Online* (*EEBO*) presents two digitized versions of the second, 31 July impression, one of which has a striking image next to the title page: a portrait of Surrey himself stares back from the screen! The image, almost surely based on a Holbein portrait of Surrey from 1541,[34] was not printed in the 1557 edition. Instead it was tipped in to the miscellany sometime before 1874, and was probably created in the late-eighteenth or early-nineteenth century. It was then removed from the copy after being microfilmed. A similar case exists in the title page to the British Library's copy of Surrey's translations from *The Aeneid*, also visible in the *EEBO* copy, and also first printed by Tottel in 1557.[35]

These examples show *Tottel's Miscellany / Songes and Sonettes* to be a fluid, constantly updating collection in which subsequent reproductions include all sorts of variations, both to the poems and to their surrounding paratextual material. Critical editions such as Rollins's or Marquis's represent only one kind of variation; the tipped-in portraits are another. This fluidity of both addition and subtraction is crucial to our understanding of the reproduction of *Songes and Sonettes*: both loss and conservation figure into all of these examples. But crucially, Tottel's text itself both enacts and reflects the opposing impulses to conserve and annihilate. I am especially interested in pursuing the coincidence of this opposition in both the poetry and in its material, reproduced form, as the following examples demonstrate.

The elegies printed in *Songes and Sonettes* make it clear that one primary function of the collection is memorial. Especially in the elegies for Sir Thomas Wyatt, we find all that can be expected: praise, lament, and the halting reassurances that though he is dead, he nevertheless lives both "there" and "here" – both in heaven, and in the very pages the reader is now perusing. Yet we should examine how Wyatt is said to live on in textual form – how it is that he has been reproduced in this verse miscellany. One peculiarity of the collection is that a brief elegy to Wyatt was added to the second, Q2 printing of the 1557 *Songes and Sonettes*: a short poem entitled "Of the death of sir Thomas wiate the elder." In just seven lines, it hits all the marks of lament, praise, and reassurance. In five of the seven, the author reassures us that Wyatt either lives or shall live: "Lo dead he liues," the poem begins, and it ends "Though he be dead, yet liues he here aliue. / Thus can no death from Wiate, life depriue."[36] It is Wyatt's "liuely name" that this poem promises to conserve through reproduction, and that the title of the poem delivers. But in light of this poem's medium, this miscellaneous section in which Wyatt's name appears among other names, that promise should be reexamined. The title of the very next poem assures us "That length of time consumeth all thinges," while other poems nearby immediately plunge us into other subjects: lovers' pledges, Penelope and Ulysses, and immediately prior to the poem, "The louer declareth his paines to excede far the paines of hell." The elegy's immediate context, then, both assures Wyatt's fame and changes our sense of Wyatt simply by placing him in among these other poems. The poem immediately preceding the short elegy finishes by pleading "So helpe me soone to haue / My parfect earthly blisse." The poem immediately following it finishes more flatly: "By proofe wherof we see, / Time geues the greatest dint." The elegy promises us that though Wyatt is dead, "yet liues he here aliue." But *where* is the textual "here" which Wyatt occupies? The collection answers this question by placing him just between the lover's desperate exaggerations and pleadings for present pleasure, and the moralist's sober lesson that nothing will last.

We should also pause over the name itself, here rendered as "sir Thomas wiate the elder," and elsewhere as "sir. T. w. the elder," "the same sir. T. w.," and then just "the same" in a trio of poems in the Surrey section of *Songes and Sonettes*. We have just seen how Wyatt's name gets somewhat dissolved into the miscellaneous context of the poems with which it is surrounded. And above, we saw how the legal reproductions of statutes gradually filed down the particulars of Henry VIII's sordid divorce proceedings into phrases like "if a king did marry" and digests of the results of the statutes and proclamations and court proceedings from this time. Here, it is worth noting that "the elder" is a critical phrase, since it differentiates the Wyatt of these elegies from Thomas Wyatt the younger, who was executed for his part in the rebellion of January and February 1553/4. By late 1554, the story had already been published in an account by John Proctor that narrates the rebellion, forcefully arguing Wyatt's heresy.[37] This Wyatt really was effaced from his country's ground; his corpse presumably was cut into pieces and never reached the ground intact, unlike the elder's. But Proctor's history also effects a memorialization of the younger Wyatt even though Mary Tudor's purpose, in exacting the punishment for traitors, was to do just the opposite: to render him annihilate and unburiable in England's ground. Thus, even though there might be good reason for *Songes and Sonettes* to print the poet's name followed by "the elder," nevertheless both Wyatts are the recipients of a textual reproduction that marks their bodily effacement. The result is that their memorializations are not nearly as different as the politics might require. Given the reversals of laws, religious articles, and personal fortunes in mid-Tudor England, the potential confusion of Thomas Wyatts may even signal the unexpected survivability of a name that had otherwise been supposedly expunged from memory.

What happens to "Wyatt" in the course of the most important elegies to him, the two by Surrey beginning "Dyuers thy death doe diuersly bemone" and "Wyatt resteth here, that quick could neuer rest," is that it is preserved and effaced simultaneously. The paradoxical textual action fits well with both elegiac poetry and with successive reproductions of the poem in multiple manuscript and printed editions. In fact, Wyatt's presence is visibly attenuated from an earlier form of the poem through to the form in Tottel's *Songes and Sonettes.* The poem beginning "Wyatt resteth here" first appeared in print in a small pamphlet of poems that was probably published shortly after Wyatt's death in 1542.[38] There, as in the Latin pamphlet of praise poems to Wyatt published the same year,[39] both Wyatt's name and the image of his face are prominent: Wyatt's "vysage sterne and mylde" appears in profile just under the title (see figure 1.1). Surrey's poem, which has justly received much critical attention, is in part an encomiastic blazon, listing Wyatt's body parts and noting each one's relation to his noble soul, which, with his body now reclaimed by the earth, is reclaimed by the heavens. The poem has been taken to signal Surrey's high regard for Wyatt. Even more strikingly, for some critics it comprises an attempt to "capture the presence of Wyatt."[40] William Sessions goes so far as to say that this elegy "will have the effect of an innovative holy relic, available through printing-presses now, but just as capable of continuous intercession through continuous reading by thousands of readers through centuries."[41]

Yet loss, even more than presence, is the subject of Surrey's poem; loss is also what happens as Wyatt's praise and name are reproduced in successive editions. The visual representation of Wyatt in portrait, his name, and Surrey's blazon all work together to mark his effacement from the temporal world.

In *Songes and Sonettes,* gone is the portrait of Wyatt, as well as Wyatt's full name. Instead, Tottel's edition titles the poem "Of the same," since it follows "Of the death of the same sir T.w.," which itself follows "Praise of certaine psalmes of Dauid, translated by sir T. w. the elder." The poet here undergoes a diminution from full portrait and name, first to his initials only, then to "the same," and finally to the single initial "*VV*":

VV. Resteth here, that quick could neuer rest:
Whose heauenly giftes encreased by disdain,
And vertue sank the deper in his brest.
Such profit he by enuy could obtain.[42]

The rest of the poem, which adapts the blazon tradition for the purpose of lament, magnifies the losses by accumulating praises connected to Wyatt's head, visage, hand, tongue, eye, and heart. Yet against the regularity of this blazon, Surrey's celebrated regular iambic pentameter is never so interrupted as in that first line, at the exact point when Wyatt's name occurs.

An excellent Epitaffe of ſyr Thomas Wyat, with two other compendious dytties, wherin are touchyd, and ſet furth the ſtate of mannes lyfe.

What reſteth here, that quicke could neuer reſt.
Whoſe heuenly gyftes, encreaſed by dyſdayne
And vertue ſanke, the deper in his breſt
Suche profyte he, of enuy could optayne

A Head, where wyſdom myſteries dyd frame
Whoſe hammers beat ſtyll in that lyuely brayne
As on a ſtyth, where ſome worke of Fame
Was dayly wrought, to turn to Brytayns game

A Vyſage ſterne and mylde, where both dyd groo
Vyce to contempne, in vertues to reioyce
A.i. Amyd

Figure 1.1 *An excellent Epitaffe* (c. 1545), sig. A1r. This item is reproduced by permission of The Huntington Library, San Marino, California

Wyatt's visible reduction is even stranger if one reads the poem aloud. For what is that first syllable? Even when "Wyat" is fully written, it does not scan regularly, but in Tottel's version, the name is reduced even further to just this initial. The "T. w." in the title of the previous poem need not be spoken. But this *VV* letter must be spoken, and yet cannot. It is unpronounceable. Yet we know that the editor of the poems in *Songes and Sonettes* often corrected with an ear for regular meter.[43] In this same poem, he corrects line 7, adding a syntactically unnecessary "that" in order to bring the syllable count to ten. But no such expedient solution is applied in this first line, and this broken reproduction of Wyatt's name is entirely appropriate, because Wyatt does not in fact "rest here" at all. Expedience, and seamless integration of the man into a poem, are precisely what Surrey's poem resists. Instead, the poem professes the impossibility of a mark – an initial, the praise of a body part, the praise of virtue, a portrait, or an entire elegy – standing in for a person. "*VV.* Resteth here" simultaneously states the truth and a falsehood: Wyatt, the dead man, does not rest here; but the letter that now must stand for him does. It rests in the "here" of the present poem, which is all that is possible.

At the same time, this initial capital letter regularizes Wyatt into the context of Tottel's *Songes and Sonettes*. All of the poems surrounding this elegy begin with larger initial capitals, setting the first two lines off from the others. In other words, this poem looks like all the others that surround it, unlike the poem in its original printed context, where it was combined with the striking portrait of Wyatt. Here, "Wyatt" has become fully dissolved into the tissue of Tottel's *Songes and Sonettes*, so that the name is simultaneously effaced and reproduced. This textual action is one of the hallmarks of Tottel's collection. Wyatt, Surrey, Grimald, and the other authors are all subsumed under the name of "The Lover." The addition of the lover to the titles of the poems in *Songes and Sonettes* is one of its most widespread textual interventions. Along with "The Printer to the Reader" and the index added to the Q2 edition, it is one of the few textual interventions which we can probably credit to Tottel. (Neither Rollins nor Marquis definitively ascribes metrical changes, deletions and additions, or changes to the order of poems to Tottel.) As a name, "The Lover" also appears far more often than Surrey, Wyatt, Grimald, and all the other specific personal names combined. His is the dominant voice of the collection, despite the emphasis on Surrey in the title, and despite the elegies to Wyatt. To fill the void left by the effacement of Surrey and Wyatt, *Songes and Sonettes* presents the lover.

One might object that Tottel's stated conservative, preservational goal is foremost. This goal is most conspicuous when Tottel refers to "the honorable stile of the noble earle of Surrey, and the weightinesse of the depewitted sir Thomas Wyat the elders verse." Surely Tottel does not desire, or even assume the posture of desiring, the kind of annihilation that we saw expressed in *A colleccion*? While

Tottel does not specifically attend to the annihilation of the authors he professes to preserve, nevertheless the operations of the miscellany itself tend towards a levelling of authorship and style, so that the "honorable stile" of Surrey and the "weightinesse" of Wyatt blend together by virtue of their occupying pages in the same book. The title page may emphasize Surrey, but it also encourages readers to attend to the generalizability of the poems *across* authorship, rather than to divide the collection into distinct areas based on either author, theme, or some other criterion. As they are all songs and sonnets, we should be less inclined to think of the book as broken into four sections, Surrey-Wyatt-Grimald-Uncertain Authors. This sectioning, to be sure, does occur in the text. But it is not nearly so conspicuous as the levelling of authorship caused by reading title after title, in any given section, that contains "The Lover." In fact, in both the Q1 and Q2 texts of *Songes and Sonettes*, Surrey's name and Wyatt's appear only at the end of their sections, while the running title is almost invariably "Songes and Sonettes." Thus if the book were unbound, or if a reader were casually to flip through the pages, the chances of seeing "The Lover" would be far greater than those of seeing Wyatt's name, or Surrey's or Grimald's, or a more "uncertain" attribution.[44]

The currency of "The Lover" is perhaps its most important property. The titles do not perform the documentary or narrative work of describing the poet Surrey's poetic achievements, now past and needing to be preserved. Rather, they present the poem as occurring now, in the present. This currency is most apparent in titles that combine "the lover" with an action verb: "The lover describeth ..." or "The louer comforteth himself." But it also occurs when the title simply states what the poem is, or what it does, usually by identifying its subject. The first few poems of Surrey's perform this task, identifying the poems as "descriptions" or "complaints" – "Descripcion of the restlesse state of a louer, with sute to his ladie, to rue on his diying hart," for example, or "Complaint of a louer rebuked."

Tottel's printing of Surrey's poem beginning "From Tuskane came my Ladies worthy race" demonstrates the tension. This poem details places from Surrey's own life as well as that of the woman whom the speaker calls "my Lady," even though she is "chase[d]" from his sight; these places include Tuscany, Florence, Hunsdon, Hampton, and Windsor. As Rollins discusses, the legend of Surrey's love for Elizabeth Fitzgerald of Ireland sprang up soon after his death, and was quite tenacious. Tottel gave this poem the title "Description and praise of his loue Geraldine," and almost 200 years later, in 1728, Henry Curll used this name as the basis of the title of his second reprint of *Tottel's Miscellany*.[45] But in the printed context of the 1557 *Songes and Sonettes*, when we read "his loue Geraldine," we might reasonably ask, "whose?" In other nearby poems (the opening of sigs Aiiiiv – Bir of the 1557 Q2), the antecedents of "his" all refer us to the lover: "a louer" [rebuked] and "the louer" [disdained] also speak from these pages. Tottel's reproduction, insofar as it retains references to specific places, preserves Surrey's presence in the poem. But within the larger text, Tottel's reproduction tends to annihilate Surrey's presence and replace him with The Lover.

The situation on this particular page is slightly more complex, because "Complaint of a louer rebuked" is itself a translation of Petrarch's #140, beginning "Loue, that liueth, and raigneth in my thought" in Surrey's translation. The learned reader thus is confronted with a chain of effacements, linking together a set of potentially equivalent figures. The lover is understood to be Surrey, but also Petrarch, whose poem beginning "Amor, che nel penser mio vive et regna ..." Surrey translates and adapts. Moreover, the lover must be equated to Wyatt, since thirty-one poems or ten pages later, we come to the end of the Surrey section, where we find *SVRREY* in a larger, italic font. The first poem in the next section is "The louer for shamefastnesse hideth his desire within his faithfull hart," and it is also a translation of Petrarch's #140. The same lover offers another version of a familiar poem, and the presence of the lover here thwarts any desire to replicate either Surrey or Wyatt exactly. Instead, they are both subsumed into a more generalized and generalizable textual figure.

The figure of the lover thus attenuates the presence of Wyatt or Surrey in many of the poems usually read as topically significant to their lives, even as the collection extols them individually and reproduces their names at key moments. Arthur Marotti proposes two possible purposes of Tottel's titles: they either "recreate the text's social context" (by referring to original occasions and authors or recipients), or they help to liberate the work "from some of the constraints that affected its original function and meaning." For Marotti, "one practice … shades into the other."[46] Even more than this, however, Tottel's Lover illustrates a central tension present in both elegies and in the texts that reproduce them. Even when the title and poem appear designed to preserve the originary occasion, both elegies and Tottel's reproductions of them insist on the production of a new textual object.

A final example of this bifurcated reproduction is Surrey's poem beginning "So cruell prison, how coulde betide, alas," which has primarily been read for its reflection on Surrey's imprisonment in Windsor castle.[47] In *Songes and Sonettes*, the place name but not the personal name is reproduced: "Prisoned in windsor, he recounteth his pleasure there passed." The poem mostly describes the speaker's happy childhood spent "With a kinges sonne," and in the last lines complains of the speaker's loss of his friend, and of his own freedom, in the same castle where he was once so happy. One way to read these lines is as a poetic reproduction of the imprisonment of Henry Howard, Earl of Surrey and his grieving of the loss of Henry Fitzroy. Yet Tottel's title adheres to this poem's own rules concerning who and what gets named. At a space of years, the speaker does not name his lost childhood playmate, nor the songs "Of pleasuant playnt, and of our ladies prayse" that they sang. Instead, we read only of a king's son, a telling phrasing – he is not a prince. The combined generality and specificity of this phrase should remind us of the phrase "yf the kyng dyd mary a woman" in *A colleccion*. There, as here, the text preserves and effaces its subject's name. Surrey's and Fitzroy's exploits as children are recorded here, as is their friendship; the poem also specifically names the place where all these things took place. But the name of the companion is unmentionable in the lyric moment. The title preserves and even solidifies this rule by diminishing the name of the author as well, reducing that name to the same "he" of the surrounding poems. The lover, as "he," is able constantly to speak in this present lyric moment, and thus simultaneously to efface and preserve.

II The Law and the Lute

The law of *A colleccion* is an ever-changing thing, particularly if viewed through the prism of mid-Tudor England, when laws about the succession, about religion, and about tyranny were all being changed rapidly in the reigns of Henry VIII, Edward VI, Mary, and Elizabeth I. However, as we have seen above, the law in *A colleccion* not only changes, but it is reproduced in such a way as to accent the new laws even as it both reproduces and purports to annihilate certain older laws that have been repealed. The right versions of religious adherence, sovereign succession, and treason depend on a complex stance with regard to the chronology of the law. This stance, as we see it in *A colleccion*, allows for simultaneous reference to at least three separate times. There is first the present moment, during which the laws are being changed and defined. There is also the recent past, which receives both suppression and preservation by having its annihilation announced and specified. Finally there is the more distant past that is being recalled to life. The new, present versions of the law require Edward III's definition of treason or Henry VIII's definition of the succession and the supremacy of the sovereign. In the pages of *A colleccion*, all three of these times are made to operate in close proximity to one another. The resulting text is understandably blurred along the lines of chronological order, even as it organizes each subject heading into a supposedly chronological scheme.

This chronological complexity, coupled with definitive statements about the error of prior versions, can help us to reevaluate a key charge against *Tottel's Miscellany*: that Tottel adulterated his text, particularly the earlier, manuscript versions of Wyatt's poems. As I have discussed above in the introduction, the "copy-text" of Greg and other exponents of critical editing practices requires an editor to choose one version of a given poem or work as the best available, and to compare that version to all available variants. This totalizing comparison is in the pursuit of the best text, and contains an underlying assumption: that textual transmission should operate faithfully, reproducing the best text with the fewest errors, ideally zero. Given the standard of faithful transmission of the poet's original (or in some cases, final) conception of the poem, editors must find a way not to adulterate the poem, or find the least adulterated version.

For adherents of eclectic editing, who search for the best text on the basis of the author's intentions, this much is self-evident. Why do an edition of Wyatt's poetry and introduce substantial changes to the poems as they exist in manuscript? How could one not, in Dawkins's genetic terms, aim at the extreme "copying fidelity" of the gene? Tottel's texts fall far short of the bar of total fidelity. His changes include widespread adjustments of individual word forms, changes of individual words, and sometimes of portions of a line. There are seldom more sweeping changes, such as modification of an entire stanza or section of a poem. But as we have already seen, in his edition each of the poems has a title; in the manuscripts the poems are seldom titled. Perhaps predictably, Tottel's word and line changes have been widely attacked; many critics agree that they destroy, attenuate, or contradict the essence of individual poems. Most forcefully, Joost Daalder argues that Tottel's changes to Wyatt's poems constitute a "falsification of Wyatt's intentions."[48] Both Rollins and Daalder also note that Tottel was adjusting the poems to the tastes of a different time, especially by regularizing the metre of some of Wyatt's poems. But Daalder also argues that such adjustments simplify complex poetry, and that there are sometimes changes that have no effect on the metre, and instead can be better explained by the desire to reduce irony or paradox, to depict a narrator who is overly involved in himself and in love, and to reduce political content.

No one who has read deeply into Wyatt's poetry will deny the force of Daalder's examples. In one of Wyatt's most famous poems, beginning "They flee from me," Daalder calls attention to the way in which the ironic and subtle "kyndely" gets changed into the unironic and unsubtle "unkyndely." There are many other examples, but this one captures the spirit of the objections, since he argues here that metricality is not as much a concern as eliminating irony and reducing complexity. The underlying assumption is that irony and paradox are what make Wyatt's poetry good, and that it is therefore wrong to create and transmit adulterated versions like those in *Songes and Sonettes*. This assertion is steeped in New Critical values regarding textual complexity: the complex, ironic, potentially ambiguous poem is a mainstay of New Critical close readings. But it also assumes something else: that seeking the best poetic state requires us to seek the earliest version. The assumption is that Tottel's versions are to be discarded in favour of the prior, better ones.

We ought to scan such judgments. As Daalder himself notes, judgments about what makes good poetry led to the changes in *Songes and Sonettes*. Nor can we say with any surety that Tottel's changes were the first. Quite the contrary: it appears that during his lifetime, soon after his death, and in Tottel's case some fifteen years after his death, there were many hands copying, compiling, and adjusting Wyatt's poetry. In other words, Tottel and other poetic reproducers actively resist faithful copying. Instead, they pursue what Peter Shillingsburg has called the "aesthetic orientation" towards editing, in which it is possible, and desirable, to improve on the author's work.[49] Tottel's versions of poems often involve substantial changes, which are in the spirit of the "unquiet state" of the lover, who vacillates between Petrarch, Wyatt, and Surrey. The poems themselves are unquiet states, resistant to existing in a single time or a single version. Chief among these unquiet states is Wyatt's "My Lute Awake."

There are versions of this poem in the Egerton, Devonshire, and Blage manuscripts, and in three different printed books by 1565. The first printed version probably appeared in *The Court of Venus* around 1535, which was also published under the title *A Boke of Balettes* around 1547 and again in the 1560s.[50] In *A Boke of Balettes* (extant only as a fragment), "My Lute Awake" is preceded by a similar lyric, in which the poet exhorts his pen to "write no more." This renunciative sentiment may be seen as the central conceit of the poem as it exists in *Songes and Sonettes*, as evidenced by the first stanza:

My lute awake performe the last
Labour that thou and I shal wast:
And end that I haue now begonne:
And when this song is song and past:
My lute be stil for I haue done. (sig. I.i verso)

In the version Tottel prints, this poem works against its own central conceit of discarding the lute and giving up on singing. Instead, the continual complaint of the speaker is evident as he describes past, present, and future versions of himself and his cruel, unrequiting lover. Each stanza ends with some version of "I have done" or "my lute and I have done." Then the poem continues. Of course, it does eventually end, but as it is being read or sung, the effect of these repetitions is just the opposite: the speaker says he has done, and then continues his complaint.

The poem's claim to a continuous present triumphs over its initial, more resigned statement. In a self-indulgent fantasy that stretches far into the future, the speaker imagines that the "she" of the poem will share the regret that he now feels:

May chance thee lie withered and olde.
In winter nightes that are so colde,
Playning in vaine vnto the mone:
Thy wishes then dare not be tolde.
Care then who list, for I haue done. (sig. I.iir)

The fantasy is both vindictive and empathetic; she will sing complaints and will "wish and want as I haue done." At the centre of this poem is the imagination of reproduction. That which the speaker is supposedly ending will continue: the plaintive, moaning song. The mere act of singing leads to the reproduction of song in other, imagined registers and future times. So much for putting the lute to sleep.

The poem's continual present, and its generalizability, are heightened by Tottel's title, which could apply to just about any love complaint of the period: "The louer complaineth the vnkindnes of his loue." This title occupies the present, and coupled with the poem's relentless continuation, the supposed completion and renunciation of "I have done" is rendered into a much less believable, even ironic, statement. An earlier printed version in *A Boke of Balettes* is much shorter. This version ends with a rhyming couplet, rather than the standard "for I have done." This couplet appears at the middle of Tottel's version (and several manuscript versions), and reads "And then may chaunce the to repent / The time that thou hast lost and spent[.]"[51] At this point, *A Boke of Balettes* prints a manicule, marking the couplet as memorable, copiable, and potentially useful in other contexts.[52] In the *Boke of Balettes*, pens write no more and lutes sing no more. Together, these two poems accumulate a set of expressions of resignation, somewhat in the style of a commonplace book or breviary. Wyatt's poem is thus reproduced for its iterability; ironically, the iterable statement is one about closure. In Tottel's version, we see instead a fuller commentary on resignation itself. The lover may cleverly complain and pretend to put down his lute, but the lovelorn state is one which really is hopeless, eternal, and widely generalizable.

John Hall's 1565 collection *The Court of Vertue* takes issue with such poems, and thus also adopts the "aesthetic" orientation to textual reproduction. The prologue to the collection reveals its purpose: to supplant the lecherous and ungodly *Court of Venus*, and others of its kind, with a book of holy songs:

A booke also of songes they haue,
And Venus court they doe it name.
No fylthy mynde a songe can craue,
But therin he may finde the same:
And in suche songes is all their game.
Wherof ryght dyuers bookes be made,
To nuryshe that moste fylthy trade.[53]

Hall in fact creates an extended, revised version of Wyatt's poem. We should see Hall's version as an attempt both to reproduce and annihilate Wyatt's. The lines above signal the anxiety that poems like Wyatt's are proliferating, although his own poem is part of this proliferation. Hall reproduces the metre and rhyme scheme of "My lute awake," but changes nearly everything else:

This pleasant song shall not song be,
To the goddesse of lechery:
Nor to nothyng under the Sunne,
But praysing of the almighty,
My lute and I tyll we haue done.[54]

The renunciation of Wyatt's poem is thus reappropriated in Hall's, even while Hall's version reminds us of the other, more pleasant song. The past participle "song," appearing in all the printed versions but variously in manuscript versions, shows the paradox involved in simultaneous reproduction and denial: the "song" is no song at all, unless it is sung anew, with a difference. In Hall's version, the pleasant song is thereby repealed, marked to be of no effect, and even denied existence as a song. The new version is meant to extirpate the errors of the previous ones, and it both repeals and renews them.

Thus, as with other judges of Tottel, Hall would probably consider Tottel a disseminator of error, but for a different reason: Tottel is replicating the licentious poems in *The Court of Venus*. Hall is extremely careful in his own editorial changes: he edits away Tottel's errors line by line. But in doing so, he inevitably calls attention to the original, faulty version. If modern readers and critical editors would not consider Hall's poem a variant version of Wyatt's, nevertheless its relationship as a copy is clear. Hall might even consider it a "fair copy," if by that term we understand an improved version, from which error has been extirpated. Hall's process is therefore very much in the same spirit as the legal changes we have seen in *A colleccion*. These also seek to mitigate fault by repealing erroneous statements. They also reproduce those original erroneous texts and in the process, correct them according to their new standards. But Hall does not simply deny the force of lecherous verse; he also returns us to a moment in the distant past, just as *A colleccion* often returns us to the past when laws are repealed. Rather than the lecherous songs of Wyatt, Surrey, Petrarch, and all the others in *Songes and Sonettes* and *The Court of Venus*, Hall gives us "Dauid the Kyng," who "With harpe and lute geue God praysing."[55] David, of course, is the exemplar of penance and renunciation, who eventually sang the right songs and renounced those which Hall claims are proliferating today, and are lecherous perversions of his example. When Hall marks the songs of *The Court of Venus* as being repealed and of no effect, he also reinstates the penitential songs of David, the original lyrics, as those that should be sung and reproduced hereafter.

One common thread in all the above examples is the presence of the impulse to reduce, label, and then dispense with an individual item, or even an entire collection. We see this process in its simplest form in the rejection of the definition of treason that begins "yf the kyng dyd mary a woman ..." The statute is reduced to a paragraph in Rastell's *A colleccion* in order for its formal rejection to be recorded and codified. We also see the same process occurring to Wyatt himself, when he is reduced first to an icon and a strangely un-memorializing elegy by Surrey, then even further to the single letter "*VV.*" Surrey and the other poets receive the same treatment within *Songes and Sonettes* when they collectively become "The Lover" even in the titles of their most famously personal poems. Here, Hall essentially reduces the whole *Court of Venus* to a single judgment (lechery). This reduction serves him well, for it allows him to create his own, new version of that collection, and its individual items.

The modern judgment of *Songes and Sonettes* harshly assigns it a double status: it is among the most important of books for the study of English lyric poetry, but its individual versions of poems are not to be trusted. In fact, this unreliability is precisely its value in reflecting the state of poetry and reproduction in mid-Tudor England. This collection glaringly presents to us the multiplicities that are newly inherent to collections of printed poetry. From its dual titles, to its multiple stances on authors, to its multiple versions of poems both within and without the book, to its several distinct printed versions, Tottel's collection continuously exhibits the paradox of collecting and preserving occasional, ephemeral poetry. *Tottel's Miscellany* does not just preserve or reproduce Wyatt and Surrey; it preserves *and* effaces them. It presents the speaking voice of the author, and it collapses this voice among throngs of others. It changes poems, and it is itself changed by others. There is no way out of these contradictions; indeed, the poems themselves encourage us to consider them. What happens when authors recognize this condition of reproducibility – multiplicity – and begin to exploit its potential? This is the subject of the next chapter.

2

"Nedelesse Singularitie": George Gascoigne's Strategies for Preserving Lyric Delight

Tottel's *Songes and Sonettes* exemplifies a central tension of textual reproduction: copying a text often both preserves and effaces the earlier version. In the previous chapter, I have shown how lyric poets are deeply invested in the opposing impulses of currency and preservation. Poems like "My Lute Awake" renounce the present even as they imaginatively occupy past, present, and future. But the medium, Tottel's mid-century printed miscellany, also deepens and complicates these temporal disjunctions. Tottel's Lover is forever experiencing the present passions of lyric expostulation, even as Tottel's book professes to preserve the works of poets who have passed.

In *Songes and Sonettes*, then, the present-minded actions of printers and compilers like Richard Tottel and William Rastell reside in print alongside anxieties of death or annihilation expressed by poets like Wyatt, Surrey, and John Hall. What I am calling "fair copies" are, in these cases, anything but the stable and enduring monuments printed books are often taken to be. *Songes and Sonettes* reproduces by mutating, updating, rearranging, and proliferating poetry, some of which had already existed in multiple versions in manuscript. George Gascoigne's *A Hundreth Sundrie Flowres* (1573) is a watershed moment in the printing and reproduction of English lyric verse, because this collection, and many of its most famous poems, demonstrate an increased awareness on the part of printers and poets that the poetic creative process is changing.[1] Gascoigne's collection is endlessly playful and contains personae who seem aware of both the pitfalls and the advantages of textual reproduction. Gascoigne builds on *Songes and Sonettes* by crafting poetry that seems multiply authored, diversely sourced, and reproduced from the outset. At issue in *A Hundreth Sundrie Flowres*, then, are the proliferation and multiplicity inherent to human intercourse, whether social, sexual, or textual.[2]

Gascoigne's collection is also among the most miscellaneous of early miscellanies printed in England. It contains two dramatic texts, a prose romance that is arguably England's first novel,[3] and more than seventy pages of poetry ranging from short lyrics to poems of more than three hundred lines. Judging from the attributions in the title page, front matter, and throughout the volume, the collection has almost as many authors as genres: the first play, *Supposes*, was "written in the Italian tongue by Ariosto and Englished by George Gascoygne," *Jocasta* was "written in Greke by *Euripides*, translated and digested into Acte by George Gascoygne, and Francis Kinwelmershe," *The Adventures of Master F.J.* is credited to a man by those initials but also contains text written by a "G.T.," while the poems, or "Devises of Sundrie Gentlemen," are either anonymous or credited to Gascoigne.[4] *Songes and Sonettes* undoubtedly significantly influenced the miscellaneous form of *A Hundreth Sundrie Flowres*. As we have seen in chapter 1, this collection was in fact multiply authored, with poetry by the Earl of Surrey (the only author mentioned on the title page), Sir Thomas Wyatt, Nicholas Grimald, and other poets. But other than the authors whom Gascoigne translates, the multiple authorship of *A Hundreth Sundrie Flowres* is a façade. Despite paratextual material that cites a range of agents, Gascoigne seems to be its sole author.[5]

This solipsism is vexing, both to critics and, it seems, to Gascoigne. His multiple personae, the extreme miscellaneity of the collection, and its two very different early editions (1573 and 1575) imply multiplicity rather than singularity, and have provoked diverse critical responses. For example, critical editors address the multiple states of the text in order to establish how it was printed originally, and how it can be edited and reproduced today. For G.W. Pigman, *The Posies of George Gascoigne* (1575), with its classification of each item in the miscellany as either a "flower," "weed," or "herb," and other substantive changes, should be considered a different work, rather than a reprint or different version of the 1573 *HSF*.[6] Cyndia Clegg examines the apparent censorship of the 1573 edition, the documented censorship of the 1575 edition, and the changes between the two.[7] Other critics examine Gascoigne's posture of penitence with regard to the revised edition, or note the multiple motivations of the characters in the prose tale *The Adventures of Master F.J.*, or call attention to Gascoigne as an author who inhabits the persona of "G.T." in order to critique his own poems.[8] These critical efforts signal a robust poetic principle in Gascoigne's work, in which he eschews what he calls "nedelesse singularitie," in favour of multiple representations of similar events, poems, and characters.

Why does Gascoigne eschew singularity in favour of multiplicity? Especially with regard to his lyric poetry, we should pursue this question by attending to Gascoigne's strange textual situation. He is a self-anthologist. Perhaps for the first time in English letters, Gascoigne can not only imagine the proliferation of copies of his work, but actively facilitate it. Anthologizing poetry is the tricky business of rendering evanescent delight permanent, or at least purporting to do so. Anthologies, literally "flower collections," are founded either on the idea that poetic flowers can be preserved, or on the knowledge that like flowers, poems are apt to wither and die. It is no accident that Gascoigne's collections are named *A Hundreth Sundrie Flowres* and *The Posies of George Gascoigne.*[9] The inherent paradox in these titles is that the delights of poetry, which are inherently ephemeral and evanescent, can be instantiated into a more permanent form, such as the collected book. The social and biographical answer to the question of why Gascoigne creates so many authorial personae in the 1573 *HSF* may be that anonymity and semi-anonymity were powerful textual strategies for negotiating the stigma of print, and especially printed non-sacred poetry.[10] But Gascoigne's career shows not a shadowy anonymous author, but repeated, careful attempts to create an authorial self-image of both military and poetic service to the queen. As participant in the festivities at Kenilworth, and as humble supplicant to the queen's patronage, presenting her with a fair copy of his writings, with the motto "Tam Marti quam Mercurio," Gascoigne would have needed to show both deference and forwardness.[11] If so, then the allegations of either slander or lewdness which may have attended *HSF* and *The Posies* would obviously have worked against Gascoigne's career, and he may have been shrewd to diffuse the authorship of his first collection into many seeming agents.

Linking Gascoigne's career trajectory to his literary output, Richard Helgerson, Richard McCoy, and Wendy Wall have commented on the theme of disillusionment and reversed fortune in Gascoigne's work. While Helgerson numbers Gascoigne among his "Elizabethan prodigals," McCoy argues that Gascoigne's literary output changed to a plainer style that adjusted the courtly ambiguities of *HSF* in a bid for patronage and stability.[12] Gascoigne's "creative autonomy diminished as his proximity to power increased" according to McCoy, and his later writings reflect a self-conscious turn to "works which were either grimly moralistic or insipidly occasional."[13] Certainly Gascoigne's later works, such as *The droomme of Doomes day* or *The Steele Glas* (1576), seem to reinforce this judgment. But the most frequently cited evidence for Gascoigne's savvy consciousness of this transition is the phrase "poëmata castrata," invoked by Gascoigne to describe the supposed vast changes he wrought upon the second edition. Gascoigne explicitly links both delight and preservation with these changes, even as he invokes the violent terms of castration:

> But I delight to thinke that the reuerend father Theodore Beza, vvhose life is vvorthily become a lanterne to the vvhole vvorlde, did not yet disdaine too suffer the continued publication of such Poemes as he vvrote in youth. And as he termed them at last *Poëmata castrata,* So shal your reuerend iudgements beholde in this seconde edition, my Poemes gelded from all filthie phrases, corrected in all erronious places, and beautified vvith addition of many moral examples. (*Posies*, sig. ¶iiiir)

Both McCoy and Alan Stewart have argued persuasively that in using this phrase, Gascoigne is referring to Théodore Beza's substantial changes to his own *Poemata*. Gascoigne, however, playfully signals his awareness that he is not, in fact, changing the poetry in *A Hundreth Sundrie Flowres* much at all – certainly not gelding or castrating it.[14] For McCoy, this ironic phrase nevertheless presages a significant development in Gascoigne's artistic output: poor poetry from thenceforward. Stewart argues instead that when they move from manuscript to print, Gascoigne's works have already been gelded. For Stewart, all Gascoigne's assertions, ironic or not, that he has gelded his own poetry (by getting rid of objectionable phrases) overlook the fact that the process of print is much more destructive to his autonomy than he allows. For Wall, Gascoigne's textual transformations from *HSF* to *The Posies* comprise a consolidation of his authority, since Gascoigne forgoes the trappings of anonymity and multiple authors in favour of a single, stable authorizing figure to whom the text can be attributed. She also argues that in *The Adventures of Master F.J.* and Gascoigne's account of the 1575 entertainment of Elizabeth at Kenilworth, Gascoigne conflates martial, poetic, and phallic actions as a way of simultaneously expressing his own unrealized ambitions and desires, and enacting an ambivalently submissive and aggressive gesture of self-presentation to the queen.[15] While Wall provides a convincing reading of the gender dynamics of Gascoigne's authorial self-construction, she overstates the force of his textualized renunciations, especially in *The Posies*. Gascoigne's poems, especially when we medium-close read them in their printed contexts, suggest that the delights of amorous and miscellaneous verse cannot be suppressed or denied. Instead, these delights escape suppression and control: they seek, and find, reproduction in multiple copies.

Gascoigne's depictions of failed textual and sexual control, and the conflation of these two capacities, for delight and for reproduction, are key to my inquiry into his poetry. Gascoigne questions and explores, more explicitly than any other Elizabethan poet, the textual, authorial, and interpretive confusions that arise when poems delight, and by delighting ensure their own reproduction. In Richard Dawkins's terms, such delightful textual objects constitute memes which are well-suited to survival, because people want to reproduce them and reconstitute them either in their own brains, or in written form. In Elaine Scarry's terms, the beautiful object inspires care and a desire that contact with it be prolonged. Gascoigne, by referring to the "gelding" of his own poetry, would seem to be signalling a fantasy of total reproductive control over his poetry. However, the opposite sense arises from the poems themselves, and from the fictional situations of *The Adventures of Master F.J.* In these texts, bodily and textual delight are often combined or confused, while the reproduction of those delights occurs beyond the controls and boundaries of established systems, whether manuscript or print. These confusions and combinations of delight and reproduction are what make *HSF* such a groundbreaking and fascinating collection of poetry.

Although Gascoigne's work continually explores the connection between bodily and textual delight, and their preservation, Gascoigne also uses "delight" in its most conventional sense: paired with "profit" as a rhetorical goal. This pairing appears frequently in contemporary title pages and front matter – "thine owne profite and pleasure" (*Songes and Sonettes*), "to stir up thy pleasure and further thy profit" (Barnabe Googe, *Eglogs, Epytaphes, and Sonettes*, 1563), the posthumous *Pithy pleasaunt and profitable workes of maister Skelton, Poete Laureate* (1568), and Thomas Tusser's *A Hundreth Pointes of Good Husbandry* (1570): "What looke ye for more in my booke? / Things nedefull in tyme for to come? / Else misse I of that I do looke / If pleasant thou findest not some." Rooted in Horace's *dulce et utile*, and in Cicero's earlier, tripartite formulation of "ut et *concilientur* animi et *doceantur* et *moveantur*,"[16] the phrase "pleasant and profitable" often simply reassures readers of early modern English miscellanies that the contents of the book are beyond reproach.[17] Both the 1573 and 1575 editions of Gascoigne do make such conventional assurances. The title page of *HSF* promises that its contents will be "bothe pleasaunt and profitable to the well smellyng noses of learned Readers," while the address "To al yong Gentlemen" in the revised 1575 *Posies* qualifies this promise by categorizing the contents into flowers, weeds, and herbs. The flowers are "more pleasant than profitable," the herbs "more profitable than pleasant," and the weeds are "neither pleasant nor yet profitable," and yet still have some "medicinable" qualities (*Posies*, sig. ¶¶iiiir).

Gascoigne thus refers to a solidly established rhetorical tradition on delight in poetry. However, in his own poetry, Gascoigne makes it clear that for him, delight poses more essential questions: does poetry capture the experience of delight? How should the poet portray that experience, and how preserve it? Tellingly, there is never a single answer to such questions. In fact, the concept of singularity itself immediately comes under scrutiny, in the opening passage of the collection, when Gascoigne creates an entire textual prehistory for *The Adventures of Master F.J.*[18] But even before this moment, the full title of *HSF* helps to emphasize Gascoigne's concern with singularity and multiplicity. There, "A Hundreth Sundrie Flowres" have been "bounde vp in one small Poesie," and yield "sundrie sweete sauours of tragical, comical and moral discourse, bothe pleasant and profitable to the well smellyng noses of learned Readers." The term "a hundreth" was conventionally used to signal a large, indeterminate number, but Gascoigne's title calls attention to the conflict between unity and miscellaneity with the phrase "one small Poesie." The collection is a single mass, but it is also a set of individuated items, each perhaps separable from the others.

The term "singularitie" occurs soon after, in one of the most intriguing moments in the miscellany, when we learn of the (fictional) textual transmission of *The Adventures of Master F.J.* and the other "devises of sundrie Gentlemen." In a letter to the reader, the figure H.W. describes how he received the text we are about to read from his friend G.T., calling the text "divers discourses and verses" by various authors:

> And herewithal my said friend charged me, that I should vse them onely for mine owne particuler commoditie, and eftsones safely deliuer the originall copie to him againe, wherein I must confesse my selfe but halfe a marchant, for the copie vnto him I haue safely redeliuered. But the worke (for I thought it worthy to be published) I haue entreated my friend *A.B.* to emprint: as one that thought better to please a number by common commoditie then to feede the humor of any priuate parson by nedelesse singularitie. This I haue aduentured, for thy contentation (learned Reader.) (*HSF*, sig. Air)

Gascoigne here portrays the opposed wishes of two agents: G.T., who has collected and organized texts from a variety of sources and who wants to control their circulation, and H.W., who instead immediately both copies and distributes them.[19] H.W.'s bias is against restricted coterie exchange, as seen in the phrase "particuler commoditie," in contrast to the more public model of "common commoditie." This bias leads H.W. to wrest control over what he then terms "the worke," which he gives the name *A Hundreth Sundrie Flowres.* H.W.'s use of the terms "original" and "work" and "copy" are very nearly the opposite of present-day usage. H.W. uses "copy" in its earlier sense of an original, a pattern or exemplar from which copies, in our later sense, can be made. The "work" here is what we would call a copy; the term calls to mind the labour and activity of making a new copy. The new work is therefore the reproduction, that which H.W. has dispersed among many, rather than that which G.T. would like to restrict, in a singular "originall copie," for the few.

I *F.J.* and the "secrete entre comoning of ioyes"

H.W.'s impulse is to disperse textual pleasure, to "please a number," and this action provides a pattern for other experiences of delight in the collection. That pattern is one in which there is a short-lived, and ultimately futile struggle to reserve for oneself a private, personal moment of delight. Only when that experience is transmitted, or revisited, or even reconceived, is this futility forestalled. While the delights are usually bodily and amorous, the strategies for transmission and reconception are all textual strategies. One such pivotal moment occurs in Gascoigne's tale of *The Adventures of Master F.J.*, on the morning after F.J. and the married Lady Elynor have spent a delightful night of illicit passion together. The narrator has related the entire episode, and proceeds to describe these events as the conditions under which F.J. composes a poem:

> At the last *F.J.* awaked, and apparreling himselfe, walked out also to take the ayre, and being throughly recomforted aswell with remembraunce of his ioyes forepassed, as also with the pleasaunt hermony which the Byrdes made on euery side, and the fragrant smel of the redolent flowers and blossomes which budded on euery braunche: hee did in these delightes compyle these verses following. (*HSF*, sig. Eiir)

F.J.'s method of poetic composition, or "compiling," recasts and reproduces the previous evening's dalliances as a narrative poem, which has as its central conceit the moon's vanishing, and how that vanishing facilitated their sexual encounter. G.T. takes care to tell his readers that F.J. was still experiencing sensual delights when he composed this poem. His Proustian experience of the "remembraunce of his joyes forepassed" is one among other, more immediate pleasures: the "pleasaunt hermony" of birds and the "fragrant smel" of flowers. F.J.'s delights at this moment of composition both surround and infuse him. He sees, hears, and smells delightful natural objects while he is remembering the previous night. He thus compiles and writes from an actual *locus amoenus*, a place that is "in these delightes."

With F.J. in this state of sensory overload, his next few poems all continue to praise Mistress Elynor and relate with much bravura their romantic exploits. "A Frydayes Breakefast," for example, drolly figures another tryst as a breakfast, while a poem beginning "As some men say there is a kind of seed" uses several different cuckold euphemisms to laugh at Mistress Elynor's husband by sharing a secret sonnet behind his back. Here, we can see that the same issues of delight, poetic composition, and the dispersion of texts referred to in the paratextual material also apply to the fictional world of F.J. If any poetry should be tightly controlled, certainly these lyrics should. Gascoigne playfully explores the restriction of manuscript poetry, first by having G.T. comment on the relative worth of each one, sometimes saying that F.J. himself had performed them to small audiences. But against these instances of coterie publication (performance and circulation in private groups), Gascoigne also has G.T. advance an intentionally confusing explanation as to why the majority of F.J.'s most delight-filled poems have not made it into this printed volume:

> Well, thus these two Louers passed many dayes in exceding contentation, & more than speakeable pleasures, in which time *F.J.* did compyle very many verses according to sundrie occasions proffred, whereof I haue not obteyned the most at his handes, and the reason that he denied me the same, was that (as he alleged) they were for the

> most part sauced with a taste of glory, as you know that in such cases a louer being charged with inexpriuable ioyes, and therewith enioyned both by dutie and discretion to kepe the same couert, can by no means deuise a greater consolation, than to commit it into some cyphred wordes and figured speeches in verse, whereby he feeleth his harte halfe (or more than halfe) eased of swelling. For as sighes are some present ease to the pensife mind, euen so we find by experience, that such secrete entre comoning of ioyes doth encrease delight. (*HSF*, sig. Fiiiv)

G.T. continues at some length with his analysis of affect and expression, coming to the same conclusions already apparent here: that the recording of such delights may help to prolong and preserve them, but these records should be kept entirely private. Examining this passage, Elizabeth Heale focuses on the bodily implications of expressing passion: "The dissemination of F.J.'s verses beyond the bed closet threatens to dissipate his inner self, to diminish his real presence through language. The only solution to F.J.'s dilemma, caught between the need for bodily relief and fear of bodily loss, is private writing, verse as a form of autoeroticism."[20] Heale's analysis is acute, but in focusing on the pen / penis wordplay (and the related semen / dissemination pun), she emphasizes expulsion and dissipation over contrasting references here to collection, prolongation of delight, and remembrance in posterity. The passage is also full of words like "reteyne" and "kepe," where those verses that F.J. does not share with G.T. nevertheless can provide a "pleasaunt record" that is like a "hidden treasure" that helps him to "record vnto him selfe in the inward contemplation of his mynde the often remembrance of his late receiued ioyes," and even "ad vnto the mynd a fresh supplie of delight" (*HSF*, sig. Fiiiir). Heale's analysis describes a solitary, jealously guarded version of poetic creation in which pleasure, self-conservation, and artistic output all combine in a single act. But the overarching frame of the miscellany, especially Gascoigne's inclusion of G.T.'s commentary in this scenario, immediately calls into question the supposed privacy and solitude of F.J.'s poetic composition.

G.T. himself emphasizes delight's privacy, even as his actions prolong that delight by means of a more public, textual form. His statement that "secrete entre comoning of ioyes doth encrease delight" accents reproduction ("encrease") as a result of the sharing of delight between two people. Yet the secrecy here accents both the illicit nature of this affair and F.J.'s private reproduction of his own joy into the form of figured, even ciphered, verses. Gascoigne accents the paradoxes of reproducing F.J.'s delights by dramatizing a second conflict: one between F.J.'s attempt to "commit" his own delight to the form of verse, and G.T.'s attempt to distribute F.J.'s poetic delights, making them more common, and less secret. Both agents aim to increase delight, to prolong it and change its form, yet their desires are clearly at odds with one another. The complex layout of *HSF* as a printed book, including several typefaces, helps the reader to visualize the contrast between these varied textual reproductions. At the opening Fiv–Fiir for example (1573 *HSF*; see figure 2.1 below), different typefaces punctuate the actions of the different agents involved in F.J.'s delight. At left, G.T. narrates the delightful occasion that led to the poem titled "a Frydayes Breakefast." The poem then narrates another tryst between F.J. and Lady Elynor. But G.T. also relates to the audience F.J.'s delightful remembrance of this episode, and then presents another poem in which this remembrance spurs more poetic creation on F.J.'s part. Finally, at right, F.J.'s verse includes the experience of being overcome by his lady's beauty: "The wyndowes of myne eyes, are glaz'd with such delight, / As eche new face seemes full of faultes, that blaseth in my sight." Simultaneously, then, we are confronted with no fewer than three versions of F.J.'s delight. In this context, the "entre comoning of ioyes" takes on a new meaning, as the joys themselves begin to interact with each other on the facing page.

However, F.J. must eventually revisit these joys in a much more downcast mood, once his love affair has gone awry. The narrative of *The Adventures of Master F.J.* ends badly for F.J., with the discovery that Elynor's infidelity *with* him has changed into what he perceives as an infidelity *to* him. His last three poems ruefully echo the words that she has most recently spoken to him, and tellingly, they gradually lose their instrumental poetic force. That is, each successive poem fails F.J. more grievously than the last in his immediate, amorous purpose. With the first of the three, he attempts unsuccessfully "to recouer some fauor at her ha*n*ds" (*HSF*, sig. Liiiiv). The second poem quickly escapes his control: "he lost it where his Mistresse found it, and she immediately emparted the same vnto Dame *Pergo*, and Dame *Pergo* vnto others: so that it quickely became common in the house" (*HSF*, sig. Miv).[21] This commonality, we should recognize, is precisely what F.J. was avoiding, and what H.W. was seeking when he reproduced the text of F.J.'s story and poetry. Now the same lesson occurs again: F.J.'s delights will be shared and multiple, despite his attempts to keep them to himself. F.J., unaware of the irony of his situation, becomes embittered that his own joys have been shared with the whole household. With that bitterness, his poetic output changes to complaint, and the third poem reaches no audience at all (in the tale's world).

These last poems force us as readers to reevaluate F.J.'s earlier, manic, delight-filled moments of poetry. F.J. himself reevaluates them, when he finds himself in a state of jealousy, and then in a state of being quite plainly rejected by his former lover. F.J. just as plainly asks for a reprise of his textual-sexual delights, via a letter "thrust ... into her bosome, wherein he had earnestly requested another mooneshyne banquet or frydayes breakfast to recomfort his dulled spirits" (*HSF*, sig. Liiiir). And when she repels this request, it is clear that all that remains of his delight is the textual version. However, by the end of the narrative, it is not at all

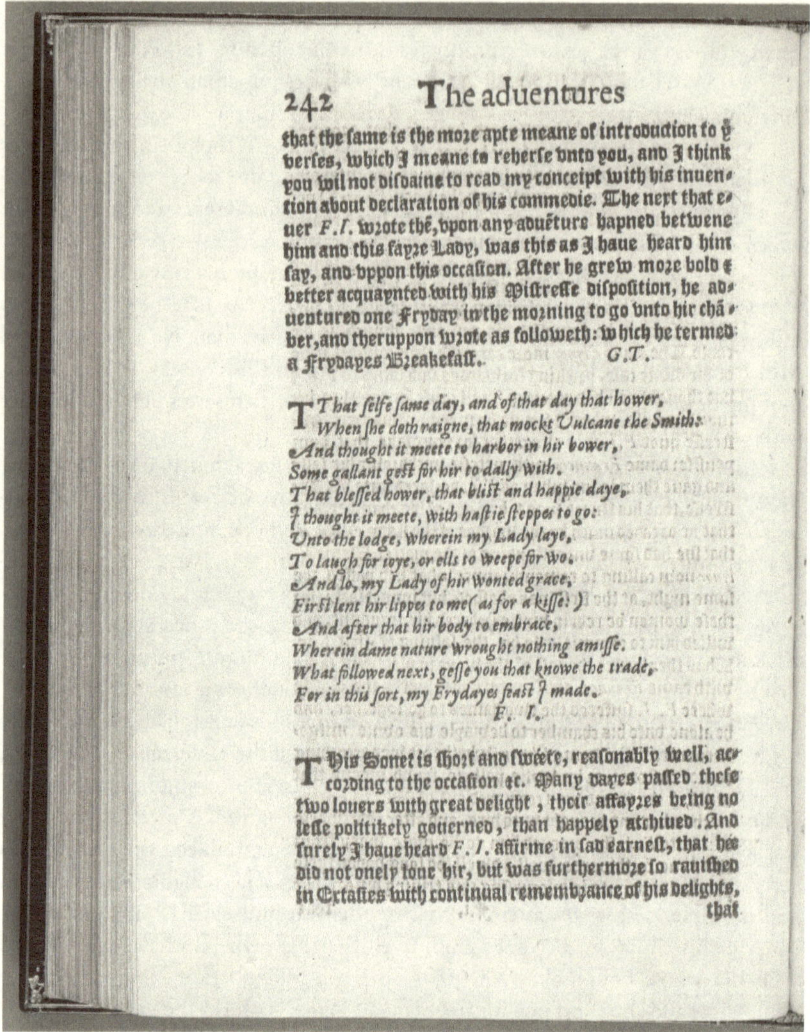

242 The aduentures

that the same is the more apte meane of introduction to ye verses, which I meane to reherse unto you, and I think you wil not disdaine to read my conceipt with his inuention about declaration of his commedie. The next that euer *F.I.* wrote thẽ, upon any aduẽture hapned betwene him and this fayre Lady, was this as I haue heard him say, and uppon this occasion. After he grew more bold & better acquaynted with his Mistresse disposition, he aduentured one Fryday in the morning to go unto hir chãber, and theruppon wrote as followeth: which he termed a Frydayes Breakefast. *G.T.*

That selfe same day, and of that day that hower,
When she doth raigne, that mockt Vulcane the Smith:
And thought it meete to harbor in hir bower,
Some gallant gest for hir to dally with.
That blessed hower, that blist and happie daye,
I thought it meete, with hastie steppes to go:
Unto the lodge, wherein my Lady laye,
To laugh for ioye, or ells to weepe for wo.
And lo, my Lady of hir wonted grace,
First lent hir lippes to me (as for a kisse:)
And after that hir body to embrace,
Wherein dame nature wrought nothing amisse.
What followed next, gesse you that knowe the trade,
For in this sort, my Frydayes feast I made.

F. I.

This Sonet is short and sweete, reasonably well, according to the occasion &c. Many dayes passed these two louers with great delight, their affayres being no lesse politikely gouerned, than happely atchiued. And surely I haue heard *F. I.* affirme in sad earnest, that hee did not onely loue hir, but was furthermore so rauished in Extasies with continual remembrance of his delights, that

Figure 2.1 George Gascoigne, *A Hundreth Sundrie Flowres* (1573), sigs Fiv–Fiir. This item is reproduced by permission of The Huntington Library, San Marino, California

clear that F.J. can return to these textual witnesses of his delight, for he never relives these moments by poring over his poems. Instead, he reconstitutes Lady Elynor's last, challenging words to him ("And if I did so [leave F.J. for another lover] what than?") into an acidic, self-pitying poem (*HSF*, sig. Miir). F.J.'s delights do

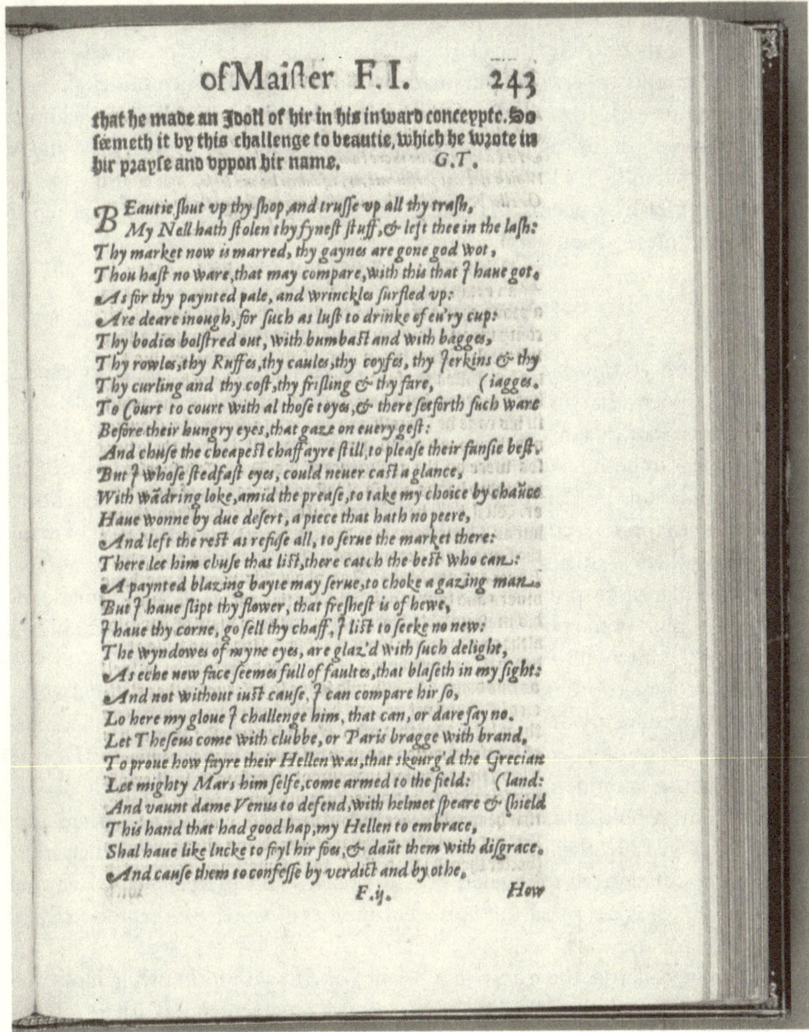

of Maiſter F.I. 243

that he made an Idoll of hir in his inward conceypte. So ſeemeth it by this challenge to beautie, which he wrote in hir prayſe and uppon hir name. G.T.

Beautie ſhut up thy ſhop, and truſſe up all thy traſh,
My Nell hath ſtolen thy fyneſt ſtuff, & left thee in the laſh:
Thy market now is marred, thy gaynes are gone god wot,
Thou haſt no ware, that may compare, with this that I haue got.
As for thy paynted pale, and wrinckles ſurfled up:
Are deare inough, for ſuch as luſt to drinke of eu'ry cup:
Thy bodies bolſtred out, with bumbaſt and with bagges,
Thy rowles, thy Ruffes, thy caules, thy coyfes, thy Jerkins & thy
Thy curling and thy coſt, thy friſling & thy fare, (iagges.
To Court to court with al thoſe toyes, & there ſetforth ſuch ware
Before their hungry eyes, that gaze on euery geſt:
And chuſe the cheapeſt chaffayre ſtill, to pleaſe their fanſie beſt.
But I whoſe ſtedfaſt eyes, could neuer caſt a glance,
With wādring loke, amid the preaſe, to take my choice by chaūce
Haue wonne by due deſert, a piece that hath no peere,
And left the reſt as refuſe all, to ſerue the market there:
There let him chuſe that liſt, there catch the beſt who can:
A paynted blazing bayte may ſerue, to choke a gazing man.
But I haue ſlipt thy flower, that freſheſt is of hewe,
I haue thy corne, go ſell thy chaff, I liſt to ſeeke no new:
The wyndowes of myne eyes, are glaz'd with ſuch delight,
As eche new face ſeemes full of faultes, that blaſeth in my ſight:
And not without iuſt cauſe, I can compare hir ſo,
Lo here my gloue I challenge him, that can, or dare ſay no.
Let Theſeus come with clubbe, or Paris bragge with brand,
To proue how fayre their Hellen was, that skourg'd the Grecian
Let mighty Mars him ſelfe, come armed to the field: (land:
And vaunt dame Venus to defend, with helmet ſpeare & ſhield
This hand that had good hap, my Hellen to embrace,
Shal haue like lucke to foyl hir foes, & daūt them with diſgrace.
And cauſe them to confeſſe by verdict and by othe,

F.ij. How

Figure 2.1 *Continued*

seem to exist multiply, in many private poems, only a few of which have escaped singularity by being reproduced. But here, in the face of F.J.'s obsessive, myopic concentration on the most recent event, we are forced to acknowledge how the delight of these poems survives into the present. Primarily, Gascoigne makes it clear that this delight passes out of F.J.'s experience, and into textual circulation. F.J.'s delights need the meddling of G.T. and H.W. in order to be preserved beyond their brief moment. Gascoigne dramatizes both the evanescence of delight, and its preservation. F.J. feels the loss of control and pleasure implied by "gelding," when he loses both his capacity for delight and his ability to control his texts. At the same time, in G.T.'s storytelling, and especially in his narrative of the textual reproduction of F.J.'s poems, Gascoigne carefully includes the subsequent reproduction and preservation of F.J.'s pleasures as well.

II Gascoigne's Various and Sundry Devises

The Adventures of Master F.J. ends with the conversion of rueful amatory experience into a poem that at last recognizes the passing of F.J.'s evanescent delights. Gascoigne's paratextual material, especially the commentary of G.T., makes it clear that F.J.'s fear of both textual and sexual infidelity is also what saves F.J.'s delights from annihilation. In "The deuises of sundrie Gentlemen," the more straightforwardly miscellaneous section that follows, Gascoigne increases the length of many of the parenthetical titles so that the resultant text is halfway between *Songes and Sonettes*, which often provides brief descriptive titles that purport to mark the original occasion of the poems, and *The Adventures of Master F.J.*, in which poems are absorbed entirely into the larger narrative work. In the "The Deuises" as well as *F.J.*, Gascoigne continues to work on the principle of "nedelesse singularitie," in part by reproducing the events and textual / sexual problems of *F.J.* in a more telegraphic series of poems with little connective narrative. These are Devices 15–20 (Pigman's numbering), which include verses written into a lady's book, her answer, and a whole dinner sequence which chiefly involves lots of meaningful looks exchanged silently among the various characters. As in *F.J.*, short narratives explain the situations to the reader; here, the poems take precedence. When read alongside *F.J.*, it is clear that this episode is meant to evoke, even reproduce, that narrative.

Gascoigne collapses the narrative substance of *F.J.*, with its knowing looks and secret assignations and midnight walks, into just a few sentences. Whereas "contentment" and "contented" are charged and vexed terms in *F.J.*, here the lover uses the word to signal patience, and perhaps even the experience which F.J. lacks. The scenario Gascoigne creates is of a potentially illicit affair, again begun in a banquet situation when meaningful glances and riddling poems are being exchanged. This lady proffers a riddle that seems to slyly refer to the would-be lover, at which

> He held himselfe herwith contented: and afterwardes when they were better acquainted, he chaunced once (groping in hir pocket) to find a letter of hir old louers:

and thinking it wer better to wincke than vtterly to put out his eyes, seemed not too vnderstand this first offence: but soone after finding a le*m*man (the which he thought he saw hir old lemman put there) he deuised therof thus, and deliuered it vnto hir in writing.

I Groped in thy pocket pretty peat,
And found a Lemman which I looked not:
So found I once (which now I must repeat)
Both leaues and letters which I liked not.
Such hap haue I to find and seeke it not,
But since I see no faster meanes to bind, then
I will (henceforth) take lemmans as I find them.

The Dame within very short space did aunswere it thus.

A Lymone (but no Lemmane) Sir you found,
For Lemmans beare their name to broad before:
The which since it hath giuen you such a wound,
That you seeme now offended very sore:
Content your self you shall find (there) no more.
But take your Lemmans henceforth where you lust,
For I will shew my letters where I trust. (*HSF*, sigs Oiiiv–Oiiiir)[22]

This, we should recognize, is *F.J.* redux. There is a gentle reworking of the same problems F.J. encountered: the transitory quality of his pleasure, the discovery that his leman has other lemans of her own, and the mutual accusations that result from such discoveries. In both cases, the male lovers expect a faithfulness that is impossible, given that their relationship was a secret and illicit one to begin with. Here, in this condensed version of the same problems, there is not as much time for the pathos of discovering faithlessness, and experiencing disillusion. Instead, the more light-hearted leman-lemon pun serves as the fulcrum on which the poems of both the lover and the "Dame" turn. She answers his single rhyme royal stanza with one of her own. Within those seven lines, all three of his points are economically answered: the pun, his suspicious searching of her pockets, and the results of that search. The last three lines, in which we see the use of "contented" in its negative sense, demonstrate that the loss of the lover's delight is again accompanied by a loss of control over circulation. But rather than F.J.'s situation, in which his writings were dispersed against his wishes, here "The Dame" exerts control over her writings by taking them out of circulation: "For I will show my letters where I trust." In this version, then, each poetic response recuperates from the bitterness in *F.J.* by looking forward rather than backward. The male lover looks forward to new "lemmans," while the female lover looks forward to a situation in which she can trust her lover not to question the past. Both these responses mitigate, and provide a new perspective on, the bleak picture of delight drawn at the end of *F.J.*

Beyond the running title promising poetry by "sundrie Gentlemen," the titles and connective tissue of this section maintain the fiction of miscellaneity and multiple authorship: "*Now to begin with another man*" (sig. Pir), "*An absent Dame thus complayneth*" (sig. Piiiiv), "*A strange* pa[ss]ion *of another author*" (sig. Qi verso), and many other descriptive titles in the style of *Songes and Sonettes*, in which "a lover" or "the lover" performs his lyric duties – bewailing, pleading, riddling, bidding farewell, and so forth. After a few of these, the text suddenly declares "I will now deliuer vnto you so many more of Master Gascoignes Poems as haue come to my hands" (sig. Siiiiv). Gascoigne's name is then attached to each poem's title, until the last sequence (the poems and story of "Dan Bartholmew of Bath"). Further, the prefatory paragraph stresses the importance of the "posies" attached to each poem, where in this usage "posy" means a motto, riddling phrase, or epigram, such as "Euer or neuer," "*Haud ictus sapio*" ("though struck, I am not wise," or simply "*Sic tuli*" (thus have I borne / thus have I written). A miniature sequence within this section asserts that five gentlemen required Gascoigne to write on five different themes in order to be accepted into their fellowship – a kind of entrance test to a coterie of textual and social companions. In other single poems, he writes epitaphs and praise poems to nobles and potential patrons. Throughout these sections, it seems that Gascoigne is striving to name as many names as possible: Lord Gray of Wilton, the "right honorable Viscount Mountacute" (Montague), captain Bourcher, Bartholmew Withipoll, and many others. *A Hundreth Sundrie Flowres* ends, however, with an unfinished sequence of poems by one "Dan Bartholmew of Bath" (sigs Eeiiv–Ii.iiir).

When taken together with *The Adventures of Master F.J.*, and with "The deuises of sundrie Gentlemen," the section of poetry attributed solely to Gascoigne has a paradoxical, double effect that we have already seen in *Songes and Sonettes*. On the one hand, the prefaces and titles relentlessly refer to ostensible specific events and people in Gascoigne's life, making this section a kind of preservation of the man through his poems and other works. On the other hand, because of the many textual echoes, both in narrative situations and in lyric passions, "Gascoigne" as an authorial presence is subsumed into the larger collection, and his individual works are dissipated into the many poetic personae who are operating in ways very similar to those in poems credited to Gascoigne. That is to say, "Gascoigne" and his passions sound very much like F.J. and his, Dan Bartholmew and his, and the other sundry gentlemen and theirs. Gregory Kneidel has argued persuasively that Gascoigne's multiplicities serve an ambitious rhetorical program: to demonstrate his capacities to fulfil the discursive requirements of any given courtly situation, including, but not limited to, statements of prodigality and reform.[23] The miscellaneity of *HSF* does indeed flourish Gascoigne's writerly versatility to his audience. But Gascoigne does more than hint that all personae are really, at the core, reducible to him. In addition to reducing multiple personae to the single, author-functioning label of "Gascoigne," his best and most evocative poems demonstrate the diffusion of a singular author within the context of a variegated miscellany. In other words, after seeing how Surrey and Wyatt become dissolved into the all-purpose "Lover" of *Songes and Sonettes*, Gascoigne willingly dissolves himself from one into many, and shows that the future of his poetry lies in its further dissolution among the reproducing audience. He shows that in poetic production, fair copies are those that reduplicate beyond the singularity of the author, occasion, and recipient.

Masterminding this tension between singularity and multiplicity, George Gascoigne reveals the depth to which the new conditions of reproducible poetry have affected his poetic production. Gascoigne seems to know that on the one hand, he *does* produce occasional poetry for specific readers; yet on the other, these poems will be bound into a new, reproductive system in which both authorial and readerly parameters will continually change. I turn now to three of Gascoigne's finest and most anthologized lyrics, in order to demonstrate how Gascoigne examines the evanescence and reproduction of delight within single poems. However, the singularity of these poems is ultimately a fantasy, like the singularity of "Gascoigne" himself. We ought to read these lyrics against the grain of traditional close reading, which treats each poem as a hermetically sealed, unified, and singular product. Instead, these lyrics especially should be "medium-close read" alongside others in the miscellany. Not only do they appear in the same miscellaneous printed book, but Gascoigne's depiction of delight is relentlessly self-aware, and each poem's delights resonate and concatenate with those of other poems and other poetic speakerly personae. Likewise, Gascoigne's special brand of delight insists on a constant appraisal and reappraisal of one's own inward state. The three best lyrics to show this pattern are "Gascoignes Lullabie," "Gascoignes passion," and "Gascoignes vvodmanship."

"Gascoignes Lullabie" is a masculinized and uneasy entrance into the lullaby tradition.[24] "And lullabie can I sing to / As womanly as can the best," boasts the speaker in the first stanza (*HSF*, sig. Uir). The bawling child he must quell, we find out in successive stanzas, takes multiple forms: Gascoigne's youth, his "gazing eyes," his "wanton will," and finally his "louing boye" or his "little Robyn," a figure for his penis, his reproductive capacity, and his own offspring. These four aspects of Gascoigne's earlier, delight-filled wanton days are supposedly put to rest by Gascoigne's lullaby; night-time squawking and middle-aged lust are thus conceived to be of a piece.

If any poem in Gascoigne's oeuvre could be said to be a gelded or castrated poem, it is this lullaby. Gascoigne seems to be in the process of systematically reducing himself and renouncing the pleasures of his former days, right down to the pleasure organ itself. Yet the instruments of youthful delight survive, precisely because the poem follows its conceit to a logical, if unexpected, conclusion. Having anatomized himself and attempted to quell each aspect of his earlier days, the final stanza begins with a formulaic recapitulation of the verses that have come before:

Thus Lullabie my youth, myne eyes,
My will, my ware, and all that was,
I can no mo delayes deuise,
But welcome payne, lette pleasure passe. (*HSF*, sigs Uiv–Uiir)

In each previous stanza, the lines that would come next employ "lullabie" in a refrain that forms a repetitive and hypnotic couplet, such as "With Lullabye bee thou content, / With Lullabye thy lustes relent ..." Each of these stanzas furthers the sense that youth is being successfully quelled, rocked to sleep both by repetition and persuasion. One logical end-point to the poem would be here, at sleep. The infant is finally rocked to sleep, just as Gascoigne finally bids farewell to all that his youth entailed. But Gascoigne instead ends the poem not with sleep, but with waking. In the final stanza, the "you" of the poem, which by now entails all the previous aspects of Gascoigne's life, takes over:

With Lullabye nowe take your leaue,
With Lullabye youre dreames deceyue,
And when you rise with waking eye,
Remembre *Gascoignes* Lullabye.
Euer or Neuer (*HSF*, sig. Uiir)

Though the commands from the speaker of the poem continue in these lines, Gascoigne himself has ceased to be the subject. Instead, all the elements of youth and sexuality show themselves capable of surviving beyond the song that was supposed to lull them to sleep. The song may help against bad dreams, but ultimately Gascoigne's youth survives the song – that is, it survives his own attempts to quell it. The bawdy image of a single, "waking eye" combines with the final command to "remembre" this song, ending the poem with a sexualized dawn rather than a gelded, lustless sleep. But it is not Gascoigne, the singular author, who rises at the end of the poem. That would entail an impossible re-dawning of his past youth and his wanton ways. Instead, "when you rise" refers to those youthful, anatomized elements of Gascoigne which the speaker addressed throughout, and which he was trying to quell.

Perhaps these elements will be "remembered" in some other, hapless young lover. Or perhaps Gascoigne's attempts continually to rid himself of these elements nevertheless continually fail, just as infants are bound to wake again and wail again. In any case, the poem effects its own preservation, and thus the preservation of lyric delight: the song itself, Gascoigne's singular lullaby, will replicate – or "remember" – itself in all of these future instances.

Despite the many references to conditions and habits of manuscript circulation in *HSF*, virtually none of his poetry survives in manuscript, and it is not clear whether all the references to writing poems in various social situations to various recipients are false, exaggerated, or if these manuscripts are simply not extant. However, a copy of "Gascoigne's Lullaby" is copied in Folger MS V.a.339, a miscellaneous compilation of verse and prose, the earliest contents of which were probably copied in the 1630s and 1640s. However, "Gascoigne's Lullaby" and many other poems in this collection were written by John Payne Collier c. 1860, and comprise a part of what has been labelled Collier's "Great Forgery" by one critic.[25] Gascoigne's poem, here renamed "The louer his Lullabie," is one of a few which Collier copied from other sources; the rest he appears to have composed himself, and inserted into the blank pages of the miscellany. (See figure 2.2.) Dawson calls Collier's actions forgeries in part because Collier imitates a seventeenth-century mixed secretary and italic hand, and cites the poems (which he himself copied into this miscellany) as the sole exemplars, in his *Extracts from the Registers of the Stationers' Company . . . 1557–1570*, and vol. 2, *1570–1587*.[26]

Charges of forgery notwithstanding, Collier's reproduction of this particular poem is entirely appropriate. It constitutes a "fair copy" of the poem because by creating a mutation, Collier remains faithful, in a way, to the poem's themes and concerns. Especially given Gascoigne's central, playful messages about both its escaping the original time, and the original author of composition, Collier admirably fulfils the poem's central concerns. In the miscellaneous context of the 1573 *HSF*, Gascoigne is already playing with multiple authorship and the escape of the poem as a semi-autonomous, reproduced text. In this manuscript, the poem indeed has escaped Gascoigne's grasp; the last line now reads "Remember this same lullabie," a pointed reminder that the poem both retains its identity and is irrevocably changed through reproduction. It is, and is not, "this same" poem. Collier copies the poem into blank pages that are surrounded by genuinely early modern text – sandwiched between recipes for potted or bottled fireworks and for black ink in this case, but with many other diverse texts. Regardless of Collier's intentions regarding authorship, his copying releases this lullaby back into a textual world that is limited neither by date nor author. As in the poem itself, Gascoigne's lullaby somehow survives by being recopied in a new context. Collier has perhaps even done the poem a favour by attaching the notoriety of the charge of "forgery"

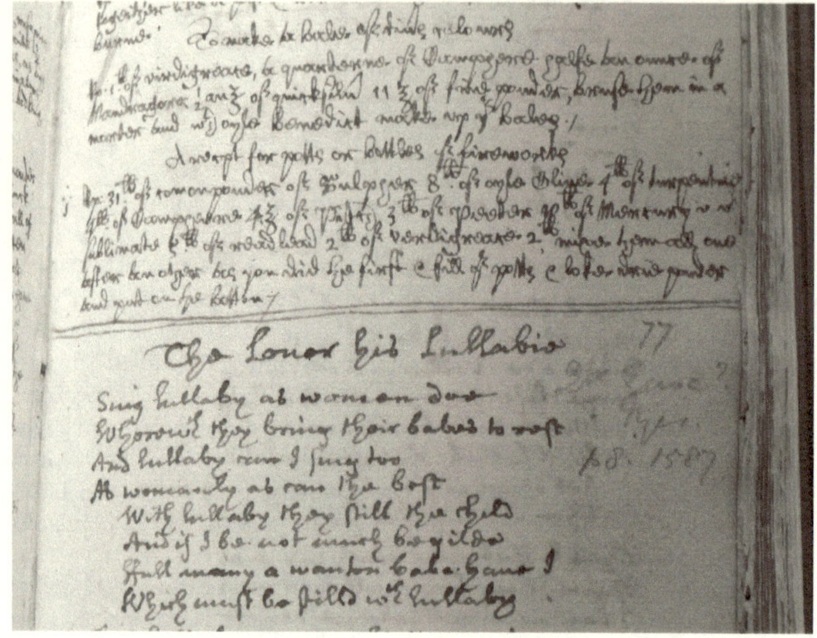
The Louer his Lullabie

Sing lullaby as women doe
Wherewith they bring their babes to rest
And lullaby can I sing too
As womanly as can the best
With lullaby they still the child
And if I be not much beguild
Full many a wanton babe have I
Which must be stilld with lullaby

Figure 2.2 detail from Folger MS V.a. 339 (fol. 176r), including the first stanza of "Gascoignes Lullabie" in John Payne Collier's nineteenth-century hand, and "A recept for potts or bottles of fireworks," and other recipes in a seventeenth-century hand. By permission of the Folger Shakespeare Library

to this poem (and others in the manuscript). The poem is not his, certainly, nor Gascoigne's, but a free-floating and self-spawning lullaby of a nameless lover.

"Gascoignes passion" also addresses the paradox of how poetry can extend, preserve, or reproduce experiences that are fleeting. This time Gascoigne addresses *poiesis* itself, especially the pleasures and pains associated with a specifically Petrarchan mode of expressing passion. At first, Gascoigne seems simply to be taking other, lesser poets to task for parroting Petrarchan conventions in poor, derivative poems. Their pangs are "passing," a fine pun: both surpassingly exaggerated, and fleeting. To these, as expected, Gascoigne contrasts his own true passions. Yet these are expressed in similarly hackneyed terms: he enjoys "No quiet sleepe," he has a "feuer … caught by wanton will," and he experiences the same "heate … And shiuring cold" described by other poets (*HSF*, sig. Tiiiv).[27]

Gascoigne's speaker seems stuck in older modes of poetry, despite his cognizance of the differences between himself and superficial, unthinking Petrarchan imitators. But that is his point here: his poetry cannot escape the same tropes and conceits of those other poets. In the lullaby, we saw that an effort to bid farewell to youth and sexuality was thwarted by the implications of the form in which that farewell was couched. Here, an effort to change the nature of expressions of passion gets thwarted by the inevitable somatic similarity with which all feeling bodies respond. Poetic fevers, burning and freezing, happen to Gascoigne in his passion just as to any other poet, and his attempt at cognizance is subsumed under the strength of these sensations. Gascoigne's own vaunted singularity, which is the subject of the poem and which the title reinforces, dissolves in the very same urgent pangs he had set out to mock. It is as though Gascoigne is simultaneously coming to terms not only with the pleasures and pains of loving, but also with his own inability, as a poet, to do anything but reinforce and reproduce the expression of these pleasures in Petrarchan metaphors. The final lines of the envoy encapsulate this predicament, since Gascoigne can neither escape his own passion, nor convincingly differentiate it from that of other, lesser poets: "And though fond fooles set forth their fitts as fast, / Yet grant with me that *Gascoignes* passion past. / *Euer or neuer*" (*HSF*, sig. Tiiiir). As in the "lullaby," the final tag line expands the poem's timeline, from the momentary to the eternal. This poem, like the lullaby, will continue to survive for "ever." But he also embeds the opposite into the posy, the negative "never." Again we see that in place of singularity, here the supposed singularity of "*Gascoignes* passion," there arises a productive poetics that allows for reproduction and continuation. Within the lines of this poem, that passion itself never passes. Rather, it is ever passing.

"Gascoignes passion," like "Gascoignes Lullabie," refuses the singularity of authorship and of pleasure which its title seems to promise. Both poems insist at first on singularity of feeling and text, only to have this singularity revoked. That singularity is revoked in the process of poetic reproduction, since poems like the lullaby are released into a world of other textual possibilities and contexts. But the structural terms of Gascoigne's *HSF*, its miscellaneity and its playful accretion of authors and commentators, already require us to read its contents as non-singular items: even in the first edition, the poems are already reproductions that have escaped their initial contexts. This is true even in Gascoigne's most famous lyric, "Gascoignes vvodmanship." If any poem can said to be truly singular and attachable to Gascoigne, it is this one, since in the lengthy preceding material, the (singular) occasion of the poem is set out in detail. It involves Lord Grey of Wilton, who has been doing some winter hunting, and has given Gascoigne a crossbow, "calling him one of his vvodme*n*" (*HSF*, sig. Cciv). But Gascoigne's ineptitude at hunting causes Grey to laugh at him, and he composes the poem to "excuse" his actions.

The poet naturally responds to this occasion with a poetic conceit: his shooting awry should not surprise Lord Grey, for Gascoigne has had this little problem for some time: "First if it please your honour to perceiue, / What makes your wodman shoote so ofte amisse, / Beleeue me *L.* the case is nothing strange, / He shootes awrie almost at euery marke …" (*HSF* Cciv–Cciir). The poet then elaborates these "marks" in succession: he has failed at attempts to be a man of law, a courtier, and a soldier. As Gascoigne lists these marks, however, he makes them seem much less desirable targets to attain. The law books studied nowadays allow no room for artful phrasing (25–30), the courtier's clothes bankrupt him with no discernible gain (42–56), and the soldier can only succeed by cheating those under him and greedily despoiling innocent people (73–86). Gascoigne initially changes the poem's specific occasion, his missing Lord Grey's actual marks, into its central conceit. But that central conceit has, by the middle of the poem, been turned on its head. Those who hit their marks "spoile the simple sakeles man," or "pinch the painefull souldiers pay …" (*HSF*, sig. Cciiv). The specific objection turns out to be a more general, robust error. So much for Grey's objections to missing the mark.

But Gascoigne pursues Grey's laughter further. He also needs to address Grey's other objection, the tendency to let deer pass by without even attempting to shoot them. He answers that he is lost in thought – "rapte in contemplation" – at the prospect that many men have hit the marks he has missed, even though they are far less worthy. While he muses, the deer escape without his ever letting an arrow fly. The interaction between poem and occasion complicates this moment. We should recognize that this complication constitutes another, more masterful instance of the principle of "nedelesse singularitie." In this instance, Gascoigne forces his reader to attend to the multiplication that is inherent in the act of imagination, which requires only a word or a phrase to muse upon and reduplicate in a new context. The repeated event of Gascoigne missing actual deer leads him to excuse this tendency by musing poetically on the similar events from his life. But that musing itself now causes another instance of missing. This instance differs in quality: he not only fails to hit, but fails to shoot. Here, as in *F.J.*, "Gascoignes Lullabie," and "Gascoignes passion," poetic composition and subsequent reproduction seem to happen simultaneously. Specifically, this poem as it appears in *HSF* first announces its occasion, which is presented as actual, but past. But then the events of the poem itself, which are presented as imaginary, but current, begin to have influence outside their poetic purview. The figure "in" the poem, the musing Gascoigne, lets pass the real deer that Lord Grey has already laughed at him for missing. The occasional world and the poetic world thus reflect and reduplicate each other: missing leads to musing, musing to missing. This reduplication seems to be another kind of textual reproduction, earlier labelled *encrease*, when G.T. and H.W. circulated, reproduced, and thus effected the continuation of F.J.'s most private, singular delights. Here, a more pensive Gascoigne wonders how to move forward, how to escape this cycle of seeming failure, a failure that he implies affects him singularly.

Given this focus on never-ending poetic increase, the final lines of the poem evoke a strange new poetic situation, this time phrased as a hypothetical:

> But since my Muse can to my Lorde reherse
> What makes me misse, and why I doe not shoote,
> Let me imagine in this woorthlesse verse:
> If right before mee, at my standings foote
> There stoode a Doe, and I shoulde strike hir deade,
> And then shee proue a carrion carkas too,
> What figure might I fynde within my head,
> To scuse the rage whiche rulde me so to doo? (*HSF*, sig. Cciiiv)

Why does Gascoigne's woodmanship never succeed, even when the poem's speaker is himself imagining another occasion, and thus another poem? The imaginary situation is nearly indistinguishable from the accounts of what has happened previously. When faced with yet another hunt, the imagined homunculus within the poem also chooses incorrectly, since the doe turns out to be another "carrion carkas."[28] The ideal situation, Gascoigne finally hitting a mark, defies imagination even in the poem-within-a-poem. By now, an acute reader knows that hitting would be missing, and thus missing is a proper response. Equally important, however, to Gascoigne as the maker of this poem, is how to react to this familiar situation, and to "the rage" that accompanies this act. In answering the question posed above, Gascoigne discards the option of "playne paraphrase," in favour of a more divine intervention: "I saye *Jehoua* did this Doe aduaunce …That by the sodaine of hir ouerthrowe, / I myght endeuour to amende my parte …" (*HSF*, sig. Cciiiv). As the poem ends, the only situation in which the Gascoigne figure does not make a mistake is in the interpretation of his mistakes. On the face of it, Gascoigne's woodman seems to be one of Helgerson's traditional Elizabethan prodigals, repenting of his ways and professing amendment. But as we have seen before, Gascoigne recuperates this self-effacing process in order to accomplish the production and reproduction of delight. Indeed, metaphorical delight and sexual reproduction close the poem, with bawdy references to his inability to "hitte the whytes," with the exhortation "olde babe nowe learne to ſuck" (here, the printed character ſ must be noted), but also with the speaker seeing "the milk hang in hir teate" (*HSF*, sig. Cciiiv). His admission of failure is simultaneously an enactment of textual and sexual success; what comes out of his failures at traditional professions is poetry itself. Mimesis, imagination, and the reduplication of Gascoigne's successful failure are the real actions of the poem.

I dwell on this poem's successful failure because it represents a subdued, though equally forceful example of Gascoigne's lyric method in *HSF.* In contrast to earlier examples, it is neither brash, sexual delight nor clever, conversational delight that the poet seeks to retain, and prolong, but instead the delight of *poiesis* itself. That kind of delight is what he longed after in all his earlier attempts at law and soldiering: if the law had been written "by arte," he could have learned it "with pleasure." Those who do succeed lack this artfulness, and continually demonstrate that they "can nor speake, nor write in pleasant wise." Gascoigne's version of woodmanship, however, prolongs the delight of making poetry by exemplifying those delights within the poem itself. Unlike F.J.'s mischievous editor, or the lullaby song that survives after Gascoigne himself is gone, Gascoigne's poetic delight in "wodmanship" is preserved without seeming to need any outside forces to prolong its existence. Rather, it sustains itself by continually reproducing the paradox in which the only way to succeed is to continue shooting awry, and by continually spawning imaginative acts of *poiesis.*

When we read "Gascoignes vvodmanship" together with his lullaby, the other devises, and the poems in *F.J.*, the overwhelming effect is accretion: individual moments, or occasions, of delight find their way into myriad textual situations. F.J.'s exuberance is quickly tempered by the complexities of textual exchange, expanding his attempts at private *poiesis* into more "common" forms. He and G.T. may think that they want such private delights, but these are shown to be illusory. Likewise, in the "Devises" I have examined, Gascoigne uses the illusory or fleeting qualities of his youthful delights to highlight the crucial importance to him of textual, poetic delights. Repeatedly, and sometimes painfully, he demonstrates that delight, whether it is bodily delight or poetic delight, cannot long be "singular," that any such singularity disappears with its occasion.

Given the concerns that I have outlined above, the second edition of *A Hundreth Sundrie Flowres*, which is renamed *The Posies of George Gascoigne Esquire* (1575), might necessitate a full rereading of the poems above, since they have now been reproduced in a new context. However, as many commentators have noted, the changes to *HSF*, while readily apparent, are far from comprehensive. Instead, they create a thinly veiled claim of reformation and change, whereas much less substantive textual change really exists.[29] To be sure, this collection has a different spirit than *HSF*, primarily because it does away with G.T. and H.W. and F.J. as fictions of textual distribution and reproduction. Instead, Gascoigne as author comes to the fore, and the "sundrie gentleman" of the earlier, miscellaneous fiction are now absent. However, we should not necessarily view *The Posies* as the next step in the imposition of the author-function, the solidification of "George Gascoigne" as the singular agent in the construction of these texts. Quite the opposite: this George Gascoigne is yet another of the multiform authorial characters in both *HSF* and *The Posies* – another instance of how needless singularity really is.

This reading squares with Gascoigne's ironic cognizance that he does not qualify as a typical prodigal, and that his poems are far from *poëmata castrata*. The more recent view of the censorship controversy surrounding *HSF* and *The Posies* is that Gascoigne probably achieved his goal of patronage because of these poetic efforts rather than despite them, since preferment soon followed. He dedicated *The Glasse of Governement* to Sir Owen Hopton, acted the part of a "savage man" in the 1575 entertainment of Elizabeth by Leicester, and presented *The Tale of Hemetes the Heremyte* to Elizabeth at New Year's 1575/6; a flurry of similar efforts followed in 1576 (*The Steele Glas*, *The Droomme of Doomes day*, and others), and he received his desired employment in the same year.[30] By his own admission, these are the poetic efforts of a middle-aged man who has atoned for his youthful missteps, and who would be absorbed into society rather than continuing his rampages. His classification of the poetry in *The Posies* as "flowers," "weeds," and "herbs" comprises a self-consciously retrospective judgment on earlier works. These earlier works, in the fiction of Gascoigne's prodigality, are over. They are useful only if they can warn others about the dangers of amatory poetry and courtly failures.

However, the gardening metaphor belies Gascoigne's fiction of prodigality, one which implies renunciation and textual oblivion. Instead, the very nature of his flowers, weeds, and herbs is that they are forever growing.[31] Gascoigne is thus updating and engaging with the ageless activity of anthologizing, and he does so in a typically playful and deceptive manner. That is to say, his absorption, resignation, and correction come at a cost that he is willing to address, but not willing to pay. Although it seems clear that he did in fact resign amatory verse and the gross ribaldries in *F.J.*, he nevertheless holds out the possibility that his verse will be reproduced by younger men than he. He creates this possibility by appearing to argue against it, in the address "To al yong Gentlemen, and generally to the youth of England" (*Posies*, sigs ¶¶iir–¶¶iiiiv). On the face of it, this address is a perfectly straightforward and conventional monitory address, of one who has erred in his youth and wants others to avoid his mistakes. He calls himself "a man of middle yeares," and wants to "serue as ensample to the youthfull Gentleman of England." But the longer this address wears on, the more apparent it is that he wants his poetic example to live on in them. For he addresses these gentlemen excitedly, not soberly as would fit the occasion: "Gallant Gentlemen, and lustie youthes of this my natiue Countrey," he opens. He addresses them as "my lustie youthes" a bit later, "my lustie Gallants" towards the end, and finally "my yong blouds." This is perhaps what they are to Gascoigne: preceding Jonson, they are potentially the "Sons of George," something akin to his poetic offspring, even if not directly in his bloodline. Likewise, of the poetry itself, he reminds the reader that "my Posies hath beene verie much i[n]quired for by the yonger sort." Most tellingly, he reveals a state of mind very much like F.J.'s, after he has been disillusioned in his love affair, and must settle for contentment rather than delight. That contentment, as we have seen, depends on both the remembrance of joys past, and on the fact of their dispersal to a new audience. Gascoigne realizes that this new reprint might brand him as a man "rather desyrous to continue in the freshe remembraunce of my follyes, than content too cancell them in obliuion by discontinuance" – and yet the work is reprinted, and the lusty young gentlemen are left to pursue these delights, Gascoigne's and yet their own. It is no wonder, then, that in the 1575 *Posies* he refuses to excise or even significantly change his poems, for to do so would prevent these flowers' perennial bloom.

3

Solitude, Poetic Community, and Lyric Recording in Spenser's *Shepheardes Calender* and *Colin Clovts Come home againe*

In Lodowick Bryskett's *A Civil Discourse* (published 1606 though perhaps written much earlier), there is a rare account of the circulation of Spenser's poetry. "Master Spenser" is one of the interlocutors in Bryskett's conversation, and Bryskett appeals to him to speak on the subject at hand, which is moral philosophy, and how one's time ought to be spent to best benefit mankind. "Spenser" at this point demurs, saying that he has "already vndertaken a work te*n*ding to the same effect," and instead wishes to hear Bryskett recite the translation he had already accomplished, of Giraldi's dialogic version of Aristotle's *Ethics*. Following this counter-request, Bryskett narrates the reaction of the rest of the company:

> After some few speeches, whereby they had shewed an extreme longing after his worke of the *Faerie Queene*, whereof some parcels had bin by some of them seene, they all began to presse me to produce my translation mentioned by M. *Spenser*, that it might be perused among them ; or else that I should (as neare as I could) deliuer vnto them the contents of the same, supposing that my memory would not much faile me in a thing so studied, and aduisedly set downe in writing, as a translation must be.[1]

Spenser here participates in a continuing colloquy centred on civic duty, and on the role of poetry in society. Not only are a group of interlocutors and fellow poets and translators requesting Spenser's work, but he also encourages the recitation, in a communal setting, of Bryskett's translation. This Spenser, who creates his poetry within a community of writers concerned with their civic duties, is the focus of this chapter.

As the previous chapters have shown, in mid-sixteenth century England, printers and poets were experimenting with the creation of a new work of art, the printed book of lyric poetry. Not only were lyric poets faced with a potentially wider audience and a larger number of copies of their works, but also with a situation in which the poet's creative cohort was expanded. Wyatt and Surrey and other poets, writing in manuscript coteries and addressing specific audiences, perhaps also considered the role of copying in the circulation of their individual poems. But as George Gascoigne's collection has shown, by the 1570s poets were facing a situation in which printed copying and collaboration with a range of agents including printers and manuscript collectors were inescapable facets of the initial creative process. Gascoigne addresses this situation somewhat playfully, by multiplying himself and declaring the needlessness of singularity; but his characters face a serious situation in which desire, and textual productions, circulate into new contexts, out of their author's control. Tottel in fact epitomizes the passing of this textual and contextual control; his *Songes and Sonettes* evinces a sophisticated attention to the dual task of marking the specific, original occasion and addressee, but also, of introducing "the lover" as a kind of lyric Everyman, and thereby continuing the present life of the poem, even when the author is long gone.

Spenser's deep engagement with conception, marriage, offspring, bastardy, virginity, dynastic succession, and a range of related issues, throughout his poetic career, has been well-documented. Most recently, Elizabeth Spiller and Tom MacFaul both examine how early modern scientific, social, political, and theological imperatives regarding biological reproduction can be traced in *The Faerie Queene*.[2] But Spenser also treats his own role as textual reproducer with great care, throughout his career. Spenser's poetry, especially *The Shepheardes Calender* (1579) and *Colin Clovts Come home againe* (1595) demonstrate a sophisticated response to this new condition of *poiesis*, in which solitary lyric production is impossible, since the lyric collection is created by both the poet and a wider community, who are from the first concerned not only with production, but with lyric reproduction as well. The complexity of the *Calender* as a printed book of poetry has been widely recognized. Its terms are extensively and sometimes mystifyingly glossed by the unknown E.K., who may or may not have been Gabriel Harvey, or Spenser himself, or another unknown person.[3] The book is also filled with woodcut images that comment on the poetry both emblematically and analytically. Even the use of typography appears to achieve a complex statement of English identity among continental precursors and authorities.[4] In other words, medium-close reading is not new to the *Calender*; it has always been read with close attention to its printed medium, because its printed elements demonstrate great care by all agents involved. But less attention has been paid to the ways in which Spenser's fictional and semi-fictional moments of poetic reproduction mimic and elaborate the collaborative production and reproduction of these printed books. All of the printed textual effects in the *Calender* and *Colin Clovts*, achieved by multiple agents, are in the spirit of the fictive situations of these works, where poets continually negotiate their roles in a communal creative process.

Spenser's response to the new poetic situation is complex and multifaceted. He assumes the humbling pseudonyms of "Immerito," "Ignoto," and Colin Clout, even as he announces his laureate ambitions.[5] As Marcy North and others have shown, these pseudonyms work both to insulate Spenser against blame and to announce his poetic abilities to those who would recognize the more learned or private references.[6] References to Chaucer, Theocritus, and Virgil both assume a posture of humility and enact Spenser's entrance into this synchronic community of master poets.

At the same time, the most vivid and perhaps emblematic picture of the poet in *The Shepheardes Calender* is a picture of withdrawal: Colin Clout, breaking his bagpipe and refusing to sing his pastoral poems, the most highly valued in all the community of shepherd-poets. Colin Clout's actions and his creative process are key to a revision of our understanding of Spenserian poetics. Spenser, I will argue, is not only thinking deeply about the role of the poet in his society, but is also weighing the relative merits of complete withdrawal into solitary creative endeavours, versus a more community-based model of poetic production. Retreating from the creative community, emblematized in the breaking of the bagpipe, is an impossible dream, one which pastoral poetry is primed to query and investigate, since it is already based on the country-city divide. In this chapter, I first reformulate Colin Clout's breaking of the bagpipe to be a positive and forward-looking action, rather than a simple and unproductive withdrawal. I then show the repercussions for this reformulation in the *Calender* itself, which models the reproduction or "recording" of poetry by the larger poetic community, rather than simply focusing on the laureate Colin Clout. Finally, I move to a reevaluation of *Colin Clovts Come home againe* as an example of how Spenser's critique of community-driven poetics can work in a positive way, by questioning the place of the poet and of poetry in society, and then depicting an actual solution. Crucially, this solution involves other agents, it involves the reproduction of poetry, and it involves the other half of the volume: *Astrophel*, a set of elegies for Sir Philip Sidney. The dual volume must be repositioned as a major statement by Spenser on the production and reproduction of lyric poetry, rather than as one more version of Spenser's increasingly embittered withdrawal from the English courtly poetic scene of the 1590s. Spenser, at this later point in his career, effects his own absorption into a larger community of re-creating poets.

I Breaking the Bagpipe

Colin Clout's solitude in *The Shepheardes Calender* confronts the reader in *January*, at the end of the collection in *December*, and in episodes throughout the rest of the months. Although the correspondence is complex, Spenser and Colin are intimately connected – by Spenser himself and by the glosses to the *Calender* – to the extent that the cover of *The Spenser Encyclopedia* pictures the image of Colin

Clout, who, having broken his bagpipe, gazes up at the sky in lovelorn angst (figure 3.1).[7] E.K.'s prefatory materials and glosses assert that his is the name "vnder whose person the Authour selfe is shadowed" (sig. ¶iiir).[8] Even before the eclogues proper begin, Spenser's self-conscious echo of Chaucer's "Go little book," and E.K.'s listing of Theocritus, Virgil, Mantuan, Petrarch, Boccaccio, Marot, and Sannazaro establish Colin Clout's identity through his poetic company. What does it mean, then, that he shuns his most immediate company, the rest of the pastoral shepherds who request that he sing for them?

This shunning occurs most explicitly in the *June* eclogue, when Colin's friend Hobbinoll requests a song or two, for the sheer delight of hearing his skilful poetry. Colin's response is intemperate and antisocial: "But pyping lowe in shade of lowly groue, / I play to please my selfe, all be it ill" (sig. F4r). That is, he plays alone, eschewing both the cooperative and the competitive models of pastoral singing in company. These poetic actions comprise what Paul Alpers has called "pastoral convention," in which convening is perhaps the fundamental precursor to acts of pastoral poetry: "Literary herdsmen need each other to hear their complaints and share the sentiments and pleasures that sustain them: singing for someone ... is fundamental to these poems."[9] Colin's full answer to the request for song includes an acknowledgment that he is in a fundamentally discontented state: "I am not, as I wish I were."

Together with the woodcuts showing him breaking his pipes, statements like these by Colin Clout have been taken as a demonstration that he is the quintessential lovelorn poet, scorned by his lady, and thus retreating from society. His solitude has also been read as a grander rejection of the rural piping of Pan, who stands for public poetry, so that Colin is a successful poet when playing for others in the *Calender*, but is a failure when he is alone.[10] In this reading, *April* is especially important, since it shows Colin playing for a larger consort including the queen herself. Colin's discontent has also been taken as a rejection of amateur, trifling poetry, denigrated in the *Calender* and feminized in contemporary discourse on poetry, such as Puttenham's *Arte of English Poesie* and a personalized critique by Gabriel Harvey of Spenser's poetry.[11]

However, neither the episodes involving poetic making and reproduction, nor the woodcuts themselves bear out this reading, in which solitude is fundamentally and simply a negative state. Instead, Spenser and the woodcut artist together explore a more nuanced depiction of poetry, music-making, and the place of the pastoral poet in his society. As Luborsky has shown, the unknown woodcut artist creates a complex relationship between image and text that she argues "could only have been planned by someone who knew the poem well: Spenser, or a person acting for him."[12] This complex relationship has also been posited for the glosses by E.K. and Spenser's poetic text. In other words, actual collaboration (rather than its simulacrum) is a key component of the formal aspects of *The Shepheardes Calender* that make it a distinctive and ground-breaking collection of printed poetry.

For this reason, it is important to revisit the associations of Colin's destructive action, and particularly of the bagpipe. Upon doing so, we find some complications to the seemingly malcontented action of breaking the pipe. First, the bagpipe as a rural instrument of the pastoral shepherd has a more nuanced set of associations that set it apart from other, harmonious musical instruments. Breaking the bagpipe could signal an active engagement in the debate over the poet's relationship to structures of power.

Although parts of the woodcuts are crudely done, the woodcut artist seems to have exercised care with regard to the representation of musical instruments.[13] In *January*, Colin's bagpipe is seen next to a smaller pipe, also broken. This instrument, probably a shawm or folk oboe, belongs with the bagpipe as its customary accompaniment. In *April* we see that the queen's musical consort play the stringed instruments of political harmony and power: principally the lyre and lute,[14] with a base viol, and just visible on the right side, a single flute rounding out the consort. Apart from them, a shepherd figure plays a pipe. His folk instrument thus underscores his position as an outsider with respect to this group, rather than as a full member of the consort.[15] In the woodcut to *October*, a figure who looks like Pan holds a set of pan pipes as though offering them to another shepherd. Though hoofless, he walks out of a classical background and wears the laurel garland of the master poet (see figure 3.1).

These three visual depictions of music-making inform our understanding of how Colin Clout stands apart from structures of power, and apart from his own peers, at the same time that he serves both these worlds with his poetry. S.K. Heninger demonstrates that *The Shepheardes Calender* has strong visual similarities with Jacopo Sannazaro's *Arcadia* as it was printed in Venice in 1571. These similarities involve both typography, the layout of the page, and even Colin's poetry. In the last eclogue of the *Calender*, which also pictures a broken pipe, Colin ruefully declares, "Here will I hang my pype vpon this tree, / Was neuer pype of reede did better sounde" (sig. N3r). Spenser, Heninger claims, is making a direct reference to a woodcut in Sannazaro's collection, which depicts this very action.[16] There, a lone shepherd hangs his set of pan pipes on a tree.

While the reference seems plausible, Sannazaro's instrument, and ultimate meaning of the action, seem to be at odds with Spenser's version. The "sampogna" in Sannazaro's original is pictured as the pipes that the shepherd god Pan invented after chasing the nymph Syrinx in vain. The story is Ovidian, with Virgil and Lucretius also mentioning Pan as a kind of Promethean figure in the technology of song. In Arthur Golding's 1567 translation of the *Metamorphoses*, the transformation is rendered thus:

Figure 3.1 Woodcuts from *The Shepheardes Calender* (1611; first published 1579): January, April, and October, sigs A6r, B6r, and E3r. Images reproduced from the 1611 reprint, courtesy of Anne Lake Prescott

> She piteously to chaunge hir shape the water Nymphes besought:
> And how when Pan betweene his armes, to catch the Nymph had thought,
> In steade of hir he caught the Reedes newe growne upon the brooke,
> And as he sighed, with his breath the Reedes he softly shooke
> Which made a still and mourning noyse, with straungnesse of the which
> And sweetnesse of the feeble sounde the God delighted mich,
> Said: Certesse, Syrinx, for thy sake it is my full intent,
> To make my comfort of these Reedes wherein thou doest lament:
> And how that there of sundrie Reedes with wax together knit,
> He made the Pipe which of hir name the Greekes call Syrinx yet.[17]

The illustrations in the 1571 Venice printing of Sannazaro's *Arcadia* confirm that this is the instrument in question, for we see the familiar image of multiple, bound

Figure 3.1 *Continued*

pipes in at least four different woodcuts. Moreover, chapter 10 of Sannazaro's narrative recounts Pan's story of thwarted love and musical creation in order to trace the genealogy of pastoral poetry from Pan, to Theocritus, to Virgil. That genealogy is transmitted through the pipes themselves, which pass from Pan to his human successors, each of whom in turn plays them anew.[18] This model of poetic transmission comes to Sannazaro directly from his classical pastoral models: in Virgil's eclogues 5 and 7, the pipe passes from one poet to another, effecting the transference of the songs which it has played. For Sannazaro, the pan pipes serve as a metonym for poetic power itself. When Sannazaro's shepherd bids farewell to his *sampogna* in the epilogue, then, he is placing himself into the line of poets whose breath he shares. Tellingly, in all of the woodcuts depicting pan pipes, they are held aloft, either in the moment of being breathed into or in the moment of being hung on a tree, where perhaps the wind will play them until the next ambitious poet comes along.[19]

Figure 3.1 *Continued*

The *October* eclogue of the *Calender* seems calculated to evoke the Virgilian and Sannazaran model of poetic transmission. In the woodcut to *October*, the *sampogna* hangs in the air and seems to beckon the next poet to enter agelessness (see figure 3.1), though the image contains profound ambiguities.[20] This is not, however, the instrument that Colin breaks. Instead, John Florio's 1598 Italian-English dictionary provides another, strikingly different translation of "zampogna." There, it is defined as "an oaten pipe, a shepheards pipe, a bagge-pipe. Also a bell that is hung about a goate or bell-weathers necke."[21] Another word for bagpipe in common usage, "cornamusa," Florio defines as "a bagpipe or hornet." The verb form, "cornamusare," has an added meaning that demonstrates the connotations of this instrument: "to plaie vpon a bagpipe or hornepipe. Also to call aloud to one that will not heare."[22] Twentieth-century Italian dictionaries confirm the close relationship of the zampogna to the Scottish bagpipe or hornpipe, its derivation from the pan pipes, and its many associations with all-purpose annoyance, piercing noise, and both breathing and farting.[23]

Sannazaro thus self-consciously refers his work to the classics, while *The Shepheardes Calender* makes reference both to the classical *syrinx* and the more modern, and rougher, *sampogna*.[24] In this sense, the *Calender* connects itself visually to works such as *The Kalender of Shepeherdes*, a translation of the *Compost et kalendrier des bergiers* (Paris, 1493). This work is partly a handbook for the practicalities of actual shepherds' work: it contains explanations of the signs of the zodiac, directions on what duties shepherds and plowmen should perform in each month, and figures describing the phases of the moon. But it also addresses religious life, with lengthy sections on the "tree of vices" and the tree of virtue. The hellish punishments that result from fostering the one, and the prayers that work to foster the other, combine to make this book a compendium of earthly and heavenly knowledge. English editions of the *Kalender* were published throughout the sixteenth century, including a 1503 English translation printed in Paris, probably by Antoine Verlaine, Richard Pynson's 1506 edition and Wynkyn de Worde's 1508 edition.[25] The 1506 title page, which is reproduced in new editions as late as 1656, depicts an entirely different pastoral prototype: the foolish shepherd with his bagpipe. This shepherd gazes at the stars, one hand on his bagpipe, while a wolf makes off with one of his sheep in the background (figure 3.2).[26]

The alter ego of this foolish shepherd typifies what Patrick Cullen has called the Mantuanesque shepherd, the pastoral model of Christian piety arising from the parable of the Good Shepherd.[27] "Mantuanesque" comes from the immensely popular and influential eclogues of Baptista Spagnuoli Mantuanus, characterized by antipathy towards the greedy city life and by an overarching emphasis on how poetry can teach Christian virtues.[28] The *Kalender*'s title page confronts its audience with the opposite of the good, Christian pastor, but it soon provides a corrective in the figure of the "maister Shepeherde," who appears to deliver an explication of the twelve months to come. He is also pictured holding a bagpipe, but appears to be instructing other shepherds, who lie attentively before him with their own instruments, both sheep-hooks and pipes, set down on the ground. In the *Kalender*, then, the figure of the shepherd with bagpipes can either stand for the Christian teacher, or the fool.[29] In either case, the instrument signals an immediate connection to a larger, dependent community.

Mantuan himself, in his first eclogue, depicts a striking transformation from pan pipes to bagpipe. Entitled "Honorable Love and Its Happy Outcome," the eclogue begins with the shepherd Faustus's love complaints, where he seems very similar to Colin Clout, but it ends with Faustus's happiness at marrying his love, Galla. The first word used for his pipe, "fistula," is the word used by Virgil in his

On shyppart kepāt hys sheyp in the feyldys q wych was not clerk et had no wnderstondyng of wryttys bot oonly be hys naturel wyt et wnderstondyng says how weeyl that leywyng et deyng to the playsyr et wyl of owr lord shoold man lyue naturelly vn to iii flor et xii or mor yf rayson was in so mych of tym ys that man ys to cuun to hys fors/strenght/et fayrnes i so mich they shoold be put to them for to way ald wayk et to to wyn to noght. Bot the term of growyng et cumyng of man in fayrnes/fors/et slegh/ys to xxxvi. ȝearys i so mych yt ys gha nant to hym et to wyn to noght et at lxxii. ȝearys that he shoold lyue by curs of natur. Thoys that deys befor that term ys oftymys be vyolēs: o wt trayge vyn to theyr natur/bot thoys that lyuys mor at lenght ys be good

a ii

Figure 3.2 Woodcut from *The Kalendayr of the Shyppars* (Paris, 1503), sig. aiir; image from H. Oskar Sommer's facsimile edition, 1892. Reproduced by permission of the Morris Raphael Cohen Library, City College, New York

seventh eclogue (literally, a tube or water-pipe). In Mantuan's eclogue, it is hateful ("odiosa"), as all things are hateful to him in his lovelorn state, and he casts it aside. Yet by the end of the eclogue, the Dionysian revelry of Faustus's and Galla's nuptials includes feasting, wine, and the bagpipe:

> After feasting and drinking [Tonius] took up his varicolored bagpipe, and, beginning to puff up his reddening cheeks, opened wide his eyes and when, having raised his eyelids and many times drained the breath from the depths of his lungs, he had filled the bag, the pipe, pressed by his elbow, gave out its sound.[30]

Here, Mantuan's word for the instrument is "ventriculum," literally a "little belly." The imagery is intensely bodily; Mantuan virtually invites us to picture the inflated bladder of the bagpipe and the inflated stomach of the shepherd Tonius, as well as his vigorous elbow-movements as he works the bladder of the instrument.

Given these gross, bodily associations, rejecting the bagpipe may signal Colin's gravity as a poet, which reverses Cuddie's suggestion, in *October*, that the best poetry is written while under the influence: "And when with Wine the braine begins to sweate, / The nombers flowe as fast as spring doth ryse" (sig. Liir). The woodcut artist may well have found this positive rejection of the bagpipe in a perennial favourite of sixteenth-century printers: Sebastian Brant's *Ship of Fools*, first published in Basel in 1494. This book was translated and reprinted almost immediately in England by Pynson and Wynkyn de Worde. Like the *Kalender*, it is a compendium that seeks to warn against vices and demonstrate the path to virtuous living. But it does so half-playfully, by compiling a nearly endless list of the many types of fools in the world, each one described in detail and then packed into an increasingly laden ship of fools.[31] It was published in a 1570 folio edition, which includes eclogues of the translator, Alexander Barclay.

Thus in 1570, we find an elaborate folio edition that reprints works from the early 1500s, including the first collection of English eclogues, published just as a young Edmund Spenser went to Cambridge. Though *The Shepheardes Calender* contains no direct references to Barclay's eclogues, it is quite possible that Spenser saw a copy of this immensely popular book, and even more likely that its extraordinarily popular images provided a visual, iconographic source for the woodcut artist of the *Calender*. [32]

In *The Ship of Fools* there are three representations of the fool with his bagpipes showing this instrument to signify useless action, poor judgment, and a kind of deafness to the harmonies of society and community action. In the first, a fool stands ready to exchange his horse for a bagpipe. As the rest of this section makes clear, we must understand the exchange allegorically: the journey in question is the soul's journey, and the exchange is that of worldly goods and concerns for everlasting life. The fool thus trades his useful item for the useless one, erring grossly in judgment, with the severest of consequences. And the object which the fool actively seeks is the bagpipe.

In two other representations (figure 3.3), the fool's errant judgment includes an additional element: his subjection to authority. The lone fool represents "Impacient fooles that vvill not abide correction." He is shown playing the bagpipe, with the lute and lyre neglected at his feet. The accompanying text connects musical judgment to judgments of virtue, since the fool "in his Bagpipe hath more game and sport, / Then in a Harpe or Lute more sweete of melody," and likewise "though one geue them councell sad and wise, / They it disdayne and vtterly despise" (sig. R4r). Counsel, wisdom, and physically administered correction all combine somehow in the stringed instruments which the fool disdains, so that the community itself – figured as harmony in many strings – is rejected by the oversized, but tone-deaf, ears of the fool:

> Such [fools] haue such pleasure in their mad foolishe pipe,
> That they despise all other melody,
> They leuer would dye fooles, then bide a stripe
> For their correction and speciall remedy:
> And without doubt none other armony,
> To such fooles is halfe so delectable,
> As is their foolish bagpipe and their bable. (sig. R4v)

Here, the instruments' relative placement neatly parallels the fool's inverted, errant judgment. In the *Calender*, the pan pipes and the stringed instruments are centrally placed, while Colin Clout's bagpipe (and his smaller pipes as well) lie broken at the bottom of the scene. The fool's deafness to wisdom and to his community of would-be correctors involves not only actively choosing the "mad foolishe" bagpipes, but also discarding the instruments of concord. Madness and foolishness characterize those who choose the debased sound of the bagpipe, while "armony," the sound of lute and lyre, connotes a special kind of collective interaction between members of the community, which administers a remedy to a wayward member.

There is a more sinister form of correction in the section that treats those who strive against their betters. Usually the woodcuts in *The Ship of Fools* show those fools in the act of erring, with their exploits demonstrating lapses in judgment against which the text warns. But in this instance, we catch a rare glimpse of the fool in the process of receiving brutal correction. That correction comes in the form of flaying: the fool lies bound to a rack, while two figures separate his skin from his bones, and others look on. The key word in the text of this section is "strive," for it is this word that relegates the fool to an inferior place and captures his inability, or unwillingness, to stay within the boundaries of that place. The woodcut depicts the enforcement of these boundaries, since the fool's torturers destroy the most basic, corporeal boundary between him and them: his skin. At their feet is the fool's bagpipe, unbroken but discarded to the same low position as Colin's broken bagpipe in the *January* eclogue of *The Shepheardes Calender*.[33]

Moreover, as the accompanying text explains, Brant connects this scene of flaying specifically with the fate of Marsyas, who was punished for striving musically against Apollo.[34] As in the previous example of correction, the fool's errant behaviour is compounded by an inability to recognize his flaw:

> And for his foly was fleyed being aliue,
> For that he compared to ioyous armony
> His foolishe Bagpipe voyde of all melody,
> Yet kept he still his bagpipe in his hande,
> Not willing his foly to knowe nor vnderstande. (sig. Y5v)

That lack of understanding finds its most potent emblem in the fool's beloved instrument, which simultaneously keeps him from recognizing his own faults, and provides a sign of them to others: "so hangeth on his shoulders his pipe continually, / Whereby men may his lewdnes notify." In action, his fault may be expressed as misprision of his own abilities, improper derision of his betters, prodigal spending, and even miscalculations of his own intellectual ability. But emblematically, all these errors find readiest expression in the rustic bagpipe, itself made of skin, which the striving fool plays in a vain attempt to compete with Apollo and his lyre.[35]

The above network of associations means that we should not interpret Colin's breaking the bagpipe in *January* as a straightforwardly negative action signifying Colin's lovelorn and retreated state. Rather, his rejection of the instrument is an aesthetically astute rejection of the ass-ears and the flaying of the fool figure, and the earthy, unadorned songs of shepherds. This rejection may well be an acknowledgment by Spenser that the purported simplicity or "naturall rudenesse" of speech is actually a fully wrought poetic choice. Breaking the bagpipe also can emblematize Spenser's awareness of the necessity of poetic community, and of not retreating entirely from the highest echelons of courtly power. When Colin Clout refuses to sing in *June*, E.K. reminds the reader of Pan's musical challenge to Apollo, and thus of the superiority of harmonious stringed instruments to the

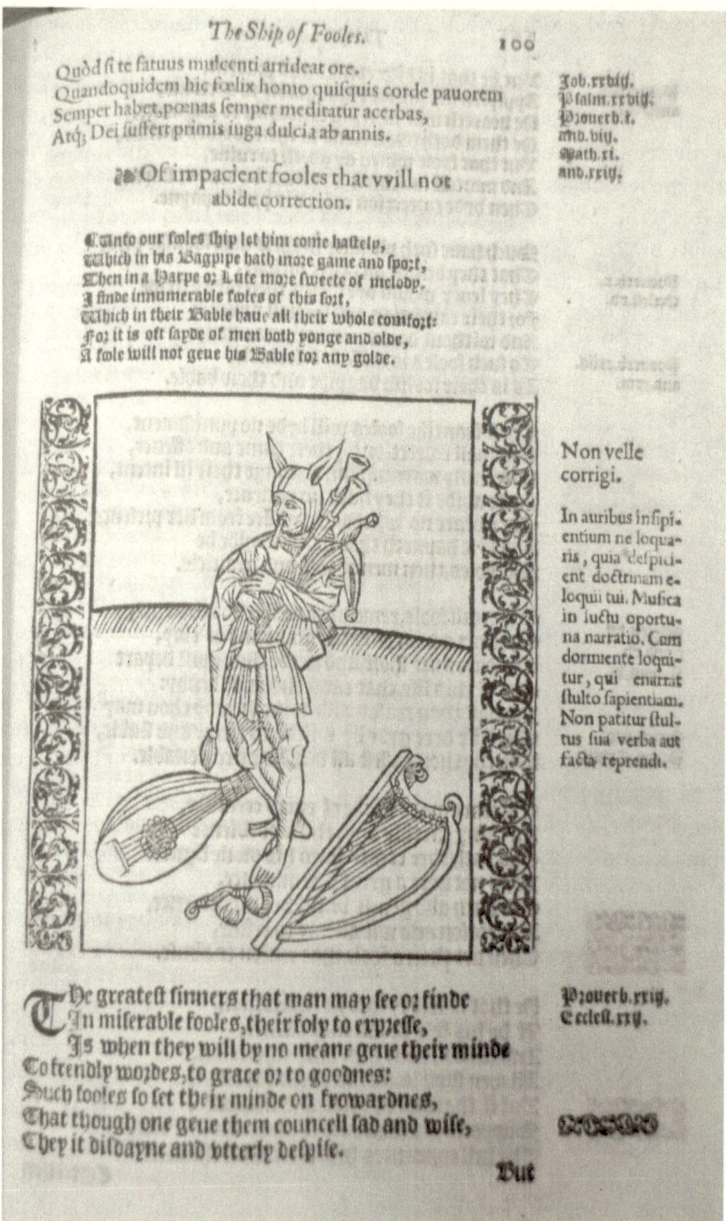

The Ship of Fooles. 100

Quòd si te fatuus mulcenti arrideat ore.
Quandoquidem hic fœlix homo quisquis corde pauorem
Semper habet, pœnas semper meditatur acerbas,
Atq; Dei suffert primis iuga dulcia ab annis.

Iob.xxviii.
Psalm.xxviii.
Prouerb.x.
and.viii.
Math.xi.
and.xxiii.

Of impacient fooles that vvill not abide correction.

Unto our fooles ship let him come hastely,
Which in his Bagpipe hath more game and sport,
Then in a Harpe or Lute more sweete of melody.
I finde innumerable fooles of this sort,
Which in their Bable haue all their whole comfort:
For it is oft sayde of men both yonge and olde,
A foole will not geue his Bable for any golde.

Non velle corrigi.

In auribus insipientium ne loquaris, quia despicient doctrinam eloquii tui. Musica in luctu oportuna narratio. Cum dormiente loquitur, qui enarrat stulto sapientiam. Non patitur stultus sua verba aut facta reprendi.

The greatest sinners that man may see or finde
In miserable fooles, their foly to expresse,
Is when they will by no meane geue their minde
To frendly wordes, to grace or to goodnes:
Such fooles so set their minde on frowardnes,
That though one geue them councell sad and wise,
They it disdayne and vtterly despise.

Prouerb.xxix.
Ecclesi.xxii.

But

Figure 3.3 Sebastian Brant, *Stultifera nauis*, or, *The Ship of Fools* (London 1570), sigs R4r and Y5v. Reproduced with permission of Columbia University in the City of New York

The Ship of Fooles.

Stultitiæ signum præbet vbiq; suæ.

Ouid de tristibus.
Prouerb. xix.

Si quis opes multas locupleti possidet arca,
Thesauros magnos & tenet in cumulo,
Hunc plures vigili cursu sectantur amici,
Semina qui cumulent ad scelus atq; nefas:
Et spoliant stultum iuuenem, vacuumq; relinquunt,
Prodigus his socijs heu bona cuncta terit.

Luke. xv.

Tullius de amicitia.

Ampliùs & vacua dum nil seruauit in arca,
Nec res occulto sensit abire dolo:
Factus inops tandem, cunctis priuatur amicis,
Et refugit fatuum perfida turba procul.
Acclamat superos, & tristia verba profundit,
Pœnituit tandem, at sera querela nimis.

L. his alimentorum. ff. vbi pub. edu. debe.
Prouer. xxviij.

Qui res tam multas vno consumit in anno,
Ad cursum vitæ quæ satis vsq; forent.
Est fatuus, vafris res compartitur, at illi
Plus nummum quærunt quàm vel amicitiam:
Ex quo paupertas, contemptus, risus, egestas
Proueniunt, stultus & sine honore sedet.

Of him that vvill not see his ovvne foolishnes, and that striueth against his stronger.

Non velle stultitiam propriam recognoscere.

Si contuderis stultum in pila quasi prisanas, feriente desuper pilo, non auferetur ab eo stultitia eius. Plus proficit correctio apud prudentem, quàm centum plagæ apud stultum. Expedit magis vrse occurrere raptis fœtibus, quàm fatuo confidenti sibi in stultitia sua.

The

Figure 3.3 *Continued*

reedy blaring of the bagpipe. Colin Clout's rejection of the instrument raises the possibility of embracing harmonious poetic production, though Colin Clout is unable to realize this goal. Pointedly, while Spenser's text in *December* specifies "Here will I hang my pype upon this tree," the woodcut image depicts another broken pipe. Sannazaro's epilogue describes and pictures the same action, with an address to the *sampogna*, in which he warns the instrument against "seeking the lofty palaces of princes," and "the proud piazzas of the populous cities, in order to have the resounding applause, the shadowy favors, or the windy glories, most vain deceits, false allurements, stupid and obvious flatteries of the faithless crowd."[36] For Sannazaro, the pastoral poet can remain in his pastoral retreat.[37] But even the *January* woodcut of Colin Clout introduces a more complicated situation for the poet. Colin is not only stretched vertically between the heavenward glancing of the lovelorn shepherd-poet, but also horizontally: between his humble shepherd's dwelling, and the looming city spires at the far edge of the picture. As we shall see in the next sections, Colin's pastoral solitude and his poetic production and reproduction depend crucially on this tension between country and city, solitude and company, plaintive poetic outpouring and recreative communal singing.

II Spenser's Recreative Solitude

The debate concerning the virtues of the active and contemplative lives, of withdrawing from versus engaging with society, are inescapable in pastoral poetry.[38] Spenser's pastoral is no exception, and historicist critics have focused on his daringly topical references, his bid for the patronage of both the Earl of Leicester and Sir Philip Sidney, and his interests in epideictic poetry at the highest echelon of society (*April*'s praise of Elizabeth) and in contemporary skirmishes between ecclesiastical and sovereign authority (especially in *July*'s covert treatment of the fall of archbishop Grindal).[39] Spenser not only appears to have felt an acute anxiety with regard to the place of poetry in English society and the place of the poet in relation to political authority; he also depicts that anxiety throughout *The Shepheardes Calender*. Pastoral personae, anonymity, and E.K.'s sometimes wilfully obtuse glosses on the identities of the poetic characters all demonstrate Spenser's facility with the terms of secret communications; this skill was of course integral to his career as a secretary, or secret-keeper, to Lord Grey of Wilton.[40]

For Spenser, real retreat from all of society may well have been both an impossible dream, and an irresponsible escape. But the link between creativity and retreat from society is a powerful one, figured not only in Ovid's exile but in Augustine's *Confessions* and Petrarch's *De vita solitaria*, and perhaps most powerfully and relevantly to Spenser, by the life and Arcadian writing of Sidney.[41]

Petrarch's *De vita solitaria* also connects solitude to production, and creation to recreation. For Petrarch, as also for Boccaccio, literary production requires the contemplative life, as opposed to the active life of a lawyer or merchant.[42] Petrarch's poet or philosopher or orator appears to occupy the same places as Colin Clout's rural retreat:

> One may be enabled to put off the burden of his weariness by having easy access to woods and fields and, what is especially grateful to the Muses, to the bank of a murmuring stream, and at the same time sow the seeds of new projects in the field of his genius, and in the very interval of rest and recuperation prepare matter for the labor to come. It is an employment at once profitable and pleasant, an active rest and a restful work, so that when he returns to that narrow and secret chamber favored by Demosthenes, he may eliminate all that is superfluous and give the desired perfection of expression to the germinating thought.[43]

In a lyrical passage laden with pastoral metaphors, Petrarch highlights the solitary act of introspection. Here, solitude involves activities that are personal, emotional, and also literary. Petrarch is writing about himself, but he also mentions Virgil, Plato, and Augustine when claiming that poets and philosophers are drawn by inclination to such natural, solitary places.

Spenser thus inherits a bifurcated intellectual tradition with regard to solitude and literary reproduction. From Petrarch and Boccaccio, Spenser is likely to have got the model of solitary artistic production seen above. But as the colloquy by Spenser's companion Lodowick Bryskett demonstrates, members of the Sidney-Spenser circle were concerned with finding a place for the virtuous poet, gentleman, soldier, and courtier in his larger society. Sidney's writings were especially influential, especially his pastoral the *Arcadia*, which was likely circulating in manuscript as early as late 1577, and it is quite possible Spenser had read parts of *Arcadia* before the *Calender* was printed.[44] Sidney may have actually composed his *Arcadia* in an idyllic retreat, but it is an open question whether this retreat was chosen, or enforced by his too closely engaging the issue of the queen's potential marriage to the Duke of Alençon.[45] Yet the opening the *Arcadia* informs our discussion of Spenser's depictions of solitary poetic production. Sidney's work begins with a famous retreat into the solitude of Arcadia: the duke Basilius flees his realm with his wife and daughter in order to avoid a cryptic prophesy. But two heroes follow them into Arcadia. Early in the action, one of these heroes, Pyrocles, presents to the other, Musidorus, a spontaneous praise of solitude. In the ensuing debate, Pyrocles delights in the flowers, echoes, and music of their idyllic spot. He then confesses that he is in love. What Musidorus wants is a debate, and he has even "framed a reply" in his mind, complete with at least four potential points against solitude. But Pyrocles is too distracted to engage in debate, and the exchange ends in a friendly, humorous manner, with the witty but impossible request for Pyrocles "ever to defend solitariness so long as, to defend it, you ever keep company."[46] Solitude is thus never really an option for these two, closely linked heroes. Sidney's central characters are princes, not shepherds. Though they discuss the nature of solitude, and retreat, they will adventure together throughout the work.

Sidney's and Spenser's views on the solitary and civil lives may also have been informed by a tract called *The Praise of Solitarinesse*, printed in 1577. One of its printers, Henry Bynneman, had printed pastoral and lyric poetry, and is connected to Spenser by virtue of some of his other recent productions: Turberville's translation of Mantuan's eclogues (1567), Spenser's translation of *A Theatre for Worldlings* (1569), and part of *A Hundreth Sundrie Flowres* (1573), among others. *Solitarinesse* is dedicated to Edward Dyer, who by 1580 or so was known to be an intimate of Sidney's; at that time, the two were "the foremost arbiters of taste in courtly poetic wit and artistry."[47]

The author of *Solitarinesse*, Roger Baynes, clearly consulted Petrarch's *De vita solitaria*, since there are passages he borrows directly from Petrarch.[48] But while Petrarch's tract is a personal, essayistic, extended treatise, Baynes takes an entirely different approach. He instead uses a colloquy form; several sides of the question are represented, though the praise of solitude is expressed by a character named Eudoxus, whose name signals that he will probably win the argument. Petrarch's treatise is couched as an extended letter, but his personal defence of a solitary, studious, beauty-driven life makes it clear that for him, both treatises and poetry require quiet waters, wandering paths, and deep groves to be written. Baynes's colloquy presupposes not a spiritual crisis or creative program, but the desire to lead a virtuous life. Eudoxus defends solitariness by creating a virtuous Everyman, the so-called wise-man. The wise-man's qualities are defined not by a single voice, but through the colloquy's conversation between Eudoxus, Lysippus, and Tales, the three interlocutors. This wise-man, according to Eudoxus, lives his life both *for* his commonwealth and apart from it:

> You see therefore, how I admit into this *solitarinesse* of ours, not onely this *wise-man* alone, but also wyth hym hys like addicted friendes, and therwithall besides a general care to benefit the whole world: for no man doubteth, but that those who in their *solitarinesse* are altogether ydle, slouthfull, and full of dumpishnesse, are of all men most miserable. (sigs L2v–L3r)

Eudoxus and Sidney share a vision of solitude which can involve radically reducing one's companions, but that cannot justify either sloth, or completely eschewing all company. Pyrocles's initial retreat to "the open wildernesse" therefore represents a more extreme, perhaps unbalanced attraction to solitude. Sidney immediately defuses this version, with Musidorus's facetiously paradoxical request that Pyrocles always defend solitude by keeping company. For Petrarch, creativity partly demands refuge in complete solitude, since this condition helps to re-create weary spirits and to eliminate everything superfluous to the creative process. Baynes and Sidney invoke solitude, but it is a cooperative and sociable solitude that is perhaps antithetical to the merchant's life, but would still not allow for the melancholy isolation which Petrarch connects to *poiesis*.

Spenser, who would have eagerly taken part in any debate on civic virtue that involved Sidney and Dyer, thus had two models of solitude available to him. Petrarch's artistic model embraces retreat and re-creation; Sidney's and Baynes's model is more cooperative and restricted to like-minded friends. In the *Calender*, Spenser crystallizes the dilemma of solitude in Colin Clout, who oscillates between the extreme, unproductive solitude which Sidney and Baynes cannot admit, and the sociable, poetic life of the pastoral shepherd. Colin actively seeks complete solitude, and refuses to sing in pastoral gatherings, dialogues, and colloquies. When singing solitary complaints, Colin's poetry is filled with the kind of rapture that renders him, in the eyes of his peers, a singular and special poet, one set apart from other poets by both his deep feeling, and his superior artistry. In this way, Colin Clout's solitude is productive. As in Petrarch's version of solitude, it promotes a lyrical frame of mind, an openness to beauty and an ability to allow deep emotion – even grief or rue – to well up in the poet and, eventually, to be sung. But unlike in Petrarch, the same solitude can also be destructive. It denies fellow shepherds the pleasure of his song. In the near term, it thus strikes at the heart of the collaborative pastoral process of singing songs, and thereby reproducing poetry. Spenser's treatment of solitude thus demands that we consider his poetry medium-closely, in the temporal sense. When shepherds re-create each others' songs, the lyric survives beyond its earliest moments. But a song piped only for oneself, alone in a solitary wild place, is lost.

As a printed book, *The Shepheardes Calender* has a complex, multilayered page layout, which reminds us constantly that it is a complex, collaborative product. It simply does not allow for the illusion that it could have been produced in the wild idylls of earlier pastorals. In the 1590s, Spenser almost certainly attended to the production of his poetry in the printing house.[49] At least one critic argues the same for the *Calender*.[50] Even if Spenser did not collaborate directly with Singleton, the *Calender* is polyvocal from the start, with glossing, illustrating, and typographical statements all occurring simultaneously with the supposedly solitary work of the poet. Spenser dramatizes this new poetic condition through

Colin Clout, whose poetry is highly valued, but whose isolation stands in the way of its being reproduced.

From the beginning, not only social textual production, but a kind of textual reproduction is a concern of this book, since E.K. categorizes the eclogues of the *Calender* into three kinds: plaintive, recreative, and moral. Of the three, the label "recreative" seems most in need of definition. The *OED* gives an example by John Skelton as the first instance of "recreative" being used in the sense of refreshing, reinvigorating, or diverting; the first instance in the sense of "creating anew" does not occur until the late eighteenth century.[51] But critics do apply this later sense of recreation to the *Calender*, with Spenser's linguistic play being an activity unto itself, or with recreative language being celebratory and harmonious, the opposite of the plaintive mode.[52] For Spenser, however, there can be no simply leisurely and cloistered poetic production; Colin Clout is also awash in the negative aspects of solitude: isolation and reclusive refusal to engage others. This problem is never fully resolved in the *Calender*, though it is somewhat mitigated by the connection between "recreative" poetry and "recording" poetry.[53] The poet's absence, his community, and the reproduction of the poem are all tightly linked for Spenser.

The clearest example of recreative recording in the *Calender* occurs when *April*'s praise of Elizabeth is presented by Hobbinoll rather than by Colin Clout, its creator. In that eclogue, the shepherds Thenot and Hobbinoll meet each other and discuss Colin's lovelorn status, eventually singing a song of Colin's. Thenot makes the request: "But if hys ditties bene so trimly dight, / I pray thee *Hobbinoll*, recorde some one: / The whiles our flockes doe graze about in sight, / And we close shrowded in this shade alone" (sig. C4r). Thenot gives no particularly compelling reason for this instance of recording Colin's poetry, other than that they are together and that their flocks need no immediate attention. The act of recording places poetry firmly in their leisurely, recreative present: they are re-chording, or singing anew, Colin's poetry. This mode of poetic reproduction occurs in Theocritus, Virgil, and other pastorals; shepherds are constantly asking for a song to be sung, or obliging the request. As Louis Montrose puts it, when Colin's song is recorded in *April*, "The poem lives in the memory of those who have heard and admired it; it is now a public trust, a document of cultural history."[54] In Virgil's eclogues, and in Sannazaro's, the process occurs without fanfare, simply by passing the song, and the shepherd's pipe, from one singer to another. But here, Colin's refusal to sing coincides with his retreat into a solipsistic pleasure-world, in which he moans the pangs of disprized love. Perhaps paradoxically, Colin's withdrawal from the community of poets effects the beginning of the process of creating what Montrose calls "cultural history." His refusal prompts their response of making copies of his poetry, and singing it among themselves.

In this first edition of Spenser's pastoral poetry, then, *poiesis* is achieved through poetic reproduction.

As we have seen in *June*, a "plaintive" eclogue, Colin's retreat to solitude is made explicit when Hobbinoll hints at his desire to hear one of Colin's songs, as part of the completely delightful season:

Colin, to heare thy rymes and roundelayes,
Which thou were wont on wastfull hylls to singe,
I more delight, then larke in Sommer dayes:
Whose Echo made the neyghbour groues to ring,
And taught the byrds, which in the lower spring
Did shroude in shady leaues from sonny rayes,
Frame to thy songe their chereful cheriping,
Or hold theyr peace, for shame of thy swete layes. (sig. F3v)

Perhaps Colin's breaking of his pipe is appropriate in January, and again in December, seasons of wintry pain. But here Colin is unseasonably sombre, and cites multiple reasons for his malcontented state, including the intrusions of a shepherd named Menalcas on his love relationship with Rosalind, her spurning of his verses, and the glancing reference to the Pan and Phoebus story, another moment of failed rustic poetry. But Colin first refers to a greater loss, as his initial reply to Hobbinoll's good humour shows: "O happy *Hobbinoll*, I blesse thy state, / That Paradise hast found whych *Adam* lost" (sig. F3r). The impossibility that Hobbinoll has actually regained paradise points us to pastoral's troubled relationship to Eden. Colin Clout seems to be sarcastically implying that Hobbinoll is lost in a dream-world, even though Sidney claims that only poetry has this productive, imaginative capacity for regaining the golden age.[55] Hobbinoll knows intuitively that to recall, record, and recreate the golden world is the collective and cooperative task of poets. But this task Colin refuses. *June* provides no real answer to the dilemma, and E.K. provides no help with his gloss explaining the word "Paradise." (He thinks it is most likely to be found somewhere in Mesopotamia, perhaps between the Tigris and Euphrates.) Colin's paradise is irrevocably lost and his poetry, unlike Sidney's, is here insufficient to re-create it.

June troubles the relationship between solitude and poetic production, but *August* makes the divide explicit. This is the only month in which two separate lyric poems are performed, and the poems are sharply divided into pleasant companionship and plaintive solitude. Examples of re-creation and recording abound in this month, beginning with its dramatic situation. In *June*, Hobbinoll tries to get Colin Clout to perform his poetry, in order both to clear his heart of love-pangs and to gratify Hobbinoll's own desire to hear the poetry. In *August*, Willye suggests virtually the same remedy for the lovelorn shepherd Perigot, only here the invitation is not for a recitation. Instead, it is for a competition: "But and if in rymes with me thou dare striue, / Such fond fantsies shall soone be put to flight" (sig. H3v). The poetry proposed is dialogic in nature, and its apparent competitive bias (the shepherds expect prizes for being the best maker) belies its essentially co-operative and collaborative nature. E.K. faithfully notes that this poetic recreation is itself a re-creation of Theocritus's and Virgil's contests; both poets, E.K. glosses, "feign pledges of their strife." Any given moment in the roundelay they sing demonstrates that the more ominous mythological references are deflated, the pangs of love are transformed into laughter, and the competition of the poets is converted into a productive, cooperative project:

Per. As the bonilasse passed bye,
Wil. hey ho bonilasse,
Per. She roude at me with glauncing eye,
Wil. as cleare as the christall glasse:
Per. All as the Sunnye beame so bright,
Wil. hey ho the Sunne beame,
Per. Glaunceth from *Phoebus* face forthright,
Wil. so loue into thy hart did streame:
Per. Or as the thonder cleaues the cloudes,
Wil. hey ho the Thonder,
Per. Wherein the lightsome leuin shroudes,
Wil. so cleaues thy soule a sonder:
Per. Or as Dame *Cynthias* siluer raye
Wil. hey ho the Moonelight,
Per. Vpon the glyttering waue doth playe:
Wil. such play is a pitteous plight. (sig. H4v)

This exchange defuses the potentially destructive romantic situation in which Perigot is embroiled. The extended simile may at first call to mind a harsher, sharp-beamed Phoebus, like that which *The Ship of Fools* uses to scare its readers straight. But the flaying knife of Apollo, through this cooperative song, is transformed into a sun-beamed love that "into thy heart did streame." When punctuated by Willye's "hey ho," Perigot's lovelorn state is transformed as well into something very similar to laughter. Unsurprisingly, no harsh judgment comes out of this competition: Cuddie deems that "ech haue gayned," and so they extend their poetic exchange into a material one.[56] Line is exchanged with line, and lamb is exchanged with mazer. Willye's social, cooperative remedy, then, works perfectly in Perigot's case.

Counter to this cooperative competitive poetic recreation is the song of Colin Clout, rehearsed by the shepherd Cuddie, who has just judged Willye's and Perigot's roundelay. His poem seems to oppose theirs in both mood and intricacy. It is a sestina, lamenting lost love, and it piles dole upon grief so relentlessly that it at first seems to threaten the mood which Perigot and Willye have just created. Fully four of the six repeated end-words accent Colin's excessive grieving: "woe," "resound," "cryes," and "augment." Yet the end-words also illustrate the tension between solipsism and community that is central to Colin Clout as a poetic character. "Sound" alternates with "resound," "part" with "apart;" the word "augment" as well shows that Colin is constantly faced with augmentation, with echoes, with re-sounding, and with the tension between being "apart" from everything and yet being "A part" of a larger whole.

The poem thus points to the extreme edge of solitude, the wish for annihilation – not only to be apart from the world, but to disappear completely. In breaking his pipe and refusing to sing, Colin Clout expresses the desire to be sequestered from society, no longer sociably to sing. Colin's self-annihilation is disguised as that of an ordinary, hyperbolic lover: "Here will I dwell apart / In gastfull groue therefore, till my last sleepe / Doe close mine eyes ..." Colin's conventional lover's death-wish is directly contradicted by its medium, however, and medium-close reading helps to reveal Spenser's emphasis on lyrical reproduction. Thematically and formally, the sestina is itself based on augmentation: it requires repetition, re-sounding, and the reconfiguration of its end-words. So Spenser's choice of "augment" and "resound" as end-words forces the reader to confront dual possibilities – either the speaker and his song waste away in solitude, or they are echoed, re-sounded, augmented, and re-created.[57]

In the context of *The Shepheardes Calender*, however, the entire sestina is already juxtaposed with a more cooperative and joyful sublimation of the same feelings of amatory destitution. When *August* is examined at all, it is usually taken to be the extreme expression of Colin Clout's extreme remoteness from his poetic community.[58] Colin's complaints, when coupled with the sing-song quality of the roundelay, change significantly in their overall meaning. Lines such as "Helpe me, ye banefull byrds whose shrieking sound / Ys signe of dreery death, my deadly cryes / Most ruthfully to tune" (sigs I1v–I2r), on their own, might seem overdone. But the song in its present form is being recorded – that is to say re-created – by Cuddie. Colin's extreme unsociability, juxtaposed with the roundelay of Perigot and Willye, becomes a coparticipant in the sublimation of love's pangs. His song echoes out of the dreary landscape and into a social present that is much more hopeful. Colin's desperate seriousness has been transformed into something else entirely.[59]

Spenser, if not Colin Clout, seems to be cognizant of Colin's predicament as a poet seeking solitude but depending upon the re-creation of his verse by others. Nearly every poem of Colin's is either recorded by another poet, or released into some other context of augmentation and modification. This release is the best and only chance for the recreative song to be re-created, and thus to outlive its momentary apostrophe to the wilderness. Poems, in Spenser's *Shepheardes Calender*, move from the solitude of pastoral streams and fields to the busy conversation and glossing of other poets, printers, and woodcut artists. But Spenser recognizes that this creative community transforms poetry as they reproduce it. So the reaction to this re-created sestina is praise for Colin's verse, and for Cuddie's performance, expressed by Perigot, and with immediate commentary by Willye, Cuddie, and (usually) E.K. As for Colin, Perigot admires "ech turning of thy verse." The verse has indeed been turned in several ways. It has been turned from a solitary, doleful complaint voiced only to the landscape, to a poly-vocal and hybrid inquiry into the nature of being lovelorn, and the various poetic responses this state can inspire. It has thus turned from solipsism to collaboration, as the possessives imply: just before reciting, Cuddie calls for attention: "Then listneth ech vnto *my* heauy laye, / And tune your pypes as ruthful, as ye may" (sig. I1v, emphasis added). The change in possessive pronouns occurs simultaneously with the reproduction of the poem.[60] Here, Spenser is showing how poetic creativity is recreative. The song, created under the conditions of solitude, nevertheless will continue under the conditions of community.

III Colin's Communities: Poetic Reintegration in *Colin Clovts Come home againe* and *Astrophel*

Throughout the previous sections I have argued that in *The Shepheardes Calender*, Colin Clout's solitude provokes serious questions about poetic production. Iconographically, the breaking of Colin's bagpipes elicits a rich set of associations, principally the fool who can neither hear properly nor act harmoniously with those around him. Intertextually, his retreat from company resonates with both contemporary and classical debates on the active and contemplative lives. Poetically, his refusal to sing forces his companions to engage in poetic recreation, so that Colin's recreative poetry is itself renewed and reconstituted by his poetic community.

The final section of this treatment examines the end of Spenser's career, which was fraught with both the dangers of overinvolvement in courtly affairs, and the rewards of a gentleman poet laureate. The focus of my attention, the combined volume of *Colin Clovts Come home againe* and the elegiac collection *Astrophel*, partly depicts a shepherd-poet who is undergoing a crisis of identity, of exile, and of poetic production. But in addition to this depiction, Spenser's book enacts a movement from solitude to community. It begins with one voice, and ends with many.

Critics usually treat Spenser's later career as demonstrating one of two extremes: disillusionment and bitterness, or renewal and hope. The *Amoretti* and *Epithalamion*, and more recently *Fowre Hymnes*, are usually taken to be part of the latter pattern, while the end of *The Faerie Queene* and *Colin Clovts Come home againe* are taken to be expressions of the bitter, disillusioned Spenser.[61] But this reading of *Colin Clovts* overestimates the role of courtly complaint, discounts the place of epideictic praise, and overlooks the fact that the book is in fact a two-part volume, which again takes on the poet's struggles with solitude and integration into a poetic community. Spenser fashions a positive model of poetic reintegration, in which his speaker willingly recites his own poetry, and even records the verses of other poets.

This positive model works in direct contrast to the perceived disillusionment of Spenser's later works, especially *The Faerie Queene* books 4–6, and the scandals aroused by *The Complaints* in the early 1590s, his return to Ireland in 1591, and the rebellion in Ireland that returned him destitute to England in 1598.[62] The most explicit and emblematic version of this disillusionment may be from *The Faerie Queene* book VI (first printed 1596), when Spenser again gives us an image of Colin Clout breaking his bagpipe. In this case, Colin's *locus amoenus* on Mount Acidale is disrupted by Calidore, the Knight of Courtesy. The scene's pleasure, grace, and beauty are all dissolved upon his approach:

> But soone as he appeared to their vew,
> They vanisht all away out of his sight,
> And cleane were gone, which way he neuer knew;
> All saue the shepheard, who for fell despight
> Of that displeasure, broke his bag-pipe quight,
> And made great mone for that vnhappy turne.
> But *Calidore*, though no lesse sory wight,
> For that mishap, yet seeing him to mourne,
> Drew neare, that he the truth of all by him mote learne. (6.10.18)[63]

This episode has not been read in the same way as Guyon's destruction of the Bower of Bliss, or the malevolent but ultimately imprisoned boar in the Garden of Adonis. These key moments of destruction and creation have been mined by historicist and feminist critics, their ore transmuted into essentially forward-looking acts, entrances into early modernity.[64] But Colin's destructive act is nearly always taken to be illustrative of a more static, dialectical relationship between the poet's dual responsibilities – to his artistic vocation, and to the world. These duties are incommensurable in this episode, richly allusive though it is. It ends with no satisfactory conclusion for either Calidore or Colin Clout.[65] The two cannot exist in each other's company; their respective worlds are delimited when they are thrust briefly together.

However we read the Mount Acidale episode, the poet's home, his place at court or in solitude or among friends, is a continually vexing question for Spenser. In *The Shepheardes Calendar*, Cuddie's "O pierlesse Poesye, where is then thy place" uses a spatial metaphor for what is essentially an aesthetic and political question: how is poetry to achieve its proper sphere in society, as an imaginative, creative action with instructive capacities? The *Calender* begins by establishing English as its poetry's sphere, from its initial invocation of Chaucer to its defence of "good and naturall English words" (sig. iiv). In *Colin Clovts Come home againe* (1595), as in *The Shepheardes Calender*, Spenser consciously interrogates the poet's place in his larger society, and especially raises the question of where Colin Clout's "home" is. Yet Colin Clout's homecoming returns him to a decidedly Irish pastoral landscape, full of cartographic clues such as the rivers Mulla and Bregog, and the mountain Mole, all nearby Spenser's recently acquired 4000-acre estate. Spenser precisely dates and places his prefatory letter to Ralegh: "From my house of Kilcolman the 27. of December. 1591."[66] According to McCabe, he thus deepens and complicates his depiction of the poet's relationship to his home by blurring the fictional and the actual: "[Colin's] voyage abroad is Spenser's homecoming, his homecoming is Spenser's exile."[67] Other examinations go even further. For Andrew Hadfield, the work is primarily a "violent pastoral," and a "bitter poem of colonial exile" through which Spenser works to craft an English identity that is paradoxically removed from England, and constructed from its margins.[68]

But as we have seen in the portrait of the solitary, malcontented Colin Clout in *The Shepheardes Calender*, we ought not to read the Colin Clout of *Home Againe* as overwhelmingly bitter, and simply exiled. There are instead a range of poetic counterstrains to Colin's apparent bitterness. Tonally, Colin's extreme unsociability is nowhere to be found in the nearly thousand lines of his poem. Instead of an embittered poetic and political exile, both the poetry and the format of this book encourage us to read it as a reentry into the contested space of late-Elizabethan courtly poetics. Just as Spenser would enter the community of the 1590s sonneteers with his *Amoretti* and *Epithalamion* (1595), in this volume he also participates in a collective movement that effects the apotheosis of Sir Philip Sidney, that aggressively establishes an emerging poetic and intellectual elite, and that adds to an evolving printed verse miscellany book format. Far from simply a *cri de coeur* from an embittered exile, the composite book moves from solitude to community, and models a positive form of lyric re-creation.

To be sure, there is plenty of the discontented exile, both in Colin's brief description of himself ("like wight forlore … where I was quite forgot") and in his description of the landscape (which by contrast to England's, seems to include both "rauenous wolues" and "outlawes fell"). However, his happiness and contentment shine through at other points in the poem. In a moment that recapitulates the cooperative song of Cuddie and Thenot in *August*, Colin describes his own happy sharing of song with the "Shepherd of the Ocean," the pastoral name for Sir Walter Ralegh, to whom the volume is dedicated:

He sitting me beside in that same shade,
Prouoked me to plaie some pleasant fit,
And when he heard the musicke which I made,
He found himselfe full greatly pleasd at it:
Yet aemuling my pipe, he tooke in hond
My pipe before that aemuled of many,
And plaid theron; (for well that skill he cond)
Himselfe as skilfull in that art as any.
He pip'd, I sung; and when he sung, I piped,
By chaunge of turnes, each making other mery,
Neither enuying other, nor enuied,
So piped we, vntill we both were weary. (sig. A4r)

This is quite a different Colin from the pipe-breaker who eschews virtually all company in the *Calender*, and who cannot be bothered to rehearse or record the songs in which others take such pleasure. But here, when Cuddie makes exactly the same request – "Of fellowship … Record to vs that louely lay againe" – Colin immediately gratifies him (A4v). He and the Shepherd of the Ocean have already performed together; they sing for mutual delight, and they occupy equivalent positions. But Spenser also depicts the reproduction of this song, which is recorded by Colin himself to a larger community of shepherds. That is, he depicts its survival into the present, through a moment of copying.

To be sure, Spenser's poet-figure also sometimes condemns excesses and corruption with the anti-courtly bitterness of Skelton's earlier Colin Clout. We hear of how only those with "deceitfull wit" are successful, how the court is a place for "faire dissembling curtesie," how the most learned are "instruments of others gaines," and how there is no place for "gentle wit, / Vnlesse to please, it selfe it can applie" (sig. D2v). The echoes of Colin piping only to please himself are unmistakable. But Spenser's goal here is not to engage in courtly, topical satire so much as to praise, by contrast, the poetry of his friends and companions. The few lines of conventional courtly contempt are outweighed by some 260 lines, nearly a quarter of this long poem, in which Colin nominates and praises a set of poets, ladies, and of course Cynthia, the queen herself.

Names dominate this section. For more than ten years, Spenser's name rested in the shadows of "Ignoto," "Immerito," and of course his pastoral name of Colin Clout.[69] In the lengthy praising section, Spenser continues to use semi-anonymous insiders' names, as he had in the *Calender*: Alcyon for Sir Arthur Gorges, Amyntas for Ferdinando Stanley, Astrophel for Sir Philip Sidney. But he also names names: William Alabaster and Samuel Daniel receive no pastoral nominative shadowing. Instead, Alabaster's *Eliseis* is praised, and deemed to be insufficiently known by the sovereign Cynthia, while Colin calls upon Daniel to "rouze thy feathers" to a higher, tragic poetry. Spenser, in other words, presents his view of the present state of English poetry, and figures himself prominently within that world. He pipes and sings on equal terms with the Shepherd of the Ocean, his poem is recited to Cynthia herself, and he sees fit to bestow praise on other shepherd-poets, and even to advise them in the pursuit of their art. If this view of poetry's "place" were unmixed with courtly complaint, it would be Spenser's most supremely confident statement of belonging, coming perhaps at the high-water mark of his career.

But Spenser, as he had in *The Complaints*, pushes his own personal loyalties to a dangerous point. Perhaps most audaciously, he figures Sir Walter Ralegh and Elizabeth Throckmorton in the long tale of the river Mulla's love for her river-brother Bregog. Ralegh's and Throckmorton's secret marriage was "descried" by the queen in 1592, with disastrous results for Ralegh. The love of the rivers, too, ends badly: their secret affair is revealed, and the father-mountain Mole scatters the unified river, which "did lose his name" as a consequence. Spenser's personal associations are staunchly defended in this section, since the lamenting tone suggests exactly where our sympathies should lie. Spenser takes care to give the queen pride of place in his praises. But his close companion Ralegh, and by extension this other Elizabeth, are given space to inhabit the same poetic realm as the queen.

These elements of *Colin Clovts* demonstrate that the poem is no mere extended complaint against courtly corruption and the lack of proper support for court poets. Spenser instead is determined to foster the kind of poetic community in which Colin Clout himself could not bring himself to participate in the *Calender*. Spenser's poetic community is enlarged in the elegiac *Astrophel*, which was attached to the 1595 *Colin Clovts*, and is, I argue, an integral part of the larger, two-part volume.[70] In this collection, Spenser depicts, and enacts, the poet's participation in an established, supportive, and reproducing community of poets. Their task involves plenty of bitterness and complaint: mourning the loss of Astrophel, one of two well-known names for Sir Philip Sidney's poetic personality. (The other is Philisides, a character in the poems of *Arcadia*.) But that bitterness is leavened in part by the elegiac mode, with its two-part structure of grief and joy.[71] Even more strikingly, *Astrophel* also demonstrates how the community of poets, praised in detail by Colin in *Colin Clovts*, acts in concert, and ensures its own reproduction and continuance.

Sidney's textual apotheosis had been going on since the day of his funeral in 1586, when the first printed collection of elegies was published.[72] Poems of praise and lament for Sidney became something of a cottage industry, and the care and feeding of his poetic legacy was contested in the early printed editions of Sidney's works, as the next chapter examines in detail. But *Astrophel* is remarkable precisely because it is commonplace. That is, rather than aggressively asserting his unique poetic contribution, Spenser's collection accents his participation in a larger poetic community, and in a poetic project that had been going on for nine years. This volume is Spenser's contribution to the larger elegiac project, and places Spenser alongside his peers. The text makes attributions to "Clorinda," "Thestylis," "Lycon and Colin," and "L.B.," with several unattributed poems. The last three poems were reproduced directly from the 1593 verse miscellany *The Phoenix Nest*; of these, the first is known to be by Matthew Roydon, the second has been judged to be by Sir Walter Ralegh, and the third is guessed to be by Fulke Greville or Sir Edward Dyer.[73]

The miscellaneity of the *Astrophel* volume means that Spenser can scatter references to other poets amid those poets' elegies. The result of these textual interactions is that rather than singing to please himself only, Colin cooperatively participates in a larger poetic community. The volume opens with an appeal (entirely in italics, thus typographically set off from the rest of the poems) that these poems be included in the larger project of praising and immortalizing Sidney. The first stanza closes "*Hearken ye gentle shepheards to my song, / And place my dolefull plaint your plaints emong.*" The speaker, who may or may not be taken to be Colin Clout, later asserts that his verses are *only* meant for their ears, and that if some "nycer wit" chances to come upon them, "*Thinke he, that such are for such ones most fit, / Made not to please the liuing but the dead*" (sig. E4r). With the calculated ambiguity of "such ones," Spenser places his verses humbly but assertively into the ears not of a shadow audience of superiors, the nicer wits, who call to mind not the deceitful carpers in *Colin Clovts*, but instead his fellow shepherds. At the head of this group is Sidney himself; the fit audience are the fellow shepherds, and the fittest audience is the deceased Astrophel. Spenser's placement of his song among other songs in honour of Sidney humbly but aggressively levels the field: no longer are they Lord Brook, Sir Walter Ralegh, and a humble former sizar whose status has been achieved by education, not by birth. Although the volume continually asserts Sidney's last position as Lord Governor of Flushing, Spenser's own voice blends in with those of higher status.[74]

This blending is most apparent in a dialogue attributed in the text to L.B., almost certainly Lodowick Bryskett, who also likely authored "*The mourning* Muse *of* Thestylis."[75] There, Colin and his anagram Lycon are the two voices, who take turns mourning the death of Philisides (Sidney's persona in the songs and poems in the *Old Arcadia*). Lycon prevails successfully upon Colin to sing with him ("Vp iolly swaine, / Thou that with skill canst tune a dolefull lay"), and we should recognize in this depiction both the cooperative, turn-taking song Spenser had created in *August*, and a conversion of the earlier, unsuccessful attempts to engage Colin's more sociable side. Here, he agrees to "make a sad consort" and to "ioyne our mournfull song" (sig. H2r–v). That which in *The Shepheardes Calendar* was an unrealized dream of harmonious poetic singing, and that which in *Colin Clovts* was a monologue praising many poets and carving out his place in their company, in *Astrophel* finally comes to fruition on the printed page. Bryskett, as Thestylis, has shared both his poetry and his grief with Spenser, and out of that shared experience he has created a blended poetic voice: he appropriates Spenser's Colin (the stanzas employ a linked rhyme scheme that may be a homage to Spenser's), and thereby re-creates Spenser's voice.

By far the most interesting and controversial blending and reproducing of voices occurs in what is now known as the "Doleful Lay of Clorinda," the second poem of the *Astrophel* miscellany, attributed there to Mary Sidney Herbert, the Countess of Pembroke, Philip Sidney's "sister that *Clorinda* hight." Clorinda is figured earlier in *Colin Clovts* as Urania. There, she is given pride of place as the most important of the maids (except, perhaps, the one to whom he has pledged his love). Here, however, she is not merely the object of praise but the speaking voice of the poem. Colin, in a poetic performance that is deeply significant, recites ("rehearses") the poem exactly as she had sung it: "in sort as she it sung," he claims. In other words, he has gone from a malcontent, whose retreat from pastoral company necessitates the rehearsing of his beloved poetry by others, to a poet whose weeping poetry is not only accomplished in the company of other poets, but even rehearses their poetry as well.

Critics currently disagree on whether Spenser or Mary Sidney is the author of the "Doleful Lay." However, the authorship controversy over this poem runs against the grain of the *Astrophel* collection itself. To print the poem as a single lyric in a collection of Mary Sidney's works (as Hannay and Kinnamon do), or to ascribe it solely to Spenser and print it alongside *Colin Clovts* but not alongside the rest of the poems (as McCabe does), changes the nature of the poem by asserting exactly what both Colin Clout and Clorinda deny: that the poem is solely theirs, rather than a multiply iterated poem reproduced within a collaborative poetic community.[76] Some critics have taken "The Doleful Lay" to indicate Spenser's appropriation of a female voice, as part of an overall poetic self-portrait as master author.[77] But the composite, multivoice text shows Spenser both asserting mastery and ceding it; his Colin professes that he is repeating Clorinda's verses as exactly as he can, in order not to mar them. In a later poem, Bryskett, in the guise of Thestylis, creates his own version of a Colin with whom he can sing a mourning elegy for Sidney. Bryskett's poem thus appropriates Spenser's Colin, and presents another voice, "Lycon," (perhaps an anagram for "Colyn"), and repeatedly asserts his inferiority to Colin in poetic skill.[78] In the *Calender*, Spenser's Colin Clout seems a figure torn between solitary feeling and collaborative song. In *Colin Clovts* and *Astrophel*, poetic production occurs in a context of collaborative reproduction that is actual, not simply idealized.

The running title pages of this volume provide a clue that Colin's long poetic monologue and the poems that follow should be seen as a multivocal, single volume. In both the 1595 quarto and a 1611 folio (the first reprint of *Colin Clovts*), the running title "Colin Clouts | Come Home Againe" appears not only over the long poem, but over Spenser's contributions to the *Astrophel* miscellany (see figure 3.4). In the 1595 quarto, the running titles seem to imply that Spenser's contributions to the volume (via Colin Clout) end abruptly with the "Doleful Lay." But in the 1611 folio edition printed by Matthew Lownes, Colin Clout's name hangs over this poem, and the ensuing pages change the running title to fit the miscellany's current poem: "The Mourning Muse of Thestylis," "A Pastorall Aeglogue," "An Elegie," and "An Epitaph."[79] These titles accentuate the miscellaneity of the volume: both the contents and authors are variegated in nature. The matter of who cooperated in the production of this book, and to what extent, is very much in dispute.[80] But both printed versions of *Colin Clovts / Astrophel* make it clear that the shepherds singing for Astrophel do so in concert with one another; they take turns singing their verses, and even reproduce one another's verses in their own voice.

Thus it is all the more striking that Clorinda, whose complaint begins by searching for a proper audience, returns us to the dilemma of Colin Clout: the broken pipe, the retreat from society, and the solipsism of self-directed singing. After asking whether she should complain to the heavens, or to "earthly men," Clorinda instead settles on an audience that is by now very familiar:

Then to my selfe will I my sorrow mourne,
Sith none aliue like sorrowfull remaines:
And to my selfe my plaints shall back retourne,
To pay their vsury with doubled paines.

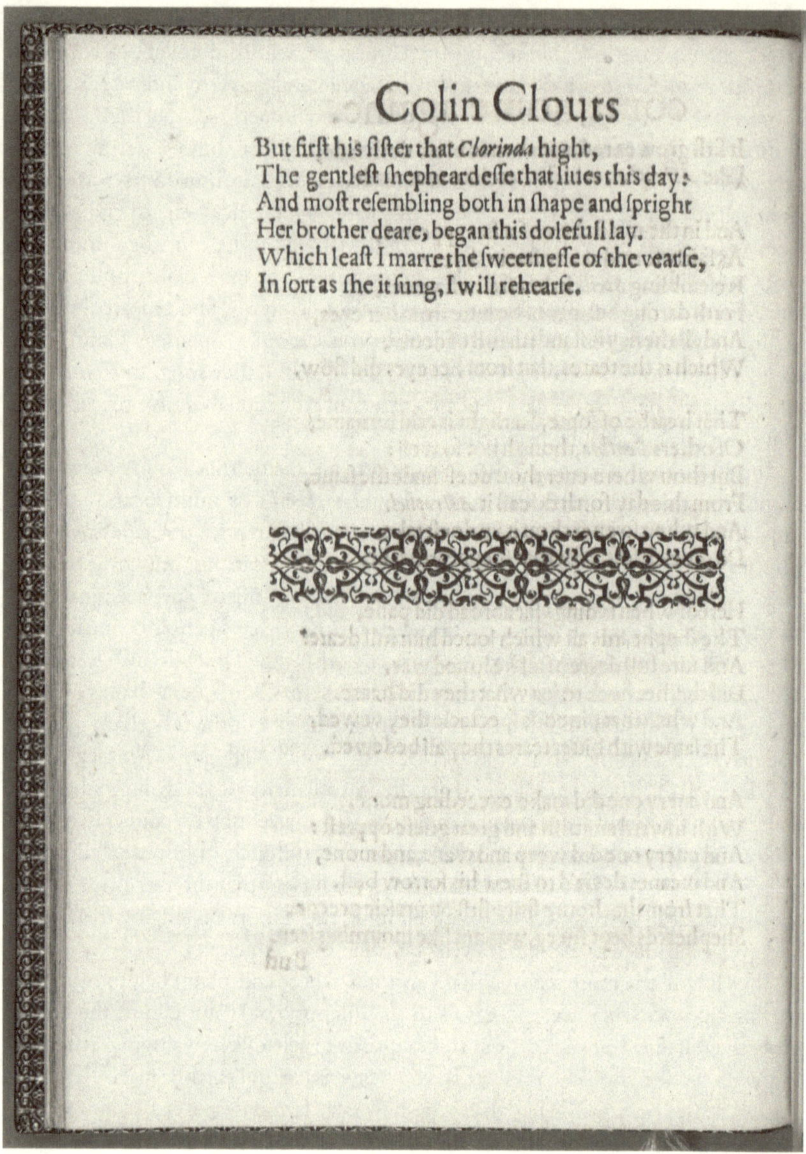

Colin Clouts

But firſt his ſiſter that *Clorinda* hight,
The gentleſt ſhepheardeſſe that liues this day:
And moſt reſembling both in ſhape and ſpright
Her brother deare, began this dolefull lay.
Which leaſt I marre the ſweetneſſe of the vearſe,
In ſort as ſhe it ſung, I will rehearſe.

Figure 3.4 "The Doleful Lay of Clorinda," in *Colin Clovts Come home againe* (1595), sigs F4v–G1r. This item is reproduced by permission of the Huntington Library, San Marino, California

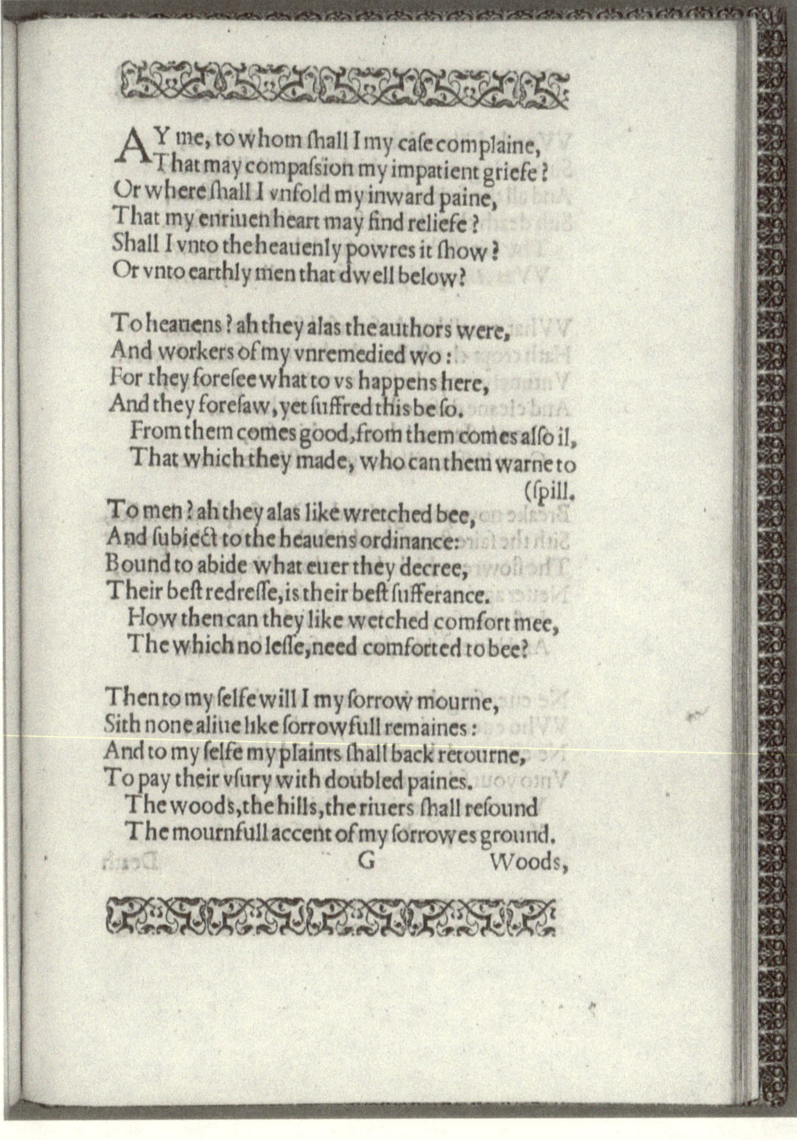

AY me, to whom ſhall I my caſe complaine,
That may compaſsion my impatient griefe?
Or where ſhall I vnfold my inward paine,
That my enriuen heart may find reliefe?
Shall I vnto the heauenly powres it ſhow?
Or vnto earthly men that dwell below?

To heauens? ah they alas the authors were,
And workers of my vnremedied wo:
For they foreſee what to vs happens here,
And they foreſaw, yet ſuffred this be ſo.
From them comes good, from them comes alſo il,
That which they made, who can them warne to (ſpill.

To men? ah they alas like wretched bee,
And ſubiect to the heauens ordinance:
Bound to abide what euer they decree,
Their beſt redreſſe, is their beſt ſufferance.
How then can they like wetched comfort mee,
The which no leſſe, need comforted to bee?

Then to my ſelfe will I my ſorrow mourne,
Sith none aliue like ſorrowfull remaines:
And to my ſelfe my plaints ſhall back retourne,
To pay their vſury with doubled paines.
The woods, the hills, the riuers ſhall reſound
The mournfull accent of my ſorrowes ground.

G Woods,

Figure 3.4 *Continued*

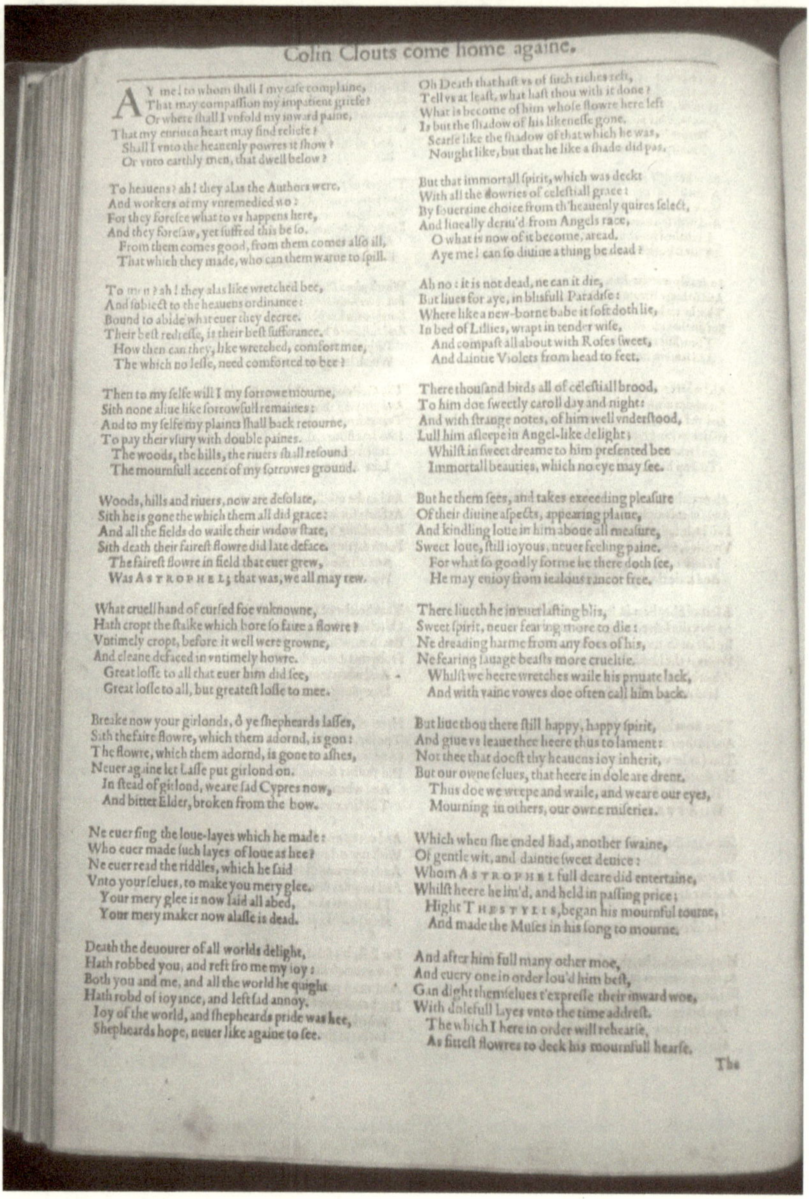

Colin Clouts come home againe.

AY me! to whom ſhall I my caſe complaine,
That may compaſſion my impatient griefe?
Or where ſhall I vnfold my inward paine,
That my enriuen heart may find reliefe?
Shall I vnto the heauenly powres it ſhow?
Or vnto earthly men, that dwell below?

To heauens? ah! they alas the Authors were,
And workers of my vnremedied wo:
For they foreſee what to vs happens here,
And they foreſaw, yet ſuffred this be ſo.
From them comes good, from them comes alſo ill,
That which they made, who can them warne to ſpill.

To men? ah! they alas like wretched bee,
And ſubiect to the heauens ordinance:
Bound to abide what euer they decree.
Their beſt redreſſe, is their beſt ſufferance.
How then can they, like wretched, comfort mee,
The which no leſſe, need comforted to bee?

Then to my ſelfe will I my ſorrowe mourne,
Sith none aliue like ſorrowfull remaines:
And to my ſelfe my plaints ſhall back retourne,
To pay their vſury with double paines.
The woods, the hills, the riuers ſhall reſound
The mournfull accent of my ſorrowes ground.

Woods, hills and riuers, now are deſolate,
Sith he is gone the which them all did grace:
And all the fields do waile their widow ſtate,
Sith death their faireſt flowre did late deface.
The faireſt flowre in field that euer grew,
Was ASTROPHEL; that was, we all may rew.

What cruell hand of curſed foe vnknowne,
Hath cropt the ſtalke which bore ſo faire a flowre?
Vntimely cropt, before it well were growne,
And cleane defaced in vntimely howre.
Great loſſe to all that euer him did ſee,
Great loſſe to all, but greateſt loſſe to mee.

Breake now your girlonds, ô ye ſhepheards laſſes,
Sith the faire flowre, which them adornd, is gon:
The flowre, which them adornd, is gone to aſhes,
Neuer againe let Laſſe put girlond on.
In ſtead of girlond, weare ſad Cypres now,
And bitter Elder, broken from the bow.

Ne euer ſing the loue-layes which he made:
Who euer made ſuch layes of loue as hee?
Ne euer read the riddles, which he ſaid
Vnto your ſelues, to make you mery glee.
Your mery glee is now laid all abed,
Your mery maker now alaſſe is dead.

Death the deuourer of all worlds delight,
Hath robbed you, and reft fro me my ioy:
Both you and me, and all the world he quight
Hath robd of ioyance, and left ſad annoy.
Ioy of the world, and ſhepheards pride was hee,
Shepheards hope, neuer like againe to ſee.

Oh Death that haſt vs of ſuch riches reft,
Tell vs at leaſt, what haſt thou with it done?
What is become of him whoſe flowre here left
Is but the ſhadow of his likeneſſe gone.
Scarſe like the ſhadow of that which he was,
Nought like, but that he like a ſhade did pas.

But that immortall ſpirit, which was deckt
With all the dowries of celeſtiall grace:
By ſoueraine choice from th'heauenly quires ſelect,
And lineally deriu'd from Angels race,
O what is now of it become, aread.
Aye me! can ſo diuine a thing be dead?

Ah no: it is not dead, ne can it die,
But liues for aye, in bliſfull Paradiſe:
Where like a new-borne babe it ſoft doth lie,
In bed of Lillies, wrapt in tender wiſe,
And compaſt all about with Roſes ſweet,
And daintie Violets from head to feet.

There thouſand birds all of celeſtiall brood,
To him doe ſweetly caroll day and night:
And with ſtrange notes, of him well vnderſtood,
Lull him aſleepe in Angel-like delight;
Whilſt in ſweet dreame to him preſented bee
Immortall beauties, which no eye may ſee.

But he them ſees, and takes exceeding pleaſure
Of their diuine aſpects, appearing plaine,
And kindling loue in him aboue all meaſure,
Sweet loue, ſtill ioyous, neuer feeling paine.
For what ſo goodly forme he there doth ſee,
He may enioy from iealous rancor free.

There liueth he in euerlaſting blis,
Sweet ſpirit, neuer fearing more to die:
Ne dreading harme from any foes of his,
Ne fearing ſauage beaſts more crueltie.
Whilſt we heere wretches waile his priuate lack,
And with vaine vowes doe often call him back.

But liue thou there ſtill happy, happy ſpirit,
And giue vs leaue thee heere thus to lament:
Not thee that doeſt thy heauens ioy inherit,
But our owne ſelues, that heere in dole are drent.
Thus doe we weepe and waile, and weare our eyes,
Mourning in others, our owne miſeries.

Which when ſhe ended had, another ſwaine,
Of gentle wit, and daintie ſweet deuice:
Whom ASTROPHEL full deare did entertaine,
Whilſt heere he liu'd, and held in paſſing price;
Hight THESTYLIS, began his mournful tourne,
And made the Muſes in his ſong to mourne.

And after him full many other moe,
And euery one in order lou'd him beſt,
Gan dight themſelues t'expreſſe their inward woe,
With dolefull layes vnto the time addreſt.
The which I here in order will rehearſe,
As fitteſt flowres to deck his mournfull hearſe.

The

Figure 3.5 "The Doleful Lay of Clorinda," in *Colin Clovts Come Home Againe* (1611), sigs B2v–B3r. Image reproduced courtesy of Roger Kuin

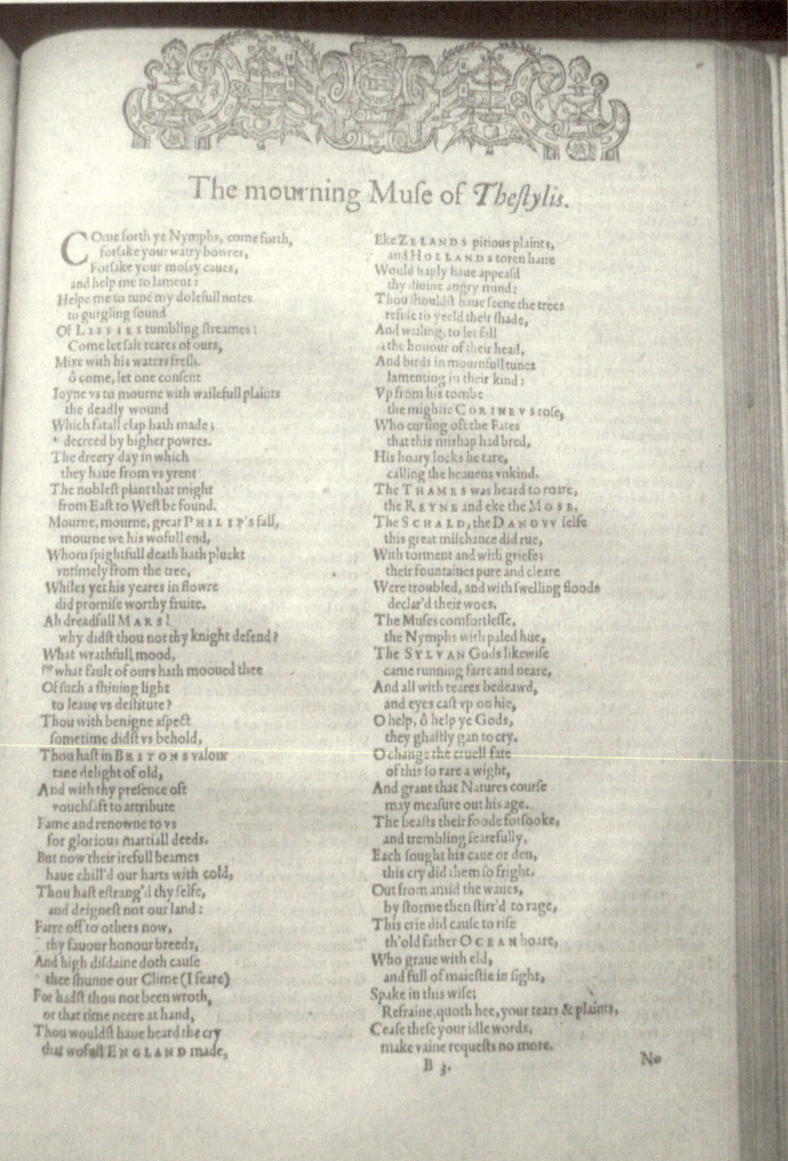

The mourning Muſe of *Theſtylis*.

Come forth ye Nymphs, come forth,
forſake your watry bowres,
Forſake your moſsy caues,
and help me to lament:
Helpe me to tune my dolefull notes
to gurgling ſound
Of LIFFIES tumbling ſtreames:
Come let ſalt teares of ours,
Mixe with his waters freſh.
ô come, let one conſent
Ioyne vs to mourne with wailefull plaints
the deadly wound
Which fatall clap hath made;
decreed by higher powres.
The dreery day in which
they haue from vs yrent
The nobleſt plant that might
from Eaſt to Weſt be found.
Mourne, mourne, great PHILIP's fall,
mourne we his wofull end,
Whom ſpightfull death hath pluckt
vntimely from the tree,
Whiles yet his yeares in flowre
did promiſe worthy fruite.
Ah dreadfull MARS!
why didſt thou not thy knight defend?
What wrathfull mood,
what fault of ours hath mooued thee
Of ſuch a ſhining light
to leaue vs deſtitute?
Thou with benigne aſpect
ſometime didſt vs behold,
Thou haſt in BRITONS valour
tane delight of old,
And with thy preſence oft
vouchſaft to attribute
Fame and renowne to vs
for glorious martiall deeds.
But now their irefull beames
haue chill'd our harts with cold,
Thou haſt eſtrang'd thy ſelfe,
and deigneſt not our land:
Farre off to others now,
thy fauour honour breeds,
And high diſdaine doth cauſe
thee ſhunne our Clime (I feare)
For hadſt thou not been wroth,
or that time neere at hand,
Thou wouldſt haue heard the cry
that wofull ENGLAND made,
Eke ZELANDS pitious plaints,
and HOLLANDS toren haire
Would haply haue appeaſd
thy diuine angry mind:
Thou ſhouldſt haue ſeene the trees
refuſe to yeeld their ſhade,
And wailing, to let fall
the honour of their head,
And birds in mournfull tunes
lamenting in their kind:
Vp from his tombe
the mightie CORINEVS roſe,
Who curſing oft the Fates
that this mishap had bred,
His hoary locks he tare,
calling the heauens vnkind.
The THAMES was heard to roare,
the REYNE and eke the MOSE,
The SCHALD, the DANOVV ſelfe
this great miſchance did rue,
With torment and with griefe;
their fountaines pure and cleare
Were troubled, and with ſwelling floods
declar'd their woes.
The Muſes comfortleſſe,
the Nymphs with paled hue,
The SYLVAN Gods likewiſe
came running farre and neare,
And all with teares bedeawd,
and eyes caſt vp on hie,
O help, ô help ye Gods,
they ghaſtly gan to cry.
O change the cruell fate
of this ſo rare a wight,
And grant that Natures courſe
may meaſure out his age.
The beaſts their foode forſooke,
and trembling fearefully,
Each ſought his caue or den,
this cry did them ſo fright.
Out from amid the waues,
by ſtorme then ſtirr'd to rage,
This crie did cauſe to riſe
th'old father OCEAN hoare,
Who graue with eld,
and full of maieſtie in ſight,
Spake in this wiſe;
Refraine, quoth hee, your tears & plaints,
Ceaſe theſe your idle words,
make vaine requeſts no more.

B 3. No

Figure 3.5 *Continued*

The woods, the hills, the riuers shall resound
The mournfull accents of my sorrowes ground. (sig. G1r)

"Then to my selfe" echoes Colin Clout's earlier "I pipe to please my selfe." But here, Clorinda's solipsism is already framed by Colin's repetition ("I will rehearse") of her song. Not only that, but the late date of this elegiac collection, nine years after the earliest elegies to Sidney were collected, means that Clorinda and Colin are rehearsing collective grief for Philip Sidney all over again.[81] They are reburying him through a productive reproduction of poetic grieving. And this collective reproduction is precisely what Clorinda arrives at, despite her earlier solipsism. As the poem wears on, instances of "I" and "me" give way to those of "we." She begins to mention shepherds and "shepheards lasses" as a collective group, and Sidney's death robs "Both you and me." Though it raises the conventional hope that Sidney's spirit is now "in blissfull Paradise," the poem concludes with a surprisingly dark message. Clorinda comes to realize that Sidney's spirit is now in heaven, "Whilest we here wretches waile his priuate lack." Thus the purpose of mourning poetry takes on a collective production, in which the focus is the larger group: "Thus do we weep and waile, and wear our eies, / Mourning in others, our owne miseries" (sig. G2v). Gone is the sense of a sole author, Clorinda, who has a unique claim to grief as the sister to the deceased. Instead, the poem ends with an attempt both to envision Astrophel, the star-lover, in his proper celestial realm, and to engage in collective consolation that de-individuates each singer so that the ownership of grief can somehow be both radically particularized and generalized to the whole of the grieving population.

As if to emphasize this turn from solipsism to collective reproduction, Colin's voice here intervenes in the text, in a two-stanza narrative link to the next poem, which is in turn connected to all the remaining poems in the volume. He says that next Thestylis began to sing, and then many others after him. Poems written by Bryskett are followed by three poems that had first appeared in *The Phoenix Nest*, so that the collective rehearsal of grieving shepherd-poets simply cannot be seen in terms of the single, laureate author. Rather, Colin's final words open up the possibility for others' words, and the "resounding" of an empty echo gives way to a more active and collective poetic resounding: "full many other moe … Gan dight themselues t'expresse their inward woe … The which I here in order will rehearse, / As fittest flowres to deck his mournfull hearse" (sig. G3r). Spenser certainly does not give up the laurel band. But his version of poetic "rehearsal" expands the theory, practice, and representation of poetic production. His Colin is now reproducing poems, just as his own poems have been reproduced. Spenser reestablishes mastery and laureateship, since these narrating verses situate him as presiding over the elegiac proceedings. But his laureateship depends radically on his community. In *Astrophel,* Colin Clout, no longer languishing in solitude, at last records and is recorded.

4

Lyric Surrogacy: Reproducing the "I" in Sidney's *Arcadia*

In Gascoigne's self-consciously arranged miscellany, and Spenser's acutely self-aware calendar of pastoral poetry, we have seen two examples of how English poets of the 1570s begin to incorporate new conditions of reproducibility into their poetic methods. Spenser's Colin Clout continually wrestles with the tension between solitude and poetic community, while Gascoigne repeatedly dwells on the futility of sexual and textual control. For both authors, reproduction is a central concern: Colin Clout gradually learns to participate in a community of poetic "recorders," while Gascoigne's lyric delights mutate and proliferate far beyond the author's control.

This chapter, on Sir Philip Sidney's *Arcadia*, continues to examine how Elizabethan English lyric poems were reproduced, and how English poets incorporate new conditions of reproducibility into their works. If we assume (with Richard Dawkins and other advocates of genetic models for cultural reproduction) that there is something compelling in certain works that causes them to be taken up and reproduced in a new host, as a virus compels its host, then Sidney's *Arcadia* is one of the most compelling of early modern English literary viruses. It went through three printings in the 1590s and many more in the seventeenth century. Prior to its first printing (1590), the work was circulated in several manuscript copies in the 1580s, and this circulation was gathering the attention of the nascent field of literary criticism of English works.[1] Its printings in the 1590s and in the seventeenth century attest to the continuing, seemingly inexhaustible interest in the work, and especially in a continuing project of adding to the *Arcadia*, completing it, enhancing it, and creating entirely new stories and poems based on its characters and tropes.

Far from reproduction being something that simply happens to the *Arcadia*, Sidney depicts poetic reproduction, proliferation, mutation, and perfection. Sidney's *Arcadia* models and anticipates, in its fictive poetic situations, a pattern of reproduction that would be carried out by his completers, re-printers, and spinners-off. Sidney previews the afterlife of his poems by narrating their first moments of being copied. He thus repeatedly depicts a program of lyric poetry in which successive generations of a poem are taken up by new poetic agents in new contexts. This lyric surrogacy emphasizes the survival of a poem as a kind of adopted offspring.

"Lyric surrogacy" is my term of use for an act of textual reproduction that does not simply copy, but instead adopts the text, producing a new and different poem. This action combines authorship, adoption, and adaptation.[2] Throughout his writings, Sidney is concerned with *poiesis*, textual "making." Although in his theoretical writings, making is both a philosophical and aesthetic problem, Sidney shows in his poetic writings a parallel concern, with re-making, that is, with the afterlife of the poem as it moves forward in time, and as its fundamental lyric terms, "I" and "you," undergo mutation.

Sidney's most famous statements on *poiesis* are suffused with both ancient and early modern theories of generation and animal reproduction. In Sidney's *Defence of Poesie*, poets are separated from other kinds of writers in part because they produce their works out of themselves: "the Poet onely, bringeth his owne stuffe, and dooth not learne a conceite out of a matter, but maketh matter for a conceite."[3] The view that making poetry involves real, physical "stuffe," and that poets make their own "matter," is firmly grounded in early modern theories in which both men and women contributed matter, in the form of "seed," to human generation. *The Birth of Mankind*, the 1540 translation of *De Partu Hominis* (1532, itself a translation of the 1513 *Der Swangern Frauwen und hebammen Rosegarten*, or *Rose Garden*), devotes several chapters to the women's "stones" and "seed-bringers," the postulated female equivalents to the male testicles and epididymis. There, we see that the women's stones and seed-bringers, while not identical to their male counterparts, are nonetheless necessary for reproduction: "On eache side of the matrix lyeth a stone: which bothe be callyd the womans stones, wherin in engendryd the seede and sparme that cu*m*meth from the woman not so stronge, ferme and myghty in operation as the seede of man: but rather weke, fluy, cold and moyst, and of no great fyrmite: howbeit as co*n*uenient, & propre for the pourpose for the whiche it was ordeynid, as the seede of man for his pourpose."[4] Without a genetic model for parental contribution, Galen, Hippocrates, Plato, and Aristotle all delineated two-parent models of varying kinds.[5]

Treatises like *The Birth of Mankind* condensed and disseminated centuries of theorizing on human reproduction, but also updated their sources, both in theory and practice. They included home remedies, recipes, and advice for midwives; at the same time, they also provide evidence for a gradual, though not necessarily step-wise, change in how male and female contributions to human reproduction were theorized. We thus see a range of theories intermixed in *The Birth of Mankind* and in Sidney's *Defence*: Galen's one-sex model for human anatomy; his two-sex model for parental contribution to offspring; Plato's accent on physical reproduction as an inferior kind of intellectual and idealized reproduction; and Aristotle's two-sex model for conception, which nevertheless differentiates male from female contributions.[6] Moreover, both these treatises reveal the intellectual and scientific climate that made treating the book as a child, and its writer as a begetter, perhaps the most pervasive metaphor for authorship in the early modern period.[7] Sidney's poet, bringing "his owne stuffe" to poetic production, must nevertheless bring both male and female stuff, according to the melange of reproductive models then current. Thus writers like Sidney and Montaigne, among others, emphasize a dual-parent model of intellectual creation. In "Of the Affection of Fathers for Their Children," Montaigne expresses the idea that writers are "father and mother both in this generation" of "the children of our mind."[8] Similarly, Sidney begins *Astrophel and Stella* "great with child to speake," and at the same time looks to his "trewand pen" as the font of production.

It is significant, then, that Sidney envisions poetic production as always already reproductive, and as involving both material and ideas, or as John Ulreich puts it, Sidney "unites the mutually interdependent processes of Platonic conception and Aristotelian embodiment."[9] However, as the earlier chapters of *Fair Copies* have shown, *poiesis* as reproduction is only the beginning. Sidney, like any other responsible early modern writer, also has the reader in mind, especially the effects of poetry on readers. As the examples of Tichborne, Wyatt and Surrey, Gascoigne, and Spenser have shown, early modern readers who are moved in some way by a piece of writing, are very often moved to copy it. This much is not new to the early modern period. But Sidney's poetic situations show that being moved by a poem now means coparenting a new, mutated work that has great reproductive potential.

This version of poetic moving stands in contrast to the traditional, rhetorically based version. Sidney's *Defence* is a rhetorical set piece, and the goals of both rhetorical and poetic productions are summarized in the Ciceronian trivium of delighting, teaching, and moving. In his initial definition of poesy, Sidney follows Horace in restricting poetry's aims to teaching and delighting. But throughout the *Defence*, Sidney also focuses on moving readers, and this raises the question of what a reader of poetry, properly moved, is moved to do. Sidney's orthodox answer in *The Defence* has to do with virtuous acts, and virtue itself: poetry is "the most familiar to teach it, and most princelie to moue towards it."[10] However, in the *Arcadia*, Sidney provides an alternative answer, one which is much more closely aligned to the delights which continually escape Gascoigne's control (see chapter 2). Although the virtue of the two heroes is very much at issue, nevertheless when lyric poetry occurs in the *Arcadia* – which it does quite often – we find that readers and listeners are instead moved to reproduce poems, and thereby to become cocreators or surrogate creators of the work. Sidney's Arcadian surrogacy is thus part of his larger poetic program, in which good poetry survives beyond its originary context because of its capacity to move, and thereby to be adopted, cared for, and renewed by readers and hearers.

The media in which Sidney's poems are produced and reproduced are critical to our understanding of Sidneian lyric surrogacy. Recent critical work on the early texts and textual afterlives of Sidney's works bears out the importance of Sidney's own fictive versions of surrogate creation. This work details Sidney's post-mortem transformation into an *Auctor* through two related actions. Most important, there were multiple printed editions of *Astrophel and Stella*, the *Defence*, and the revised, "New" *Arcadia* in the 1590s, with competing or diverging editorial aims.[11] In addition to these editions were the many productions of those who attempted to complete, or perfect, or otherwise add to the *Arcadia.* These related works – spin-offs, we might call them – often use minor characters and plots from the *Arcadia* and develop them into full, autonomous works. Examples of these additions and spin-offs include John Dickenson's *Arisbas* (1594), *Mucedorus* (1598), Gervase Markham's *The English Arcadia* (1607), William Alexander's supplement to the printed *Arcadia* (printed c. 1617), Richard Belling's sixth book (1624), Francis Quarles's *Argalus and Parthenia* (1629), and James Johnstoun's supplement (first printed 1638). These spin-offs, additions, and completions are the subject of a recent study by Gavin Alexander. Noting that Sidney's theory of literature in the *Defence of Poesie* is "all about the reader," Alexander grounds his study on the readerly responses to Sidney's *Arcadia* and his other works.[12] His work shows that the printed *Arcadia* was a thoroughly moving text, to editors and printers and to subsequent readers and writers: it cried out to readers for intervention, in the form of completion, perfection, or some other textual action combining reproduction with new production.

The fact that Alexander has so many examples to work with demonstrates the enormous influence of Sidney's writings on subsequent generations. But less attention has been paid to Sidney's repeated dramatizations, in the poetry and scenarios of the *Arcadia,* of a process in which poetry is reproduced in successive generations, versions, and mutations. Sidney's work did not inspire so many spin-offs and completions solely because it seemed incomplete, or because it was full of minor characters whose stories needed to be told.[13] Rather, Sidney models poetic reproduction in the *Arcadia* because he and his contemporaries are coming to terms with a new model of poetic production, one in which reproduction is an essential and inherent component of the process. Sidney's fictive poetic reproductions presage what will happen to his poetry because these reproductive practices are already ongoing, even before Sidney's untimely death. Sidney models poetic production repeatedly, and he depicts both positive and negative forms. When poetic reproduction succeeds, it does so because of a powerful, moving effect on the reader; readers are moved to adopt the poem as their own. When it fails, it is often because the solitary poet is paying no attention to the surrounding community of listener-singers, who might be moved to reproduce a given lyric. Sidney thus continues and develops the authorial struggles of Spenser's Colin Clout, who is constantly finding a place for himself and his poetry in a larger poetic system that he both shuns, and needs. In what follows, I track Sidneian poetic surrogacy in the dedication of the *Arcadia*, in several of Sidney's Arcadian poems, and in readerly inscriptions of Sidney's poetry in the first, 1590 edition. Each of these examples reveals a central feature of Sidney's lyric poetry: its essentially self-affirming nature, where each reproduction of the poem constitutes an assertion of the "I" rather than a slavish commemoration of the author.

I Philip, Mary, and Surrogacy

Sidney's dedication to the *Arcadia* places his sister Mary Herbert, the Countess of Pembroke into the prominent position of surrogate mother to the text.[14] Early in the dedication, Sidney strikes the familiar posture of cavalierly denigrating his work, calling it "this idle work of mine" and "but a trifle."[15] His posture of denigration makes use of the common reproductive metaphors highlighted above, which posit the author as both father and mother of the text. The *Arcadia* is not only a trifle, but a child which he says he is "loath to father."[16] At first, Sidney compares his renunciation of his work to "the cruel fathers among the Greeks," who abandon infants they do not want to "foster." Sidney also utilizes maternal metaphors by making reference to the popular idea of maternal imprinting at the moment of conception or during pregnancy. Through the powerful actions of the imagination, the mother's state of mind is imprinted onto the form of the child; the vivid imagining of beauty or deformity in the mind causes beauty or deformity in the child's body.[17] In Sidney's dedication, considerations of both poetic production and the care and feeding of the text thus coincide. The abandonment of the text by its father is accompanied by powerful, maternal terms of imagination, conception, and pregnancy: "In summe, a young head, not so well stayed as I would it were, (and shall be when God will) hauing many many fancies begotten in it, if it had not ben in some way deliuered, would haue growen a monster ..."[18] Elsewhere, Sidney is well aware of the power of the imagination to conjure monsters and hybrid beings; in *The Defence*, he mentions Cyclops and Chimeras in a list that demonstrates the power of the poet to go beyond nature in his creations. But here, Sidney's fancies, his imaginative flights and their textual counterparts, have resulted in a work that veers towards monstrousness, and thus needs an adoptive agent.[19] His sister's role as surrogate thus provides for the survival of a work which, like Oedipus, is rescued in a vulnerable and deformed state, and otherwise would have succumbed in "some desert of forgetfulness."

The manuscript and early print history of the *Arcadia* confirm that these common metaphors of reproduction and surrogacy describe actual textual practices, especially in the dispersed possessives of early copies. Perhaps most prominently, Mary Sidney's name is attached to the early manuscript and printed copies of the *Arcadia.* With the exception of British Library additional manuscript 38892, all manuscript copies of the Old Arcadia are either untitled or called *The Countesse of Pembrokes Arcadia.*[20] In the early printed versions, too, what arises is a dual textual responsibility – Philip Sidney's authorship and Mary Sidney's surrogate ownership and care – that is visible in the title: *The Covntesse of Pembrokes Arcadia, Written by Sir Philippe Sidnei.* This title helps to solidify the claims of earlier manuscript titles that while the work was of Philip Sidney's making, it belonged to Mary Sidney, and was under her care. Other printed works with this possessive form include *The Countesse of Pembrokes Ivychurch* (1591 and 1592), *The Countesse of Pembrokes Emmanuel* (1591), and individual poems published in verse miscellanies like *Englands Helicon* (1600).[21] These titles signal the enlargement of Pembroke's influence as a literary patron, and the dual "success" of the *Arcadia*: it was succeeding as an influential, proliferating text, and its succession was being steered by Pembroke, so that it had become Philip Sidney's and Mary Sidney's *Arcadia*, a kind of joint venture.

The 1590 and 1593 printed editions of the *Arcadia* retain this titular role for Mary Sidney, but they also reassess the defective or deformed state of the work, and explain their own roles in the process of its reproduction. The 1590 edition's brief preface makes reference to the "ouer-seer of the print," and primarily addresses the decision to divide the work into chapters and provide brief descriptions of the events in each chapter (sig. A4v).[22] But the writer also refers to the possibility that a "defect" might "be found in the Eclogues," since Sidney wrote the eclogues but did not provide for their precise placement in the work; this was done instead by the "overseer." The 1590 edition's preface thus explains its editorial interventions in organizational and practical terms that recall Sidney's own account of the feverish and disorganized creation process. (Sidney's dedication is printed just prior to the account of the "over-seer," on sigs A3r–A4r.) When this preface mentions "defects," we are reminded of the "deformities" Sidney has warned of already. In both its manuscript and printed versions, Sidney's text thus seems to require continual care, and to be in a state of continual need, or even danger. The language of error and defect is common to paratextual material, but here it demonstrates an intersection between metaphors of reproduction and the actions of textual editors in the process of reproducing works.

A preoccupation with the care of the text is magnified in the second, 1593 edition of the *Arcadia*. Critics have long remarked on the struggle that arose over control of Sidney's works after his death in 1586, and especially the competing visions of Fulke Greville and Mary Sidney regarding the *Arcadia*. H.R. Woudhuysen finds transition rather than conflict: with the 1593 edition, "editorial control moved from Greville to the Countess of Pembroke, yet Sidney's sister and his old school-friend did manage to co-operate."[23] The roles of author, translator, completer, and textual fosterer are also mixed in the Sidney Psalter, which combines the work of Mary and Philip Sidney.[24] Joel Davis sees Fulke Greville's involvement in editing the *Arcadia* as part of a larger program to stake his claim as a militant Protestant writer and a Neostoic, while Mary Sidney's involvement highlights the Sidney family as a collective author or owner of the *Arcadia*, and accents the pastoral elements of the work as crucial to its aesthetic impact.[25]

However we classify Greville's and Mary Sidney's involvement in the reproduction of Sidney's *Arcadia*, it is clear from the 1593 letter to the reader (from Hugh Sanford, who printed the *Arcadia* for William Ponsonby) that the tropes of disfigurement, parenthood, and surrogacy provide these textual producers with ways of understanding their actions. The 1593 edition first reprints Philip Sidney's letter to his sister, and then Sanford's letter to the reader. In the first line of this letter, Sanford renews the image of a deformed work, but this time it is the previous edition that has wrought the deformity. He claims that the 1590 version presented a "disfigured face," and that Mary Sidney's role in this version is to wipe away "those spottes wherewith the beauties thereof were vnworthely blemished."[26] The metaphor is altered somewhat: what were inherent birth defects, caused by Sidney's imaginative fancy, are now blemishes, spots that have arisen in the work due to its mishandling, a kind of allergic reaction – or perhaps a pox – that nevertheless might be healed with gentler treatment.

Sanford thus adroitly turns the deformity metaphor to his purpose: what for Sidney had been a way to strike a posture of humility is, for Sanford, a way to justify and tout this new edition. It will present "the conclusion, not the perfection of *Arcadia*," since the work could never be perfected in Sidney's absence. This work of conclusion remedies the state of the 1590 text, which prints Sidney's revised version of the story until it ends abruptly in the third book; Sanford's and Ponsonby's edition adds text from the manuscript Old *Arcadia* to round out books three through five. But Sanford has carefully read Sidney's dedicatory letter to his sister, and he renews and amplifies the metaphor whereby Mary Sidney becomes a surrogate mother for a work which Philip Sidney fathered:

> If it be true that likenes is a great cause of liking, and that contraries, inferre contrary consequences: then is it true, that the wortheles Reader can neuer worthely esteeme

> of so worthye a writing: and as true, that the noble, the wise, the vertuous, the curteous, as many as haue had any acquaintaunce with true learning and knowledge, will with all loue and dearenesse entertaine it, as well for affinity with themselues, as being child to such a father. Whom albeit it do not exactly and in euery lineament represent; yet considering the fathers vntimely death preuented the timely birth of the childe, it may happily seeme a thanke-woorthy labour, that the defects being so few, so small, and in no principall part, yet the greatest vnlikenes is rather in defect then in deformity.[27]

Sanford extends Philip Sidney's parentage metaphors by calling Sidney the father and the present work a "labour," and he later predicts that Mary Sidney will later undertake other "pains" on behalf of her brother's memory.[28] But Sanford also brings the reader into this process, and he does so expressly in language that combines reproduction and aesthetic reaction. He seizes upon "likeness" in order to link the fit reader to the present work. Those readers who are drawn to the work, who can appreciate its beauty and understand its erudition, are themselves potential parents to it. Sanford's letter to the reader thus begins to extend authorship, here figured as paternity and maternity, to the fit reader, so that it is not only Mary Sidney who is capable of surrogacy, but anyone whose liking (aesthetic or emotional resonance) argues for likeness (resemblance by consanguinity). In what follows, I will show that Sidney meditates on surrogate ownership and authorship in certain moments of the action of the *Arcadia* itself. His lyric poems undergo moments of both abandonment and adoption which demonstrate Sidney's dual concern with textual parenting and subsequent success through surrogacy. In other words, Sidney depicts in the *Arcadia* the same lyric surrogacy that his poetry would soon undergo.

II Reproducing the Lyric "I"

Ownership, authorial production, and surrogacy are not only at the centre of the early printings of Sidney's *Arcadia*; these same issues are visible in the course of the wanderings and poetic outbursts of his characters. In Sidney's version of the pastoral world, every character seems likely to sing, or wax lyrical, at any given moment in the action (although this tendency is much reduced in the New, more martial, *Arcadia*). But lyric poetry regularly occurs in two rather neatly defined contexts in the *Arcadia*. The first context, which Paul Alpers has called "pastoral convention," shows shepherds gathering together to sing for each other.[29] This lyric context punctuates Sidney's Old *Arcadia*: at the end of each book of romantic entanglement, poet-shepherds and Arcadian characters sing, recite, and perform pastoral songs with no clear distinction between performers and audience.

But Sidney also repeatedly dramatizes the opposite situation, in which the lone lyric voice cries out to an unknown, or non-existent audience. This context is particularly informative when it comes to Sidney's understanding of lyric reproduction, since lyrics in this situation comprise an extreme case, in which the poem is thrust out into the wilderness, with perhaps no expectation of being heard, or transcribed, or someday printed. In two of his poems, "Over these brooks" and the more well-known "What tongue can her perfections tell," Sidney shows that the lyric poem's ephemerality – one consequence of this solitary context – is an illusion, since another agent witnesses the poem, and takes ownership of it. In doing so, that agent asserts his or her "I," simultaneously reproducing the poem and producing himself or herself.

At base, these are instances of poetic succession, since each poem survives into the next generation. But because the poem undergoes iteration – transferral into another context, voicing, and author – it can also be seen as an example of a lyric fair copy, which is and is not the same poem. My first example of this kind of poetic succession occurs in an episode that is central to the narrative of both the Old and New *Arcadias*. Pyrocles, disguised as an Amazon woman named Cleophila, writes a lyric complaint in the sand. He supposes himself to be alone, and so this poem seems to operate as a standard complaint by the solitary, suffering lover:

OVer these brookes trusting to ease mine eyes,
(Mine eyes euen great in labour with their teares)
I layde my face; my face wherein there lyes
Clusters of clowdes, which no Sunne euer cleares.
In watry glasse my watrie eyes I see:
Sorrowes ill easde, where sorrowes painted be.

My thoughts imprisonde in my secreat woes,
With flamie breathes doo issue oft in sound:
The sound to this strange aier no sooner goes,
But that it dooth with Echoes force rebound.
And make me heare the plaints I would refraine:
Thus outward helps my inward griefes maintaine.

Now in this sande I would discharge my minde,
And cast from me part of my burdnous cares:
But in the sand my tales foretolde I finde,
And see therein how well the writer fares.
Since streame, aier, sand, mine eyes and eares conspire:
What hope to quench, where each thing blowes the fire?[30]

Within the confines of this poem, there are only glancing references to Cleophila's audience; it is an audience of none, at least no one human. In the second stanza, she says that her thoughts "with flamy breath do issue oft in sound," and in the third, that she would "discharge [her] mind" in the sand.[31] Though ostensibly addressing her natural surroundings, Cleophila has a great deal of trouble doing so simply and directly. The phrase "great in labour" and the verbs "issue" and "discharge" certainly remind us of the parentage metaphors used by Sidney to describe poetic production. These metaphors serve to intensify Cleophila's difficulty in speaking her hidden thoughts. Such difficulty is reflected also in the repetition of the word "would." Sidney may claim to have dashed off his disfigured child, the *Arcadia*; Cleophila finds such disburdening more difficult.

What happens to thwart the revelation and relief of her mind and heart through poetry? Tellingly, Cleophila encounters an echoic duplication of her words, her image, and her emotional state: every utterance she makes encounters a sort of instant mirroring effect from the landscape. She cannot simply voice her complaint out there, alone in the woods, and be done with it. Rather, the landscape continually presents to Cleophila the image of herself: the streams reflect her face, her voice is echoed back to her, and the sand somehow tells her about her pain even before she has written that pain into the sand. The poetic act of revelation is a vicious circle for her: there will be no quenching, discharging, freeing, or easing of Cleophila's pain through poetry. But neither is there any true pathetic fallacy: each part of the natural world mirrors and echoes Cleophila, rather than serving as an extension of her.[32] Sidney thus accents Cleophila's status as both the poet and the audience. Her poetic outcry is inherently problematic when no one is around to hear her.

Except, of course, there is someone listening. The narrative context of the poem matters; Cleophila assumes she is in the solitary, lonely pastoral world rather than the pastoral world of convening, debates, contests, and song. But the trouble with running around in the wilds of Sidney's *Arcadia* is that one can never be sure whether anyone else is around. In fact, the most solitary places imaginable are the likeliest ones to harbour eavesdroppers, a fact which Cleophila soon discovers. Philoclea has been listening to the poem all along, and she responds in a fascinating way to what she has just heard. She feels that the words of the poem "might with more cause have been spoken by her own mouth." The poem resonates deeply enough with Philoclea that she feels she could be the author. In fact, she may have more cause to speak the poem than the one who has just spoken it. Thus Sidney here creates a situation in which the poem resonates deeply with its hearer, moving her to reproduce it almost in the same way that water reflects or a landscape echoes. Yet this reproduction goes beyond mere passive reflection, to active possession, so that Cleophila's poetic effusion is immediately adopted by Philoclea.

In the Old *Arcadia*, part of the narrative importance of this poem is its demonstration that Cleophila and Philoclea, with their chiastic names, are of one mind and one heart. But Sidney also dramatizes the futility with which the plaintive poet figure might try to retain control over a lyric utterance. It thus seems quite ironic that Cleophila wants to relinquish possession of this utterance, but cannot. To emphasize the ephemerality of her complaint, she scratches the poem in sand. Yet Philoclea subverts ephemerality by taking possession of that complaint as though it were a poem from her own mouth. What Cleophila wishes to abandon in a transitory poetic utterance, Philoclea hears, takes up, and bears in mind. It is a moment of lyric surrogacy, in which a discarded poem nevertheless moves its audience, who adopts it as her own.

Sidney's concern with lyric surrogacy is even more apparent in one of the few famous poems from the *Arcadia*, which begins "What tongue can her perfections tell / in whose each part all pens may dwell?" This poem, a lengthy blazon that "tells" many parts of the female loved one's body, has received much critical attention.[33] Sidney's blazon claims a unique status for its subject's beauty and virtue, and Sidney is well aware that, somewhat paradoxically, all blazons claim the same kind of uniqueness. With all lovelorn poets writing such poetry, the potential for reproduction – especially within the manuscript context implied by the literal, non-bawdy meaning of "all pens" – seems nearly infinite.

The narrative context of "What tongue" shows that Sidney was considering the afterlives of his poems. Moreover, his fictive moments of copying seem to presage what actually happened to this poem in its earliest iterations. Here, medium-close reading of both the temporal and material sort helps us to see how fictive and poetic depictions of copying shade into actual practices. The critical response to the poem goes as far back as Abraham Fraunce and George Puttenham, who noted it in their treatises on rhetoric and poetry, which preceded the first printed editions of the *Arcadia*. The reproductive response to the poem, as Ringler notes in his edition of Sidney's poetry, was overwhelming: it "became a favourite with his contemporaries, who copied it or quoted it more frequently than any of his other verses – it was transcribed in at least eight manuscript anthologies, was printed in *Englands Parnassus* [1600], and was quoted or imitated by Puttenham, Marston, Weever, Burton, and others."[34]

Figure 4.1 provides a comparison of the text immediately preceding both the Old *Arcadia* and New *Arcadia* versions of the poem. Sidney's description lavishes attention on the context, and on the agency surrounding this poem. In both versions, he takes care to show that Pyrocles, who ostensibly occupies the poet's role, does not compose and write the poem, but instead serves as a kind of surrogate for a work that already exists. In the Old *Arcadia*'s version, Pyrocles is lifting Philoclea into bed when he is reminded of a song that seems to be perfect for his situation, and a perfect description of Philoclea. The New *Arcadia* presents a much lengthier description of the moment of inspiration, and near the end of this description we find that it is no longer Philisides who is credited with originally writing the poem, but rather Philoclea. Her beauty is such that the poem is written into her disguised lover's brain, while the body of the awestruck lover becomes a kind of resonating device, a mirror or an echo-chamber that simply reproduces Philoclea in the form of a poem.

So that, coming again to the use of his feet, and lifting the sweet burden of Philoclea in his arms, he laid her on her bed again, having so free scope of his serviceable sight that there came into his mind a song the shepherd Philisides had in his hearing sung of the beauties of his unkind mistress, which in Pyrocles' judgment was fully accomplished in Philoclea. The song was this:

What tongue can her perfections tell ...

(Old *Arcadia*, quoted from the edition of Duncan-Jones, 207)

But *Zelmane* ... had the coales of her affection so kindled with wonder, and blowne with delight, that now all her parts grudged, that her eyes should doo more homage, then they, to the Princesse of them. In so much that taking vp the Lute, her wit began to be with a diuine furie inspired; her voice would in so beloued an occasion second her wit; her hands accorded the Lutes musicke to the voice; her panting hart daunced to the musicke; while I thinke her feete did beate the time; while her bodie was the roome where it should be celebrated; her soule the Queene which should be delighted. And so togither went the vtterance and the inuention, that one might iudge, it was *Philocleas* beautie which did speedily write it in her eyes; or the sense thereof, which did word by word endite it in her minde, whereto she (but as an organ) did onely lend vtterance. The song was to this purpose.

What toong can her perfections tell ...

(New *Arcadia*, 1593, sig. N1r)

Figure 4.1 Comparison of Old and New *Arcadia* introductions to "What tongue can her perfections tell?"

In these two versions of this moment of inspiration and utterance, Sidney depicts two distinct, but related, methods of poetic reproduction. The Old *Arcadia* version gives us a model of transference, where Pyrocles remembers a song he has heard, and applies it to his present situation. But the circumstances could hardly be more different: Philisides is a bundle of distemper and complaint in the Old *Arcadia*, and he is constantly thwarted in his love pursuits, whereas Pyrocles and Philoclea are here fulfilling their desires. Yet the poem, the narrator tells us, seems to be equally serviceable in both situations. In fact, in language that reminds us of the previous example, he tells us that Pyrocles felt that this poem "was fully accomplished in Philoclea." Adoption and reproduction occur here, as in "Over these brooks." The listener becomes an active agent in the reproduction of the poem, and through that activity reaches a fuller or better iteration of that poem.

Something of the same process occurs in the text preceding the New *Arcadia*'s version of this poem. In its much lengthier, more involved description of poetic production, the process of invention seizes Pyrocles (here his alias is Zelmane) without his agency or control. Every part of his body produces the poem, in a description that reminds us of the feverishly energetic production process Sidney presents in his letter to his sister. Here, production is a sort of dictation, where Philoclea's beauty actually writes the poem, while Zelmane's whole body becomes the device whereby the poem is produced. In fact, Sidney emphasizes that unlike the Old *Arcadia* version, in this version of the poem the imagination and the utterance are practically simultaneous. Moreover, Pyrocles is released from the inventive agency of this poem through a common conceit of the blazon – that the poet is merely a passive transmitter of the beloved's beauty, and that no praise or merit should thus accrue to the poet.

Why does Sidney switch from an account of poetic reproduction to one of production, of *poiesis* itself, even as he himself is reproducing the poem in a new context, an Arcadia *altera et eadam*? The key to this change may lie in the fact that one of the many adjustments Sidney made when rewriting the *Arcadia* was to drop the character of Philisides almost entirely, even as he amplified the narrative, adding many new characters and plot-lines. In the Old *Arcadia*, Philisides figures prominently, providing a link between the world of pastoral poetry and the prose romance sequences that form the main action of each book. In Victor Skretkowicz's analysis, the disappearance of Philisides represents a change in Sidney's conception of himself, from lovelorn poet to heroic knight.[35] Clearly, even more than "Astrophil," the name Philisides plays on Sidney's own name. The Old *Arcadia* is filled with poems by Philisides that fail to be reproduced because of Philisides's inattention to, or mismanagement of, his audience. In the second book's eclogues, for example, Philisides sings an echo-song in which his tortured words are thrown back to him by the echoing landscape. This poem comprises a narcissistic travesty of the sympathy seen in the "Over these brooks" episode. No one offers to take up and re-author the echo-poem, and the prominence of Philisides gradually fades. If the Old *Arcadia*'s version of "What tongue can her perfections tell" glancingly refers back to its author in coded terms, then the New *Arcadia*'s version elides this coded reference entirely, claiming instead a new poem, an invention, even as it presents a reproduction.

In the process of reproducing his own poem, Sidney shows how one author-figure disappears and a new "I" emerges. This version of success is slightly different from the one above, in which an intense sympathy of feeling leads to surrogate care for the poem. In the case of *The Countess of Pembroke's Arcadia*, Mary Sidney's surrogacy and her status as both sponsor and possessor of the work are inseparable. In "Over these brooks," we see how an auditor can take ownership of a poem at the moment of its occurrence, simply by being moved by it. With "What tongue can her perfections tell," Sidney creates a poem that continues to exist through a variety of instantiations, each further removed from the author than the last. One indicator that Sidney is examining textual practices that both involve and succeed him is that this removal trend continues beyond Sidney's depictions. An excellent example of this process of successive reproduction occurs one year after the 1593 *Arcadia*, when John Dickenson refers to this poem in his work *Arisbas*, in a poem called "Cupid's Palace." I refer to this printed work because it demonstrates succession, through a logical extension of the disappearance of Sidney-Philisides as the author or producer of the poem. Dickenson refers to "What tongue can her perfections tell" in its printed, New *Arcadia* context:

> Pyrocles such fancie knew,
> Fancie giuing Loue his due,
> Which did on Philoclea look,
> Bathing in a Christall brooke.
> He disguisde a virgin seemd,
> And his name was Zelmane deemd.
> O how sweetly did he praise,
> In those lines those louely laies,
> All perfections in her planted?
> For his pen no praises wanted.
> Tresses of her Ambre haire,
> Wauing in the wanton aire ...[36]

Dickenson continues to rehearse an additional few poetically described body parts, though not nearly as many as Sidney's poem provides, and not in the same detail. This lack of detail in Dickenson's version is simultaneously careless and calculated. "Cupid's Palace" is not one of the many relatively faithful copies of this poem. Instead, it calls attention to the process that Sidney himself engages in when he reproduces the poem in the New *Arcadia*. Philisides (and Sidney) are entirely absent from Dickenson's retelling of this poem, and instead we see only "Pyrocles" and "Zelmane." This is not to say that Dickenson did not know or care that Sidney authored the *Arcadia* or that the fictional Philisides was originally credited with the poem. Rather, Dickenson's transformation of the poem within his own context furthers the project that Sidney himself initiates and depicts, in which each new copy of the poem is an act of surrogacy, asserting the copying "I" as much as, and sometimes more than, the inventing author. In Dickenson's instantiation of the poem, its genealogy might well be traceable (Sidney-Philisides-Philoclea-Pyrocles-Dickenson), but this succession is not rehearsed. Instead, the poem has mutated into a brief reference, which might contain a flash of resemblance to its original form, but which by now has become something else entirely. Dickenson has been moved to reproduce a version of "What tongue." But his is a fair copy, not an exact copy: Dickenson's version asserts his own poetic voice, which possesses and contains Sidney's.

III Reproducing Lyrics and Producing the "I"

Dickenson's compact, referential version of "What tongue can her perfections tell" is coded into an entirely new poetic production, which elides the Sidneian "I" by referring only to its most recent, surrogate author. This kind of reproduction is in line with the poetic surrogacy which Sidney depicts in the *Arcadia*. Sidney depicts and enacts a process of *poiesis* that includes both feverish, imaginative production and the adoption of poetic products by listeners, writers, and copiers who act as surrogates, and in their surrogacy become new owner-authors of the poem. In my final example, there is manuscript evidence of readerly surrogate care for an Arcadian poem, as well as evidence of the assertion of the readerly "I." This example involves lyric reproduction and survival in at least three ways. First, it is an epitaph, serving to memorialize the faithful love of two of Sidney's New *Arcadia* characters. Second, the poem was a part of Sidney's own revision process, appearing only in the New *Arcadia*. And third, the poem itself has narrowly survived, appearing only as a blank space at first, inviting reproduction before being first printed in 1593.

The poem has the first line "His being was in her alone," and occurs in the third book of the New *Arcadia*. Although it involves plenty of actual killing, the Old *Arcadia* is much less violent and martial than the New, in which death intrudes in many of the plots. Nowhere is death's appearance more flagrant than in the episode of Argalus and Parthenia. That episode is in the third book, in a side-plot involving the deaths of these two true lovers. Argalus dies first, slain by the champion Amphialus. So Parthenia does what any bereft true lover would do, especially one in Sidney's New, more martially heroic *Arcadia*: she disguises herself as the "Knight of the Tomb" and challenges Amphialus to a fight she knows she cannot win. Though Amphialus attempts to win virtuously, mercifully sparing the life of this knight whose identity he has not been able to ascertain, she draws his ire with ignoble insults, and falls to Amphialus's sword, just as her Argalus had.

This episode culminates with a moment of discovery: when the victorious Amphialus removes the helmet of his vanquished foe, in order to find out his identity, he sees that the Knight of the Tomb is really Parthenia. Recognition gives way to lament, and the epitaph is written on the joint tomb of the two lovers. It sums up their unity and violent deaths:

The Epitaph.

H*Is being was in her alone:*
And he not being, she was none.

They ioi'd one ioy, one griefe they grieu'd,
One loue they lou'd, one life they liu'd.
The hand was one, one was the sword
That did his death, hir death afford.

As all the rest, so now the stone
That tombes the two, is iustly one.
ARGALVS & PARTHENIA.[37]

In the text just prior to the poem, we find that the character Basilius "caused this epitaph to be written" and that he also makes "marble images" of the lovers themselves. Both the narrative justification for the epitaph, and the epitaph itself, straightforwardly perform the act of commemoration. In chapter 1 we have seen how fraught epitaphs can be with the recognition that effacement is an inevitable part of reproducing the poet following his death. Here, Basilius expresses the impulse to effect some sort of preservation. Something of Argalus and Parthenia ought to be preserved, and the text of the epitaph yields to that impetus with a short, economical encoding of the lovers' story.[38] Although in other places in the *Arcadia*, Sidney undermines the permanence of a poetic message by having his characters write poetry in sand, or on smooth marble that is smeared with ink, the epitaph here seems destined for the kind of permanence to which the writers of epitaphs and the builders of tombs and monuments usually profess to aspire.

The manuscript and printed contexts of this epitaph, however, belie this monumental permanency, and instead suggest that the poem is constantly undergoing mutation in the form of readerly participation in the process of poetic reproduction. In the sole surviving manuscript of the New *Arcadia*, there is a blank space rather than this poem. And in the 1590 first printed edition, there is a large blank space (occupying most of the quarto page) surrounded by a printed frame.[39] These blank spaces, of course, invite the reader to fill in the Sidneian epitaph, which is exactly what has happened in at least three cases (see figure 4.2 for one example). In the 1593 edition, the printed frame still exists, but the epitaph has been printed within the frame, with "The Epitaph" above the poem and "ARGALVS & PARTHENIA" below it. This state, with a printed frame filled in with a printed poem, is how the poem appears in subsequent editions.

The readerly action of reproducing these epitaphs is striking, since it is at odds with the narrative. There, Basilius is the agent responsible for the commemoration of the lovers. His epitaph, once graven in stone, might seem to close off further participation in the process of commemoration. The tension between group participation in mourning, and individual poets' efforts to distinguish their own grieving poetry, is inherent to poetic elegies in early modern England, as has been widely noted. Collections of epitaphs – especially those written about Sidney himself, but also about Wyatt, Edward King, and a great variety of noblemen and women, including Prince Henry and Elizabeth – demonstrate the degree to which the work of mourning often took the form of a collective textual effort rather than an isolated outpouring of grief.[40] Edmund Spenser, as we have seen in the previous chapter, voices a considerably conflicted and complex response to the tension between public and private grief, and to the process of creating collective poetic writing. Others, as Dominic Baker-Smith has argued, were willing to exploit the form of Latin verse compilations both in order collectively to praise and mourn for Sidney, and to pursue a political objective: "an interventionist policy in the Netherlands."[41] The efforts of the readers of the 1590 printed *Arcadia* in fact point up the failure of Basilius to achieve a solitary and permanent epitaph, engraved into stone. Some readers of the 1590 *Arcadia* are confronted by a failed epitaph: on the page, only a blank printed frame, and in the Arcadian world, one would have to imagine a blank tombstone, or perhaps one whose text time has worn away. In other copies, readers show that what fails in stone can succeed on paper.[42]

In those copies with handwritten epitaphs, obvious care has been taken to reproduce both the text of the epitaph and its celebratory, commemorative spirit. There are flourishes throughout the short poem, and the carefully penned capital letters of a fair, presentation copy. The Pforzheimer Library copy appears to have its epitaph copied in a contemporary, secretary hand. The others appear to be in later hands, although one of the Huntington copies (HL 69442, figure 4.2)

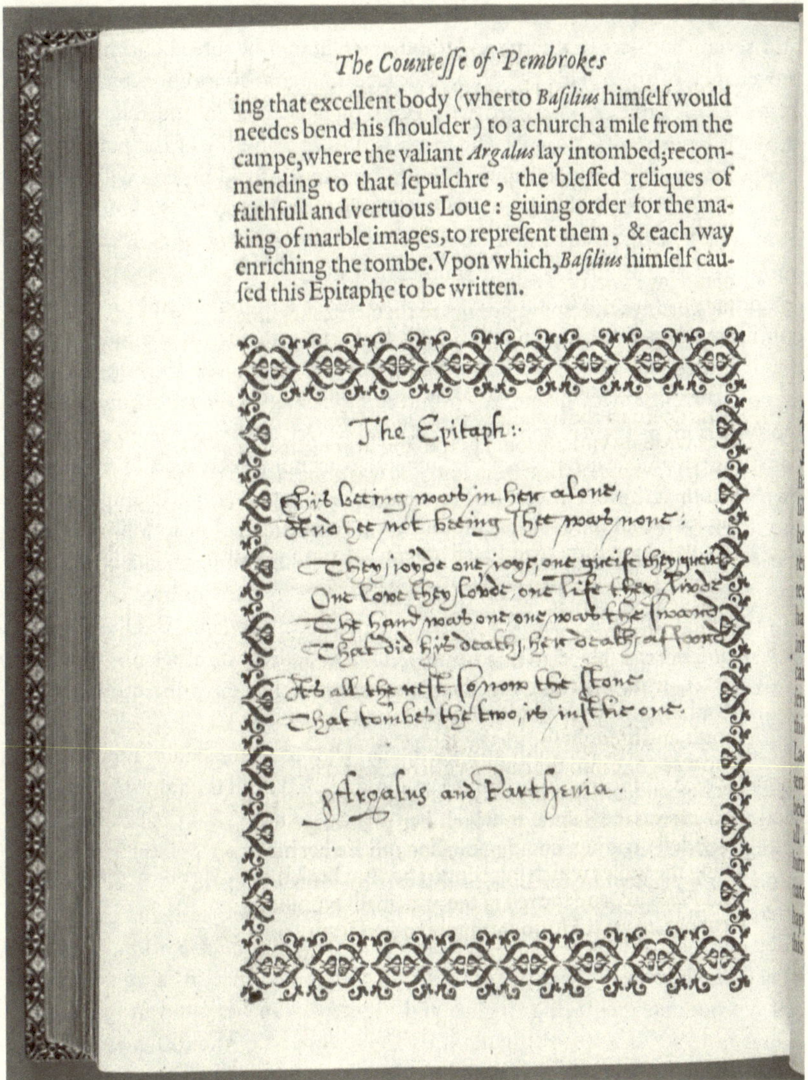

The Counteſſe of Pembrokes

ing that excellent body (wherto *Baſilius* himſelf would needes bend his ſhoulder) to a church a mile from the campe, where the valiant *Argalus* lay intombed; recommending to that ſepulchre, the bleſſed reliques of faithfull and vertuous Loue: giuing order for the making of marble images, to repreſent them, & each way enriching the tombe. Vpon which, *Baſilius* himſelf cauſed this Epitaphe to be written.

The Epitaph:

His being was in her alone,
And hee not being shee was none:

They ioyde one ioye, one greife they greivd
One love they lovde, one life they livde
The hand was one, one was the sword
That did his death, her death afford.

As all the rest, so now the stone
That tombes the two, is iust the one.

Argalus and Parthenia.

Figure 4.2 "His being was in her alone," copied into the *Arcadia* (likely in a late-sixteenth or seventeenth-century hand), Huntington Library 69442, sig. Rr7v. This item is reproduced by permission of The Huntington Library, San Marino, California appears to be written in a mixed secretary and italic hand, often characteristic of mid-seventeenth-century writers. Although we cannot be sure about the date and provenance of these hands, there is a crucial thematic connection to my earlier examples of Sidney's poetry in the process of reproduction and renewal. As in the earlier poem by Cleophila, the composition and afterlife of the poem do not cleave to any originary occasion or intentions, but instead mutate with the new copy's context. Basilius's graven poem, without completion by the reader, would instead be a blank space, and the everlasting monument and epitaph would wink out of existence as quickly as any momentary song.

Epitaphs, as commemorative texts, refuse decay, and thus attempt to effect the continuing presence of their subjects, or at least a reminder or symbolic replacement of these subjects. Such reminders ultimately have a self-affirming purpose, as do many instances of graffiti.[43] But epitaphs can never constitute a simple reproduction, or faithful copy of the dead subject. More often, the poetic epitaph constitutes a double assertion of the subject's continued existence and the author's own written "I," even if only in the form of commemoration. Examples of this motif can be found in Surrey's epitaph "Wyatt resteth here," or in Jonson's Shakespeare. So it is telling that Sidney's epitaph of Argalus and Parthenia is of a more participative kind, with Basilius attempting to demonstrate his own lavish generosity through the medium of Argalus and Parthenia's epitaph. Basilius's epitaph quickly becomes a place for the movement and activity of other reader-writers, however, when they take part in its reproduction within the printed frame of the 1590 edition.

Sidney's epitaph of Argalus and Parthenia, with its participatory model of self-expression combined with reproductive copying, makes all the spin-offs and completions of the *Arcadia* seem much less surprising. In particular, the fact that initial readers participated in copying Argalus and Parthenia's epitaph seems to presage a much more elaborate retelling of this tale by Francis Quarles.[44] Quarles's abject reference to himself as a scion of Sidney's stock nevertheless contains an authorial assertion that is more fully realized in his lengthy poetic adaptation of Sidney's brief tale. However, perhaps the most strikingly succinct instance of readerly self-reproduction regarding Argalus and Parthenia can be found in the Morgan Library's 1590 *Arcadia* (see figure 4.3). There, instead of the epitaph, is found a large handwritten flourish, followed by "Elizabeth Bastard / ow this Booke."

The writer of these lines is otherwise unidentified by this copy's other marginalia and provenance, and of course the inexpert, practice flourish makes it look as though this is merely a case of handwriting practice – a common enough use of blank space.[45] However, the same impulse that causes people to compose and engrave their epitaphs also causes them to engage in this kind of graffito. It seems significant, then, that Elizabeth Bastard does not write her name several times in the

The Counteſſe of Pembrokes

ing that excellent body (wherto *Baſilius* himſelf would needes bend his ſhoulder) to a church a mile from the campe, where the valiant *Argalus* lay intombed; recommending to that ſepulchre, the bleſſed reliques of faithfull and vertuous Loue: giuing order for the making of marble images, to repreſent them, & each way enriching the tombe. Vpon which, *Baſilius* himſelf cauſed this Epitaphe to be written.

Elizabeth Bastard
this booke

Figure 4.3 Sidney, 1590 *Arcadia*, with manuscript ownership mark of Elizabeth Bastard; Morgan Library, MS G.9, sig. Rr7v. Reproduced by permission of the Pierpont Morgan Library, New York. Photograph by Joseph Zehavi, 2007.

available blank space, as is often seen with those who are merely practising their letters. Instead, she adds "ow this Booke" (where "ow" means "owns" or "owneth"), a common but telling phrase which Heidi Brayman Hackel places in the category of "inscriptions, signatures, and other claims to ownership."[46] In the same place where Sidney shows Basilius asserting his own "I," while ostensibly commemorating the love of Argalus and Parthenia, we also see Elizabeth Bastard producing her own textual memorandum. She thus fulfils the impetus that originates in a hybrid and perpetually incomplete text, one which we have seen variously under the care of Mary Sidney, Fulke Greville, printers (like William Ponsonby), the next generation (like John Dickenson), and even Sidney's own characters. Elizabeth Bastard's version of that care does not involve copying or remembering a poem. Instead, she encodes herself directly onto the page, asserting her "I" in a self-reproduction that simultaneously capitulates to mortality – she is, after all, written into an epitaph – and denies it, since her name survives. With its disorderly hybridity, its multiple versions, and its long list of textual agents, the *Arcadia* mandates and depicts just this kind of action. Sidney's characters, readers, reproducers, and editors all demonstrate that producing poetry means reproducing the "I."

5

"All Men Make Faults": Begetting Error in *Shake-speares Sonnets*

Chapter 1 began with a reference to the proliferation of error in print. There, we saw that Tottel's *Songes and Sonettes* deploys a vexed, but productive model of error. Prior, erroneous versions of texts are incorporated into large legal compendiums and, I argue, into Tottel's miscellaneous poetry collection as well. Poetic production *is* reproduction with a difference, and that difference is often judged to be the correction of error. I end with Shakespeare's sonnets because they intensify the connections between error, reproduction, sexuality, textuality, and lyric. They do so despite the common view that the book of Shakespeare's sonnets is a vessel of preservation, and that what it preserves is beauty. This view, which gets the book titled *Shake-speares Sonnets* wrong, can be seen as far afield as an article published in 1995 entitled "Ensuring the Longevity of Digital Information," in which Jeff Rothenberg raises an alarm regarding the disintegration of texts stored in the new digital media. As Rothenberg points out, not only do magnetic tape and disks degrade and dissolve, but software and hardware readers quickly become obsolete.[1] His exemplars of longevity? The Rosetta Stone, and Shakespeare's sonnets, particularly sonnet 18's claim that "So long as men can breathe or eyes can see, / So long lives this, and this gives life to thee."[2]

But Rothenberg, like many critics and readers, misreads *Shake-speares Sonnets*. The stable arrangements of matter that are possible for stone and paper are precisely what Shakespeare's "this" and "thee" call into question. For Rothenberg, magnetic tape and hard disks are to be contrasted with paper and stone: the new technologies are dangerously unreliable compared to the old. For Shakespeare, however, the existence through time of a range of beings – human, textual, floral, and architectural, among others – evokes a wide range of potential problems, meditations, emotional responses, and rhetorical possibilities. Rothenberg takes at face value that Shakespeare's speaker *wants*, and strives to achieve, immortality for himself, for his poetry, and for his addressees. If one carefully reads sonnets

1–18, the "procreation sonnets," and reads the rest of the sonnets desultorily, this is precisely the kind of gist that is most likely to arise. But reading the sonnets for their gist is a bit like reading chapter summaries of *Ulysses*. It denies the capacity of these poems to express the very inconsistencies and volatilities, paradoxes and reversals, ruminations and declarations that are arguably the defining characteristic of Shakespeare's sonnets and of collections of amatory poetry in general.[3] Begetting, in a more capacious sense of not only human procreation but of poetic making and of being through time, is Shakespeare's constant concern not only in the procreation sonnets but throughout the collection and *A Lover's Complaint.* But Shakespeare's sonnets do not simply state that the goal is immortality, and the means is procreation. Instead, they continually discover an existential axiom that could be applied to genetics, to textual studies, to Neoplatonism and other epistemologies, and to the discourses of lovers: that there are no exact copies; there is always error, change, descent with modification, offspring with bastardy. Poetics *is* reproduction with a difference. This axiom contradicts the most well-known message of Shakespeare's sonnets: that though the young man will die, poetry will preserve his perfect copy.[4] Shakespeare's treatment of reproduction in the sonnets, however, reveals his deep interest in the imperfections of human and textual copies, and the mutation of material objects as they exist through time. A medium-close reading of early versions of the sonnets reveals that the fairest copy of this book is the one that changes it.

I begin with two relatively uncontroversial observations about reproduction in the sonnets. First, the reception history of the sonnets shows that they have been perennially viewed as a flawed text. Their precise faultiness varies from one critical moment to the next. Textual critics and editors have often focused on the 1609 quarto edition and its seemingly sloppy, error-riddled text.[5] Some critics have denied that the 1609 edition, entitled *Shake-speares Sonnets. Neuer before Imprinted.*, was authored by Shakespeare at all, while others have expressed dismay that Shakespeare wrote these sonnets.[6] Many late eighteenth- and nineteenth-century critics went to great lengths to extenuate, deny, or reinterpret the homoeroticism and heterosexual improprieties which they perceived to be both present in some of the sonnets, and unacceptable to their model of Shakespearean authorship.[7] Many nineteenth-and early twentieth- century critics found the sonnets biographically faulty and attempted to link all of the ambiguous references to a young man, a dark lady, an "onlie better," and a "Mr. W.H." to figures with whom Shakespeare interacted, or might have interacted, in his lifetime. Here, the puzzling ambiguity of the sonnets was seen as their chief faulty component: the mystery of Shakespeare's deepest personal thoughts seemed locked in the sonnets, which stubbornly refused to divulge their creator's secrets.

More recently, textual critics have examined the charges that the early printed versions of Shakespeare's sonnets were unauthorized, pirated versions of his poems – not only the 1609 quarto, but John Benson's 1640 *Poems. By Wil. Shakespeare. Gent*, and the 1599 *Passionate Pilgrime*, which contains versions of the sonnets numbered 138 and 144 in the 1609 quarto.[8] Moreover, editors since the 1980s have called for the expansion of the work we tend to call simply "Shakespeare's Sonnets" to include the long poem *A Lover's Complaint*. The corrected error here is that in editions after the 1609 quarto, *A Lover's Complaint* is often not printed together with the sonnets. Only with John Kerrigan's 1986 edition has this poem been "restored" to its place as an integral appendix to, or appendage of, the textual corpus of the book of Shakespeare's sonnets.[9] Following Kerrigan's lead, recent critics have attended to the ways in which the composite structure of *Shake-speares Sonnets* marks it as a typical, late sixteenth-century English printed sonnet sequence, with similarly composite sequences being produced by a range of authors, including Edmund Spenser, Thomas Lodge, and Samuel Daniel, and also compiled by printers and editors, such as those involved in the early printed editions of Philip Sidney's *Astrophel and Stella*.[10] Attention to these features of Shakespeare's text aims to correct previous notions, now deemed mistaken, that the final two poems of *Shake-speares Sonnets* do not belong in the sequence, or that *A Lover's Complaint* should not be read alongside the sonnets, or should even be considered non-Shakespearean.

The second uncontroversial observation is that Shakespeare's sonnets relentlessly pursue the idea of human reproduction. It has long been observed that the initial "procreation sonnets" were likely influenced by a model persuasive letter written by Erasmus and available in *The Arte of Rhetorique* (1553).[11] Many critics have also noticed that the proposed physical reproduction of the young man's beauty through procreation quickly metamorphoses into a textual reproduction of his beauty through *poiesis*. The couplet of sonnet 17 makes this equivalence clear: "But were some child of yours alive that time, / You should live twice in it and in my rhyme." As well, sonnet 11 connects the writerly implements of seals and printing presses with human reproduction in a straightforwardly positive manner: "She carved thee for her seal, and meant thereby / Thou shouldst print more, not let that copy die."[12] These, however, are just two of many kinds of reproduction treated in the sonnets. Shakespeare dwells on the ubiquitous metaphor in which the poet's creations are seen as human offspring, which I have examined at greater length in chapter 4. But Shakespeare also repeatedly refers to alternative forms of reproduction, such as grafting, coining, and imping, and to suspect versions of reproduction such as bastardy or counterfeiting. In the later sonnets, the speaker faces the challenges of making a large sonnet collection. These challenges include the reproduction of the same sentiment in multiple sonnets, the reproduction inherent in writing multiple sonnets to the same addressee, and the competitive reproduction-project of sonnet writing itself, a project which compels the writer to recognize formalized tropes of addressing the loved one even while inventing new ways of praising the addressee.

In what follows, I argue that there has been a fundamental misunderstanding of Shakespeare's poetics of reproduction. Shakespeare's speaker does not simply encourage the young man to reproduce; he also gradually explores the impossibility of extending a human identity through time. Not only are successive copies of the young man's beautiful form inherently mutating, but perfect reproductions via poetry are impossible as well. *Errata* are human occurrences, and these occurrences are bound to proliferate not only in manuscript copies and printed copies, but in human copies, and especially in sonnets.[13] This poetic concern reverses the *poiesis* of epideictic striving, in which praising the love object assumes that perfection is not only attainable, but is in fact lyric poetry's default, its aspirational norm. Certainly *Astrophel and Stella* centres around Stella's perfection and the poet's struggle to express it. Even more explicitly, Drayton's *Ideas Mirror* and Daniel's *Delia* both take poetic idealization as their fundamental goal: Daniel's Delia is an "ideal," while Drayton's poetry holds a mirror to an otherwise unattainable Platonic form. Both poets perhaps strive towards the ideal versions implicit in their titles, by creating successive printed versions of their sonnets: they add and subtract sonnets in successive editions, raising the possibility that each edition is nearer to perfection than the last.[14] Shakespeare's sonnets advance English lyric poetry precisely because they challenge the assumptions of traditional sonnet collections: a tendency towards representational perfection, a sequential progression from one sonnet to the next, and a central goal of conserving in text the essence of its addressee, primarily through praise. Instead, the sonnets reveal, through their insistence on human error and the difficulty of maintaining identity through time, that the truest and fairest copy is the mutated one, the imperfect one, the one which maintains identity not by staying the same, but by changing. A fair copy of Shakespeare's sonnets is thus a copy that mutates them.

I Poetic Increase, Material Erasure, and Making Faults

Sonnets 138 and 144 offer an instructive introduction into the myriad issues regarding the reproduction of Shakespeare's sonnets. They alone among the sonnets were printed before the 1609 quarto edition. *The Passionate Pilgrime* (1599) was printed by William Jaggard, and includes twenty poems, five of which are known to be by Shakespeare and eleven of which are of unknown authorship. This edition has often been said to demonstrate a new period of ascendancy in Shakespeare's career: after the successes of *Venus and Adonis* and his plays of the early 1590s,

Shakespeare's name was now sufficient to sell copies. Although other possibilities exist, one likely scenario for this volume's composition is that Jaggard placed the two Shakespearean sonnets at the beginning of the volume, added three songs from *Love's Labour's Lost* and poems on the theme of Venus and Adonis, and to these Shakespearean-sounding poems added other poems circulating anonymously in verse miscellanies. Going by the title page, all of the poems seem to be attributed to Shakespeare.[15] However, the volume also has a second, internal title page promising "Sonnets To sundry notes of Musicke" without specifying an author. The volume went into a second printing in 1612, and occasioned some wrangling over authorship ascription.[16]

Critics have long noted the differences between the versions of sonnets 138 ("When my love swears that she is made of truth") and 144 ("Two loves I haue of comfort and despair") as they appear in *The Passionate Pilgrime* and the 1609 quarto edition of the sonnets. These differences are substantive, and present a rare editorial quandary. There are many textual cruxes and imperfections within the 1609 quarto version of the sonnets, but no other extant early printed edition or manuscript with which to compare potential readings, except, that is, for sonnets 138 and 144, which exist in two distinct early printed versions, which for textual scholars raises questions such as which version came first, and what the relative authority of each version is. Stephen Booth calls the evidence regarding the question of chronological priority "abundant and inconclusive."[17] Elsewhere in his notes to sonnet 138, Booth brings up two distinct possibilities for how the variations arose: Shakespeare might have revised the *Pilgrime* version into the more artful and developed quarto version, or the *Pilgrime* version might represent a memorially reconstructed version of the quarto version as it appeared in manuscripts in circulation before either version was printed. He occasionally speculates on whether a line in the *Pilgrime* version sounds like a "misremembered" quarto line. Without ever making a definitive hypothesis, Booth nevertheless lightly invokes the language of reproductive error: the *Pilgrime* version is described as a "garbled version," a "patch-up job," a "mistake," or "a typical product of a memory straining to recover a poem."[18]

This language makes the *Pilgrime* sonnets 138 and 144 seem like "bad quartos." If this appraisal is appropriate, then Shakespeare's sonnets, like his dramatic printed texts, should be scanned for the author's initial and final intentions, and one of the two early versions should be adopted as the copy-text.[19] But these editorial practices do not square with the reproduction of Shakespeare's sonnets, nor with reproduction *in* the sonnets. The language of "final intentions," grounded as it is in the New Bibliography, has been challenged in several different ways over the past half-century, primarily through the recent attention to the production of both manuscript and printed texts in social and commercial systems much larger than a single author,[20] but also through recent attention to the publication of Renaissance texts online and in facsimile editions, that is, in "unedited" editions whose production aims to mirror a certain state of the text at a certain time rather than sifting through all available versions.[21] Early reproductions of Shakespeare's sonnets raise a third problem: that a definitive or ideal text runs counter to Shakespeare's fictive models of both human and textual reproduction, as well as to the actual reproduction of these texts in extant printed copies. The stable and definitive copy is an illusion; as Arthur Marotti puts it, "There is *no* text of the *Sonnets*, in either manuscript or print, that can be shown to represent the ideal of old-fashioned textual critics," and instead we should "perceive in the poems the kind of fascinating textual instability that appeals to a postmodern sensibility."[22]

This postmodern instability should not just concern editors and bibliographers, but readers of the sonnets, because it is congruent with the quandaries of Shakespeare's poetic speaker and the conditions of their initial production and early reproductions. It is fair to assume that Shakespeare wrote his sonnets with a quill pen and oak gall ink. Reading "Shakespeare's sonnets" implies reading copies of the marks that he wrote, on paper, that are now lost. Are they fair copies? Do they represent what Shakespeare wrote, or is there some distant vision of those poems that is now irrecoverable? These issues, unanswerable by textual critics, nevertheless arise in the sonnets themselves. In the first few sonnets, the relatively straightforward injunction to marry and reproduce seems to provide a program for the conservation of beauty through sexual copy-making. But there are far fewer sonnets on sexual reproduction than on textual reproduction. In asserting that the young man will live on in his verses, Shakespeare expresses a commonplace of epideictic poetry. Virtually every sonneteer (or elegy-writer) brags that the subject of the verse will live forever. Shakespeare's sonnets, too, make this claim. But they also undermine it.

Primarily, the sonnets interrogate textual copying by representing writing itself as a process of reproduction, and by meditating on the faultiness inherent in this process. If the first sonnet instills the sense that fairest creatures deserve special reproductive consideration, then the "creature" which Shakespeare's sonnets reproduce is not simply the image of the young man but the whole of their relationship – its love, friendship, advice, gifts, betrayal, failings, attempted reconciliation, and acknowledgment of change. Errors creep into this reproductive program throughout the collection, but sonnet 35 addresses them especially directly:

No more be grieved at that which thou hast done:
Roses have thorns, and silver fountains mud,
Clouds and eclipses stain both moon and sun,
And loathsome canker lives in sweetest bud.

All men make faults, and even I in this,
Authorizing thy trespass with compare,
Myself corrupting salving thy amiss,
Excusing thy sins more than thy sins are;
For to thy sensual fault I bring in sense –
Thy adverse party is thy advocate –
And 'gainst myself a lawful plea commence.
Such civil war is in my love and hate
    That I an accessary needs must be
    To that sweet thief which sourly robs from me.

The sonnet begins with aphorisms applied to the speaker's particular situation, rendered by the rather vague "that which thou hast done." We are therefore in the realm of *sententiae*, which were copied into personal commonplace books or "table-books" for future reference; for use in letters, plays, or poems; for use as ornament to conversation with others; or simply because the habit was ingrained.[23] Sonnet 35 exemplifies this type of copying because, as Booth notes, the speaker is in effect copying proverbs into the first few lines, including the particularly relevant proverb that "a fault once excused is twice committed."[24]

The proverb is relevant because Shakespeare multiplies the faultiness in this sonnet. The young man's fault is unspecified; the speaker's fault is endemic to poetry. Representation in poetry, here condensed into the single word "compare," is an error-riddled process, one which corrupts the maker even as it excuses the faults of the love object. The double fault here is thus not simply countenancing the original transgression but poeticizing it, and the urgency of this action rings in all the present continuous verb forms, which run together in the above three lines: "Authorizing ... corrupting salving ... Excusing." This faulty copying contradicts the copying in the procreation sonnets. Those contain an idealized, future-tending trajectory, in which "beauty's rose" is preserved via future generations of the young man's beautiful image. The speakers of Sidney's *Astrophel and Stella* or Daniel's *Delia* assume a posture of modesty when faced with putting the perfections of their mistresses into words. Here, Shakespeare's speaker finds the whole prospect of comparison to be inherently faulty.

Shakespeare's anti-Petrarchan "My mistress' eyes are nothing like the sun" (130) is his most famous instance of satirizing the sonnet form's tendency to praise hyperbolically and without consideration. But "No more be grieved at that which thou hast done" goes even further, by evaluating both the young man's faultiness, and the inherently faulty proposition of transmuting him into poetry. If sonnet 130 emphasizes such "true" speech, which does not sugar-coat realities with the hyperbole and ornamentation common to amorous poetry in the Petrarchan tradition, then sonnet 35 questions whether any speech at all can be linked to the young man. Even in the absence of anti-Petrarchan plain speech, sonnets like this one force a more or less immediate re-evaluation of the young man's reproduction project, and expose the fantasy of a perfect copy or unalloyed reproduction. If all men make faults, then the poet's fault is representational in nature: the creative process inherently involves reproduction, here "compare," and reproductions contain the seeds of the maker's corruption.

As if exemplifying this inherent faultiness, sonnet 35 is one of many in the 1609 Thorpe quarto presumed to have textual errors. The quarto version of line 8, "Excuſing their ſins more then their ſins are:" (sig. C4r), is usually taken to be, as above, "Excusing *thy* sins more than *thy* sins are."[25] It is probably unwise to make too much of this particular error when it comes to the sonnet's meaning, other than perhaps to note that in line 10, "Thy adverse party is thy advocate," a similar construction, with a double "thy," occurs. In fact there are eight instances of "thou" and "thy" in this poem (assuming the emendation is a good one), and the alleged their / thy fault occurs multiple times in the quarto. If this sonnet generalizes fault-making to all, then the compositor of the printed book shows that he, too, is part of the error-filled process of textual reproduction. The sheer unintentionality of this minor fault is perhaps the best demonstration of the rule that "all men make faults."

The thy / their error may be a minor one, but it raises an issue that is central to Shakespeare's sonnets. The issue is no less than the question of what constitutes a fair or perfect copy, and how beauty, truth, fairness, and kindness can be reproduced through and against time, the "eater of things." Sonnet 35 has the potential to expand its aphorism's meanings, by forcing the reader to consider "every rose," as Shakespeare does in various sonnets. There is "beauties rose," (1.2), a seemingly Platonic essence of beauty which the speaker urges the young man to reproduce by making a copy of himself. (The flower distilled into perfume is the famous metaphor of sonnet 5, in which the distilled perfume triumphs over winter as the imagined child of the young man triumphs over death.) There is also, however, 35's thorny rose, aphoristically showing that no beauty exists without fault, and serving as a reminder of the young man's faultiness. And there is "thou, my rose" (109 and elsewhere) which seems in that sonnet to signify the young man in his entirety. If one project of the sonnets is textually to reproduce him, then Shakespeare's version of copying does not essentially involve conservation, but instead proliferation and mutation.

This is not to deny the force of Shakespeare's monumental language. He repeatedly defies time, even echoing Horace's comparison of verse to the pyramids.[26] This is the material stability which Jeff Rothenberg and many other readers take to be the central message of the sonnets. Pyramids crumble and pass into dust, but not sonnet 18. However, the written word, the "material" into which the speaker knows his love will mutate, is unstable in a different way. Shakespeare explores the stability and instability of written reproductions in sonnets 77, 81, and 122, which deal with less permanent modes of reproduction than in other sonnets, with their talk of monuments and graven stones. These sonnets seem to have to do with the private gift of a blank table book, ready-made for copying snippets of text. In 77, the speaker again persuades the young man to reproduce, but this time his mind is to be copied: "The vacant leaves thy mind's imprint will bear." The speaker then more explicitly connects writing and reproduction, making reference to the very common metaphor in which writing and giving birth are conflated:

> Look what thy memory cannot contain,
> Commit to these waste blanks, and thou shalt find
> Those children nursed, delivered from thy brain,
> To take a new acquaintance of thy mind. (77.9–12)

Recent critical attention to *sententiae* has revealed the importance and pervasiveness of copying commonplaces: as an essentially humanist action, involving both attentive reading, and as a textual action oriented towards the future use of the quotations in conversation or in written texts.[27] Here, the actions of both copying and of creating are juxtaposed, such that it is not clear whether the young man is the author of the lines yet to be penned, or whether he will be copying only the aphorisms and *sententiae* of others into the blank leaves of the book. So what at first seems a romantic conception of authorship, in which a lone author toils in a labour as difficult as childbirth, and gives birth to an offspring of which he can claim sole paternity (the mother is almost always elided or discounted in Shakespeare's sonnets and in other instances of this metaphor), in actuality edges much closer to the humanist model of citational coauthorship.[28] In urging such "offices," the poet advises the young man not to reproduce only the fair copy of himself from the procreation sonnets. Rather, here the young man is urged to create a new, hybrid textual version of himself, one which circumscribes both old authority and "new acquaintance."

In this poem, the book itself fulfils an important function in the birthing and nursing process; it is the repository for those thoughts or compositions which the young man's "memory cannot contain," and it is the blank space capable of receiving his "mind's imprint." It also serves as a memento mori, and is likened both to the mirror that shows the young man's gradually wrinkling face, and to the dial's demonstration of the progress of the sun. More particularly relevant to commonplacing is the declaration that the contents of the book will "take a new acquaintance of thy mind." Ever forward-looking, Shakespeare's speaker here imagines a kind of reunion between the young man and the offspring of his brain. That reunion comes through the gradual work of compiling the book, and through the re-perusal of thoughts long since forgotten. There is none of the bravura of claiming to reach eternity here: the book is not imagined as an escape from time's progress. Instead, it is a reminder of time's progress. The self which the young man will see in it is not a physical reproduction, not the beautiful self-image the speaker refers to in the earlier sonnets. Instead, it is a textual being, including ancient sources, more recent texts by the young man's friends and contemporaries, and those of the speaker himself. What the young man will be reacquainted with, then, is himself as a composite text. It will not be an exact copy of his former self. Rather, it will present an older version of himself, a child he has borne, and a set of others' texts which he has copied and incorporated into this hybrid object.

The metaphors of copying and offspring in this sonnet are in direct contrast to those of sonnet 122, which also mentions the practice of copying and commonplacing in "thy tables." In this poem, the ostensible occasion of the poem seems to be that the young man has given or loaned his table book to the speaker, who has then given it away to another recipient. In his analysis of sonnets 77 and 122, Arthur Marotti highlights the collectibility of sonnets, and the common practice of circulating poetry on bifolia, making it likely that several poems were circulated on a single sheet. Noting that the table book would be "a convenient place in which to record the sonnets written to him," Marotti goes so far as to say that this sort of table-book "would have been just the sort of manuscript in which a holograph copy of part or all of the sonnet collection might have been made."[29] In other words, Shakespeare's speaker is referring to exactly the type of book that textual critics dream of: the ideal copy text, an early source, in the author's hand, of what would later be printed as *Shake-speares Sonnets*. Because Shakespeare accents the ability of the book to retain precious text through time in sonnet 77, it is all the more shocking that he demeans the book's physical form in 122:

> Thy gift, thy tables, are within my brain
> Full charactered with lasting memory,
> Which shall above that idle rank remain
> Beyond all date, even to eternity –
> Or at the least, so long as brain and heart
> Have faculty by nature to subsist –
> Till each to razed oblivion yield his part
> Of thee, thy record never can be missed.
> That poor retention could not so much hold,
> Nor need I tallies thy dear love to score.
> Therefore to give them from me was I bold

To trust those tables that receive thee more.
To keep an adjunct to remember thee
Were to import forgetfulness in me.

In both 77 and 122, writing and memory are brought to bear on the speaker's abiding preoccupation with the physical dissolution of death. In both cases, Shakespeare accents the impossibility of the fair, beautiful, and identical copy. In 77, the blank leaves do not receive an exact impression of the young man, but a hybrid amalgamation which conquers time, but not by retaining an exact copy of him. Here, there seems to be a slightly different accent, because the "vacant leaves" of 77 and "thy gift, thy tables" in 122 may refer to different kinds of writing, and different kinds of memory. The former seems to imply individual leaves of paper, filled with writing over time. But "thy tables," according to Stallybrass, Chartier, Mowery, and Wolfe, probably refers to a different object: a portable, erasable surface used for jotting notes, thoughts, commonplaces, or the kind of seasonal information that might be found in almanacs, or used as annotations to them. They note that "erasability is endemic to the human body," and connect this bodily dissolution to the repeated erasure of table-books.[30] Needless to say, such erasability flies in the face of sonnets that assert a timeless love that preserves the young man through the enduring power of poetry.

Sonnet 122 calls up a number of models of lasting memory, and undermines them all. In a gift economy, the gift-object serves in part as a reminder or place-holder of the relationship; itemized gift records at New Year's detail who gave what, and serve to define courtly relationships between the sovereign and the nobility. Sonnet 122 delays until line 11 the shocking "Therefore to give them from me I was bold," a statement that wittily rationalizes the re-gifting of the young man's gift, even as it destroys the material place-holder, the table book, which ordinarily would define and preserve a trace of their relationship. This action, the speaker says, is truer to that relationship because he is trusting the gift instead to his "brain and heart."

But this version of memorial retention also breaks down under pressure, and it does so in a way that again reveals Shakespeare's deep suspicion of exact copies in the sonnets. In the first quatrain, we have the assertion, so familiar from earlier sonnets, that a "full charactered" written record will not only outshine its peers (the "idle rank"), but also last "Beyond all date even to eternity." In the second quatrain, this assertion is immediately and devastatingly undermined by the prospect of death's physical dissolution: "Or at the least, so long as brain and heart / Have faculty by nature to subsist." The second half of this quatrain is no more reassuring, since it imagines each person known to the young man slowly dying off, and in doing so "to razed oblivion yield[ing] his part / Of thee ..." The last eight lines attempt to recover the textual vestiges of the young man, asserting that the "poor record" of the table book is a suspect "adjunct" to memory, untrustworthy compared to "those tables that receive thee more," presumably the brain and heart of the speaker. But this is poor reassurance indeed, since in other sonnets the speaker reminds us repeatedly that he is older and closer to death, and that he himself wishes to be forgotten. Sonnet 122 touchingly implies that the speaker's love is not bound by printed characters in a paper book, but rather alive in his memory and heart. At the same time, it calls into question the whole project of the speaker's "love," when that love is understood as a textual reproduction of these thoughts and feelings. If sonnet 77 urges the young man to engage in the humanist offices of copying and commonplacing, sonnet 122 discards such written ephemera as suspect mnemonics, a pointedly Platonic suspicion of writing. Favoured instead are the brain and heart of the poet, but these too are evanescent; they will yield up the young man's essential record as soon as the brief human life span is over. Crucially, we must hear not only "heart" in the phrase "brain and heart," but "art" as well, echoing Sidney's famous opening to *Astrophel and Stella*, "Look in thy heart and write."[31] The perfect copy of the young man is locked in the poet's brain and heart, while the written copy is as crude a record of the young man as a score-mark on a tally rod.

In addition to gifts and table books, a printing error in the quarto version of sonnet 122 brings up a third form of faulty memory: gnomic quotation marks. Double commas, often inverted and usually placed in the margins, served to call readers' attention to lines deemed worthy of quotation in personal commonplace books. As Lesser and Stallybrass have shown, in the early 1600s, a spike in commonplace markers occurs in first-edition playbooks, and this pattern is connected to poetic collections of the same period. Noting that these markers also appeared in Shakespeare's *The Rape of Lucrece*, printed in 1594, Lesser and Stallybrass connect commonplacing marks to the first quarto edition of *Hamlet*, which they argue deploys inverted commas in an attempt to render the text into a more consciously literary object rather than simply an acting version of the play.[32]

Sonnet 122 repeats the initial capital "T," and then gives a double comma in the first line (see figure 5.1).[33] The double comma, most likely a compositor's error, is nevertheless intriguing because there are so many aphoristic phrases in Shakespeare's sonnets, as well as in his dramatic works. *Hamlet*, also referring to table books, connects writing to the fluidity of human memory: "My tables, meet it is I set it down, / That one may smile, and smile, and be a villain" (1.5.107–8).[34] The staged action here is clearly similar to actions referred to in sonnets 77 and 122. Hamlet's *memorandum* has occasioned many questions, both practical and theoretical. Does he actually write this phrase down? How would this be staged? When he says "So uncle, there you are" (1.5.110), does this refer to the ghost's injunction

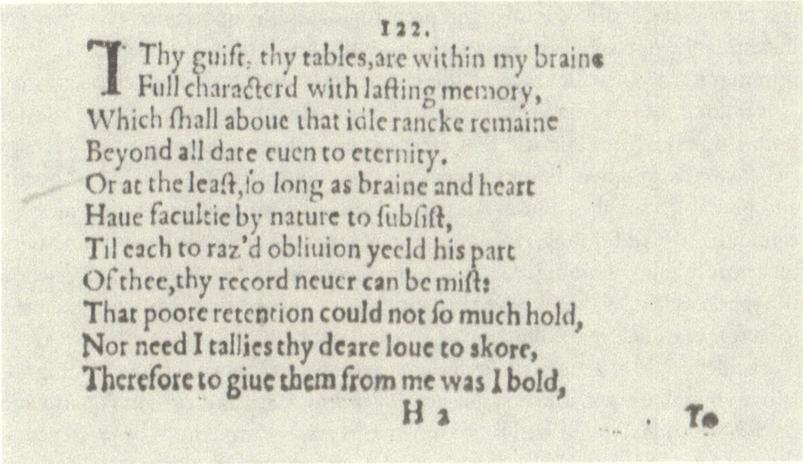

122.

THy guiſt, thy tables,are within my braine
Full characterd with laſting memory,
Which ſhall aboue that idle rancke remaine
Beyond all date euen to eternity.
Or at the leaſt,ſo long as braine and heart
Haue facultie by nature to ſubſiſt,
Til each to raz'd obliuion yeeld his part
Of thee,thy record neuer can be miſt:
That poore retention could not ſo much hold,
Nor need I tallies thy deare loue to skore,
Therefore to giue them from me was I bold,
H 2 To

Figure 5.1 *Shake-speares Sonnets* (1609), sig. H2r (detail). This item is reproduced by permission of The Huntington Library, San Marino, California

to "remember me?" How does whatever he writes relate to the next phrase, "Now to my word," often glossed as a military watch-word?[35] Even more tellingly, just before writing this word, or phrase, or perhaps merely miming writing or just referring to the action (all potential decisions of staging), Hamlet figures his own memory as an erasable table book. Everything he has written in it can be effaced in this one moment of crisis:

> Remember thee?
> Yea, from the table of my memory
> I'll wipe away all trivial fond records,
> All saws of books, all forms, all pressures past,
> That youth and observation copied there;
> And thy commandment all alone shall live
> Within the book and volume of my brain,
> Unmix'd with baser matter; yes, by heaven! (1.5.97–104)

If the printers of Q1 *Hamlet* call attention to the book's status as a literary object worthy of quotation, sonnet 122 and *Hamlet*'s erasures here register a deep suspicion that such scribbling can comprise any sort of lasting copy. The printed version of sonnet 122 makes that suspicion manifest, by seeming to deceive the reader into paying special attention to its contents. If the attentive reader sees this instance of double commas and prepares for a pithy quotation, what they get instead is the opposite instruction: do *not* write down those things that are most important; do not trust these to the characters of writing. Those characters are "trivial fond records," and the "pressures" (probably the actual pressing of a stylus onto a waxed writing surface) that exert them can have no lasting effect. Perhaps the answer is to rely only on memory and the non-material recitation of poetry and quotable thoughts. But as so many of the other sonnets insist, that message cannot be trusted for long, since textual memories are embodied truths, and bodies are only short-term objects. The truer receptacle for the young man's essence, the speaker's "tables that receive thee more," can only retain this perfect memory for a few years before the oblivion of physical decay intrudes.

Hamlet might actually write in order to preserve an aphorism about smiling villains in his table book. The first quarto of *Hamlet* (as well as the second quarto and the folio editions) might well be saying that its *sententiae* ought to be preserved in the same way. Sonnet 77 is at least in partial agreement with the procreation sonnets, since it too urges him to produce offspring, hybrid and textual though they are. But sonnet 122, and the many fault-laden sonnets examined above, call this whole reproductive project into question. One potential answer to the problem of error-laden reproductions is the kind of immateriality espoused by sonnet 122: the best reproduction of the young man, and his thoughts, is that which lives in the poet's mind. Sonnet 122 and *Hamlet* counter this answer: the poet is older and visibly closer to death, while Hamlet continually meditates on "the thousand natural shocks / That flesh is heir to." Both texts encourage a humane fostering of their respective ideas and memories. But both texts also destroy this hope, sonnet 122 with its "razed oblivion," and *Hamlet* with the initial vow to remember the ghost's command in "the book and volume of my brain" being completely undermined on a number of occasions. The most striking of these is his iconic contemplation of the brainless skull of Yorick, whose memory is retained in Hamlet's beautiful, nostalgic musings. But these memories will last only as long as Hamlet's own brain functions, and in the play's action, this time scale is very short indeed.

This is not to deny, but rather to counterbalance, the sonnets' regular and insistent emphasis on eternity and on extending memory past human life-spans. The trajectory towards eternity is matched by another, darker trajectory towards oblivion, one that sonnets 67–9 confront directly:

Ah wherefore with infection should he live,
And with his presence grace impiety,
That sin by him advantage should achieve,
And lace itself with his society?
Why should false painting imitate his cheek,

And steal dead seeing of his living hue?
Why should poor beauty indirectly seek
Roses of shadow, since his rose is true?
Why should he live, now nature bankrout is,
Beggared of blood to blush through lively veins?
For she hath no exchequer now but his,
And, proud of many, lives upon his gains.
  O him she stores, to show what wealth she had,
  In days long since, before these last so bad.

In both 67 and the companion sonnet 68, the image pattern is one overflowing with corruption, aging, and death, amid which the young man is still held to be a paragon of natural beauty. The conceit of both sonnets is that the addressee is living in a corrupt age which uses cosmetics and other beauty aids to imitate nature, while he stands apart from these counterfeiters and, in both poems, exists as a storehouse for nature. (The final couplet of 67 is nearly identical to that of 68: "And him as for a map doth nature store, / To show false art what beauty was of yore.") In these sonnets, his fault seems to be merely being alive in a faulty world. In the procreation sonnets, this status as a corruptible, mortal creature spurs artistic creation, in the poetry of the speaker. But these sonnets harshly confront the young man's susceptibility to "false art," and it is not clear whether the poet's own art can be separated from the "false painting," "dead seeing," and "roses of shadow," which recall the many roses of the procreation sonnets, and puncture their hyperbolically inflated ability to distil the young man's beautiful essence, to preserve his beauty by metaphorizing it as roses.

The young man's death, and poetic art's flawed mission of preserving his beauty, are never so apparent as in sonnet 68, which promises not the future of the young man, but the past. This past is not the golden age we might expect, but a time "when beauty lived and died as flow'rs do now" (68.2), and, in perhaps the most powerful lines in these sonnets, a time

Before the golden tresses of the dead,
The right of sepulchers, were shorn away,
To live a second life on second head –
Ere beauty's dead fleece made another gay. (68.5–8)

To grafting, usury, and imping, Shakespeare now adds another form of artificial increase, a kind of grave-robbing that steals the grave's treasure, the "golden tresses of the dead," only to weave them in among the tresses of the living. This ghoulish action is, on the surface, syntactically and chronologically contrasted with the addressee, whose beauty precedes this age of artificiality. Yet Nature here is vampiric, living on the youth and storing up his rose, so that he becomes a kind of encrypted victim, someone who has been sapped by imitation, someone from whom even the dead fleece will be stolen to adorn some other version of beauty.

This demise is not asserted outright, but creeps in as a necessary part of the addressee's living with infection. *Poiesis*, far from being the cure for this infection, is actively contributing to the young man's death. As in the examples above, textual faults in the 1609 quarto text help to remind us of the connection between the young man's and the poet's faulty reproductive image-making processes; they exemplify the actions and paradoxes described in the sonnets themselves.[36] Each instance of potential textual corruption comprises a moment in which copying goes awry, when the increase of the text coincides with the proliferation of human error. In the instance of 69.14, the congruency is particularly felicitous, since the line enacts a revelation of error even as it demonstrates that error in a different manner. The final couplet in the quarto is "But why thy odor matcheth not thy ſhow, / The ſolye is this, that thou doeſt common grow" (sig. E3r). Most editors conjecture that a simple transposition of letters occurred, so that "soyle" accidentally became "solye." The last three lines, with their *Hamlet*-like rankness of weeds and odours, certainly match this interpretation. But it could be read as "folly," which fits the overall context as well, since the addressee's growing common leads to a widely held faultiness. Correctness, either of any individual version or of the young man's actions and his heart, falls prey to both the poetic process and the process of reproducing poetry by copying. Throughout sonnet 69, there is an incommensurability – of praise to deed, of mind to action, and here, of a single word to the multiple meanings and words to which human faultiness has given rise.

Each early printed book containing sonnets attributed to Shakespeare has been viewed as faulty, though recent critics, often less invested in the ideal of Shakespeare as an Author, do not use such condemnatory terms. Given Shakespeare's accent on faulty reproduction outlined above, I maintain that John Benson's 1640 *Poems*, long accused of mutilating Shakespeare's sonnets, should be seen instead as an ideal, fair copy, since it reproduces the sonnets with significant changes. Benson's edition begins with sonnets 67–9, under the title "The glory of beautie." Other textual critics have noted that Benson's edition is a sophisticated one in both its appraisal of its audience and niche, and its eclecticism: Benson collected various printed sources of Shakespeare's poetry, including the 1612 *Pilgrime*, Thorpe's 1609 quarto, and Robert Chester's *Loves Martyr* (1601), combined them with non-Shakespearean sources and poems on Shakespeare, and created from these sources a composite volume that would be the only version of the sonnets printed for seventy years.[37] He also combined multiple sonnets into larger poems, and like Richard Tottel, assigned titles to these new creations (see figure 5.2).

Benson's title for the first poem creates a process in which editorial interaction with the text begets readerly interaction. Elsewhere in *Poems*, Benson's titles sometimes cleave closer to the titles and textual purposes favoured by Caroline and Restoration miscellanies, such as *The Academy of Complements* and *Wits Recreations* (1640), and *Fascicvlvs Florvm* (1636). These are loose but systematic gatherings of material all to do with a single theme. For example, *Witts Recreations* provides not only a large number of short, witty poems, but also as its title page advertises, "A Thousand outLandish Proverbs." The "recreations" of the wits are all compiled according to their subject matter, nearly all of them "on" a subject, or occasion. Likewise, *The Academy of Complements* provides aspiring wits a list of things to say in virtually every social situation.[38] These miscellanies thus collect and reproduce their materials in print, but with the expectation that the contents will be reproduced and reappropriated in social contexts.

"The Glory of Beautie," on the other hand, gives an active reader something to do. The strangeness of that title, and its potential application to the poem, might lead the reader to seek out a resolution. Rather than beginning, as expected, with beautiful images, the first lines foist on the reader the "infection" of the poem's subject, and the mortified images discussed above. The complex surprise that emerges from Benson's puzzling title has to do with the fact that the glory of beauty lies not in nature, which has been corrupted, but instead in a man known only as "him." To this surprise is added a further surprise about the man: his surpassing physical beauty is not matched by beauty of the mind – instead the poem dissolves back into "the ranke smell of weeds," and the accusation "thou doest common grow" (sig. A2v; see figure 5.2).

This effect arises from the fact that the poems, in Arthur Marotti's lovely formulation, are "Benson's Thorpe's Shakespeare's words."[39] Yet Benson was no postmodern editor of Shakespeare; his edition is firmly grounded in the assertion of Shakespeare's authorship of the sonnets and his role as a reproducer of Shakespeare's poetry and a liaison to Shakespeare's legacy. Benson is "glad to be serviceable for the continuance of glory to the deserved Author in these his poems," poems which Benson asserts were in "their Infancie in his death" (sigs *2r–v). John Warren's dedicatory poem likewise asserts that Benson's printing serves to revive Shakespeare's poetry and to keep his name "immortall on the earth," yet confers praise on Benson not so much as a creative textual agent but as an admirer, even a lover, of Shakespeare's works: "Tis love that thus to thee. is showne, / The labours his, the glory sti'l thine owne" (sig. *4v). Benson is to Shakespeare, therefore, as Shakespeare's speaker is to the young man: a lover and admirer, an instrument of continuation and succession, a reproducer of the beauty, glory, virtue, and here, eloquence, of the loved one.

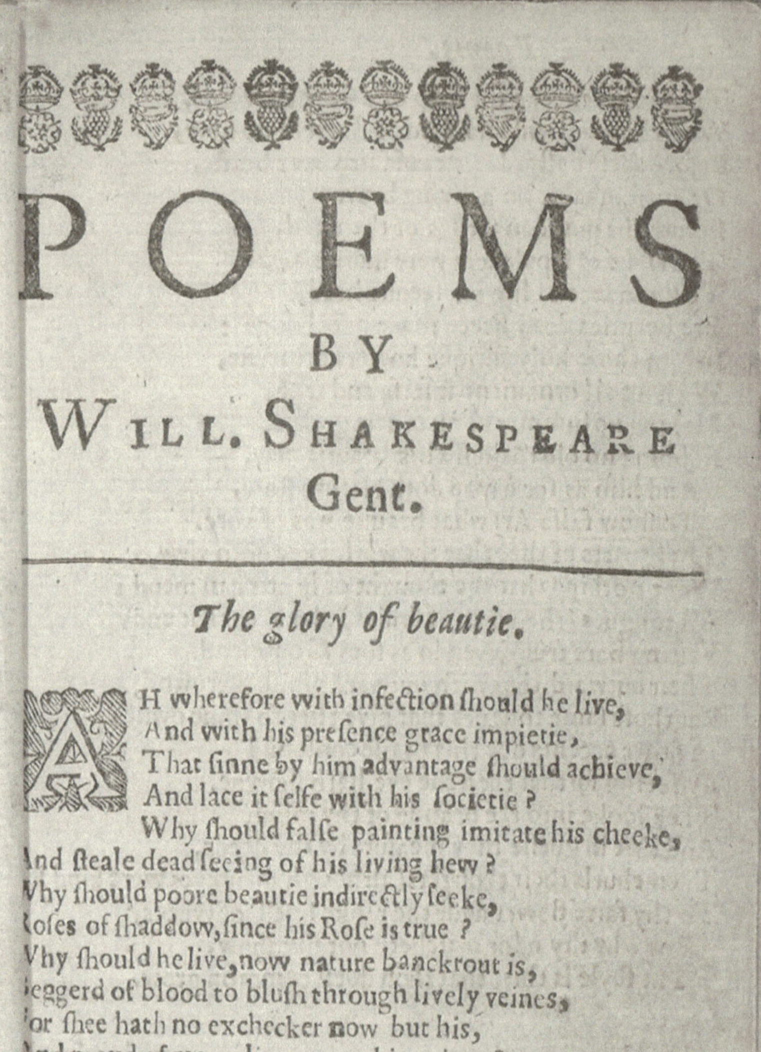

POEMS
BY
WILL. SHAKESPEARE
Gent.

The glory of beautie.

AH wherefore with infection ſhould he live,
And with his preſence grace impietie,
That ſinne by him advantage ſhould achieve,
And lace it ſelfe with his ſocietie?
Why ſhould falſe painting imitate his cheeke,
And ſteale dead ſeeing of his living hew?
Why ſhould poore beautie indirectly ſeeke,
Roſes of ſhaddow, ſince his Roſe is true?
Why ſhould he live, now nature banckrout is,
Beggerd of blood to bluſh through lively veines,
For ſhee hath no exchecker now but his,
And proud of many, lives upon his gaines?
O him ſhe ſtores, to ſhow what wealth ſhe had,
In daies long ſince, before theſe laſt ſo bad.

A 2 Thus

Figure 5.2 "The glory of beautie," comprising sonnets 67–9, from *Poems: VVritten by Wil. Shakespeare. Gent.* (1640), sigs A2r–v. Horace Howard Furness Memorial Library, University of Pennsylvania

Poems.

Thus is his cheeke the map of daies out-worne,
When beauty liv'd and dy'd as flowers do now,
Before theſe baſtard ſignes of faire were borne,
Or durſt inhabit on a living brow:
Before the goulden treſſes of the dead,
The right of ſepulchers were ſhorne away,
To live a ſecond life on ſecond head,
Ere beauties dead fleece made another gay:
In him thoſe holy antique howers are ſeene,
Without all ornament, it ſelfe and true,
Making no ſummer of an others greene,
Robbing no old to dreſſe his beautie new,
And him as for a map doth Nature ſtore,
To ſhow falſe Art what beautie was of yore.
Thoſe parts of thee that the worlds eye doth view,
Want nothing that the thought of hearts can mend:
All tongues (the voice of ſoules) give thee that end,
Vttring bare truth, even ſo as foes Commend.
Their outward thus with outward praiſe is crownd,
But thoſe ſame tongues that give thee ſo thine owne,
In other accents doe this praiſe confound
By ſeeing farther then the eye hath ſhowne.
They looke into the beautie of thy mind,
And that in gueſſe they meaſure by thy deeds,
Then churls their thoughts (although their eyes were kind)
To thy faire flower adde the ranke ſmell of weeds,
But why thy odor matcheth not thy ſhow,
The ſoyle is this, that thou doeſt common grow.

Injuriou

Figure 5.2 *Continued*

There is no question of Benson's willingness to make substantive, editorial changes to the printed object now called "Shakespeare's sonnets." Setting aside the issue of whether Benson attempted to expunge the male addressee from Shakespeare's sonnets,[40] he certainly discarded the order of Thorpe's 1609 edition, and provided commentary on the sonnets and sonnet-clusters he created in the form of their titles. "Good admonition," "Immoderate Passion," and "Fast and Loose" all demonstrate that Benson's titles are sometimes labels, in the vein of Tottel and other editors of poetic miscellanies. But these labels are analytic acts with profound consequences regarding the perception of the poems. Benson's titles, as well as his willingness to intersperse other Shakespearean and non-Shakespearean poetry throughout the volume, show him in the act of revealing the essentially miscellaneous nature of Shakespeare's lyric poetry. Benson is unmoored by ideas of strict fidelity to either printed or manuscript copies: he can move freely about among the poems, selecting, labelling, copying, and all while claiming to remain true to Shakespeare's "Seren, cleere and eligantly plaine" verse.

Benson's edition remains true to Shakespeare's sonnets precisely *because* he is willing to change and adjust his source material. Shakespeare's speaker, enmeshed in the flawed process of reproduction, and knowing that reproduction itself is an error-filled process, nevertheless forges his poetic art by continually acknowledging the changes, lies, and errors inherent in *poiesis.* Benson's most startling editorial actions, the addition of titles and the reordering of Shakespeare's sonnets, further the process of error-filled reproduction. In Benson's edition, subject matter, tone, and exemplarity are key. Shakespeare's poems exemplify "Constant affection" or "Wholesome counsell." Yet the introductory and dedicatory matter claim that these are no vague truisms attributable to everyone and no one. Instead, they are the product of Shakespeare's particular genius, a claim which destabilizes the notion of general-purpose poetic commonplaces, in which the author is less important than the distilled knowledge of the text. Even as Benson's edition praises the singularity of its author, it disperses Shakespeare's poetry into seemingly authorless, sententious exemplars, and in doing so reminds us of table books, commonplacing, and the hybrid, memory-driven copies in *Hamlet* and sonnets 77 and 122.

Likewise, Benson's reordering of Shakespeare's sonnets dissolves many of the great critical controversies that have attended the sonnets since the eighteenth century. As a miscellany, the sonnets automatically assume a form in which the author's intentions are only one of a set of concerns; the balance is tipped towards readerly and editorial interaction with poems rather than a definitive and inward statement regarding the love between the poet, the young man, and the dark lady. Benson's format also renders useless any attempt to discern the plot of the sonnets – when the moments of betrayal occur, how the love triangle develops, how the rival poet fits into the mix. Shakespeare's sonnets are not, in Benson's edition, coherent and discrete moments in the representation of a single love affair; they are clusters of sonnets lumped together to form a single, longer poem, for example, "A louers affection though his love prove unconstant" (sonnets 92–5 in the 1609 quarto). These formulations are invitations to dissolve the sequence of the sonnets, to read into and around the sonnets, rather than to treat them as a sequence of poems, a singular object that moves forward in time, that begins with the urge to procreate, muddles through some hard times between the young man and the poet, and finishes with the darkly ecstatic poems addressed to an unspecified female addressee. Shakespeare's sonnets actively recommend this kind of temporal disjunction, as we shall see in the next section. They meditate on how the love object belongs to multiple times, especially in sonnets 59, 67–8, 106, and 108, among others. They treat the beauty of the youth as something to be preserved and defended, but also something that has somehow always existed, and whose future existence must be carved out, or breathed forth, or glassed in. Every mode of poetic reproduction is bound to fail the test of fidelity, when the expansive and synchronous objects of reproduction – "you" and "my love" – are themselves constantly changing. Chiefly for this reason, Benson's willingness to meddle with Shakespeare's supposed timeline, the individuality of his sonnets, and their context (since he places them amid other Shakespearean and non-Shakespearean poetry) is perhaps his most faithful action. This meddling is itself a version of *poiesis*: a fault-ridden creative act of reproduction with a difference. It thus constitutes a fair copy of *Shake-speares Sonnets*.

II "Desire is Death": Sequence and Copulation in the Sonnets

Above, we have seen that the traditional view of the procreation sonnets, that they espouse the creation of a perfect, lasting copy of the young man, falls apart in the face of Shakespeare's many examples of the fault-ridden process of reproduction. Sonnet 35 most explicitly states that "All men make faults," but other sonnets explore both the attempt to attain a perfect copy, and the difficulties of printing, penning, monument-making, and other forms of reproducing an object, a person, a love relationship, or a poem throughout endless time. The next section considers the implications of this faultiness for an extended reading of the sonnets. In particular, it finds in the temporal faultiness of Shakespeare's poetics an imposing challenge to the many totalizing reading projects attempting to make temporal and narrative sense of the entire sonnet collection. The sonnets resist chronologizing because Shakespeare depicts and enacts an identity that exists out of time, that ranges freely into the past and the future, and is not limited either by physicality or immateriality.

Although many recent studies focus on authorship, for much of their critical history, the sonnets were deemed to be problematic in an essentially narrative way: they told either an undesirable story about Shakespeare, or an unclear one. The many autobiographical studies – the who's who of the young man, the dark lady, the "onlie begetter," and "Mr. W.H." – need not be rehearsed.[41] The sequential order of *Shake-speares Sonnets* has been central to these disputes. Hyder Rollins provides an informative summary of the numerous attempts to reorder the sonnets between the mid-nineteenth and early twentieth centuries.[42] These attempts culminated in the years 1870–1920, though the subject has been revisited since then.[43]

These studies make sense of the sonnets by changing their putative sequence. Either tacitly or explicitly, they begin with the assumption that Shakespeare's intentions were thwarted during the printing process. Usually this assumption involves the anachronistic accusation of piracy: Shakespeare's sonnets were stolen from him, and printed without his knowledge or permission, from a foul manuscript state that did not properly represent his intentions.[44] But there have also been several critical treatments that avoid the issue of authorial *imprimatur* and instead attempt to discern the compositional order of the sonnets. These studies date the creation of individual sonnets or groups of sonnets by comparing word frequency patterns in the sonnets with those plays in the Shakespearean canon that can be dated with relative certainty. They rely primarily on the stylometric evidence of rare words, and have attempted to place certain sonnets at certain points of Shakespeare's career, and even to affirm or deny Shakespeare's authorship of *The Lover's Complaint*. There is widespread agreement, among those studying stylometrics and compositional order of the sonnets, that they were almost certainly not written in the order of the 1609 quarto, and that sonnets 127–54 were most likely written first, and perhaps as early as 1591–5, while many of the sonnets to the young man, 1–126, were either composed or revised in the early seventeenth century.[45]

Other recent critical treatments of the sonnets, not addressing the question of sequence directly, nevertheless reinforce the idea that there *is* an overarching internal logic or coherence in the sonnet collection. Chiefly this coherence comes from the supposed rift between the young man sonnets and the dark lady sonnets. Most often, this rift is seen as occurring sequentially, as a development that begins with the procreation sonnets addressed to and about the young man, and that ends with the dark lady sonnets. For example, Eve Sedgwick's *Between Men* identifies a tonal rift between many of the idealized and praising sonnets to the young man, and many of the bitter and demeaning sonnets to the dark lady. Sedgwick posits that in the (numerically) early sonnets to the young man, the male-male love is "set firmly within a structure of institutionalized social relations that are carried out via women" and that the heterosexuality of the poems to the dark lady is threatening and chaotic.[46] Valerie Traub extends this observation by pointing to the sequential movement in many of Shakespeare's plays from "the relative safety, familiarity, and pleasure of male homosocial bonds into a threatening yet compelling domain of heterosexual otherness" as a way of understanding heteronormative narratives like the film *Shakespeare in Love*. Traub ultimately calls for a reading of the sonnets that eschews such narratives, and that can "disarticulate sequence from sexuality."[47]

Attention to the supposed division is not limited to sexuality studies; other critics also reinforce the division, separability, and incommensurability of the first 126 sonnets from the last 28. Because it has been so influential, Joel Fineman's book-length treatment of the sonnets is worth quoting at length:

> In short, and these examples could be multiplied, there runs through the dark lady sonnets a language of and about language which is opposed to the language of and about vision that runs through the sonnets addressed to the young man . . . It is for this reason, referring to large themes and images, that I speak of a progress from eye to tongue. Taken together, the young man sub-sequence and the dark lady sub-sequence act this progress out as a succession of opposites: from man to woman, from true to false, from fair to foul. It is a downward movement, from good to bad, from love to lust, from kind to unkind, which is developed as a progress from vision to speech. In the second sub-sequence this progress becomes explicitly the story that the poet tells about his desire, about his poetry, and about himself.[48]

Fineman's sequential terms are essential to his critique of the sonnets; for him, the emphasis is on "progress," "movement," and crucially, "story." The sonnets, formerly a story about Shakespeare himself, the pieces of which so many critics had tried to set into proper order, is for Fineman a story about the order of Shakespeare's depiction of subjectivity itself. Fineman's study can perhaps be said to be New Criticism writ large, since it treats the entirety of *Shake-speares Sonnets* as a hermeneutic object that is as complex, well-made, and worthy of scrutiny as a single metaphysical poem. This kind of idealistic reading inevitably clashes with materialist examinations of the printed book of sonnets. Specifically, if the stylometric studies are right, and the dark lady sonnets were actually written earlier than the young man sonnets, then the progressive, narrative subjectivity invented by the sonnets, and especially the story inherent in this invention, arises not solely from the intentions and poetics of Shakespeare, but also from the unknown copiers of Shakespeare's manuscripts, and from agents like Thomas Thorpe, who may well have had a hand in the arrangement of the quarto sonnets.[49] This arrangement, often called the "order" of the sonnets, is transmuted into a variety of kinds of order by the critics who discern a coherent arch-text.

Calling *Shake-speares Sonnets* a "sonnet sequence" is a disservice to this book because the sonnets, their speaker, and their mediums both muse on and enact the problems of sequentiality. Medium-close reading can reveal how thoroughly this collection disrupts notions of poetic sequentiality, especially by examining inter-sonnet relationships such as juxtaposition and coiteration. This reading strategy grows directly out of two recent trends: first, materialist hypotheses regarding the composition of the sonnets, primarily the hypotheses that they were likely composed as individual units or in twos and threes on bifolia sheets, and that the book as a whole shares many characteristics of other, semi-miscellaneous sonnet collections of the 1590s.[50] Second, Heather Dubrow's 1996 essay, which directly confronts the division of the sequence into young man sonnets and dark lady sonnets, asserting that readings which do so reveal much about their authors, but considerably less about the sonnets themselves.[51]

In most early printed sonnet collections, of course, order is imposed by attaching numerals to sonnets, and by the codex medium itself.[52] But the problem with sequence in *Shake-speares Sonnets* is that it quickly breaks down under the pressures exerted by continuous poetic representation. The "story" in the first few sonnets would be a simple one, if only it were true: a beautiful young man reproduces himself at the behest of a poet. Then, in addition to his flesh-based reproduction, he lives happily ever after, through the loving descriptions in the sonnets themselves. However, recent critics have found the richly difficult language of human sex in the procreation sonnets to be extremely problematic.[53] Moreover, we have seen above how, in other sonnets, idealized human and textual reproduction clash with protestations of faultiness, and errors proliferate both in the printed editions of the sonnets and in the human actions of saying, writing, copying, and remembering.

Sex, sequence, and writing: these are the terms through which Shakespeare approaches the formidable project of maintaining identity through time. In neither human, nor textual reproduction does perfect, unchanging copying turn out to be possible. In the sonnet that most protests invariance, an inexorable poetic variation nevertheless surfaces:

> Kind is my love today, tomorrow kind,
> Still constant in a wondrous excellence;
> Therefore my verse to constancy confined,
> One thing expressing, leaves out difference.
> Fair, kind, and true, is all my argument,
> Fair, kind, and true, varying to other words;
> And in this change is my invention spent –
> Three themes in one, which wondrous scope affords. (105.5–12)

The poem has often been taken at face value, as a straightforward, even tautological, statement of the poet's constant, identical writing.[54] Stressing constancy, the poem nevertheless confesses variation. To begin with, the three terms are somehow equated. In a trinitarian trick that was grammatically viable in Shakespeare's English, the three terms fair, kind, and true *is* "all my argument."[55] Then, the terms are repeated; this repetition varies "to other words," and this variation stretches the poet to the limits of both craft and identity: "in this change is my invention spent." In one sense, the poet's spending invests his energies in extravagant, ornamental, ever-changing sonnets. In another sense, such poetic efforts are wasted; they spend invention unnecessarily, since the poet's declared (and impossible) task is a kind of repetitive constancy of expression. In sonnet 108, the poet addresses the question directly, asking "What's new to speak, what now to register," and just as quickly answering that instead of seeking new things to say, "I must each day say o'er the very same" (108.3, 108.6). Poetic succession, especially the repetitive act of writing sonnet after sonnet on the same theme, actually opposes the natural succession of one identity or theme with the next. In other words, the sonnets have to resist narrative because narrative insists on change, the enemy of representing the young man's species or "kind," and the enemy of the constant and simple truth. What sonnet 105 discovers, counter to its own message of constancy, is that the introduction of multiple terms is bound to alter identity to form a mysterious, new entity: "Fair, kind, and true, have often lived alone, / Which three, till now, never kept seat in one" (105.13–14). The threefold repetition of this threefold list actually effects a change, the exact opposite of the speaker's protestations of constancy.

The problems of sonnet sequence, then, are codetermined by Shakespeare alongside the problems of human sequence. Combination, repetition, juxtaposition, and coitus – of terms like "fair, kind, and true," or the young man and his imagined lover, or the sonnets combined into a collection – create something new and strange. The skewed sequentiality of these combinations is most apparent in sonnet 59, which begins with a hypothetical premise, and its logical conclusion:

> If there be nothing new, but that which is
> Hath been before, how are our brains beguiled,
> Which, lab'ring for invention, bear amiss
> The second burthen of a former child!

In this sonnet, the addressee's beauty is a problem precisely because it *cannot* be new. The intertext for the opening assertion, Ecclesiastes 1:9–11, proclaims that there is nothing new under the sun; the speaker extends this principle to the young man. He too is nothing new, and has come from his own mortal and flawed parents. In the context of the procreation sonnets, the relevance is obvious: this is why the young man must reproduce. His beauty, though superlative, is only "borrowed," and it must be continued "by succession" (2.12). In these sonnets, the young man's superlative beauty must be preserved successively in time, and Shakespeare dwells on the fact that his beauty cannot be unprecedented. Instead, that beauty has to be a reproduction of former beauties. In sonnet 1 and other (numerically) early sonnets, the young man's beauty has the potential to "increase" through replication.[56] That process of increase also implies that the young man's beauty may seem unprecedented or extraordinary, but the representation of his beauty is bound to have occurred before, in other times, in other hyperbolic poetry.

If this is the case, sonnet 59 asks, and all later poets are copying earlier objects, then why bother at all with the whole poetic reproduction project? These productions are miscarriages, with the poet bearing "amiss" after "lab'ring for invention." As with other early modern authors, Shakespeare's speaker seems to be able easily to access the role of textual mother.[57] But perhaps unlike other authors, he skews the traditional chronology of creation, reproduction, offspring, and succession. Textual reproduction, instead, unmoors the poet from time, and poetic reproduction thus is equated to becoming a parent who bears "the second burthen of a former child." Margreta de Grazia playfully calls the offspring of this poem "less a child than a freak of nature … not a twin, not an aborted foetus, not a false pregnancy, but a new kind of offspring: a *pre-nati* or déjà né."[58] Throughout the poem, the speaker stretches both forward and backward in time. The poet imagines seeing "your image in some antique book," but also imagines the "old world" looking forward and commenting on "this composed wonder of your frame" (59.7–10). The chaotic synchrony of the sonnet reaches its culmination in the question of "Whether we are mended, or where better they, / Or whether revolution be the same."

The poem ends with a posture of certainty that, despite the paradoxes and chronological confusions and strange birthing processes, the addressee retains his superiority compared to other addressees in antique books: "Oh sure I am the wits of former days / To subjects worse have giv'n admiring praise." Vendler, calling this statement one of "desperate uncertainty," shows that the final couplet fails to relieve the tension between classical time, which features eternal returns, and Christian time, which moves relentlessly forward following the "unique intervention" of Christ.[59] The final "Oh sure I am" seems to be one of many brave, but self-contradicting assertions of the power of art either to achieve, or preserve, perfection. Art's ability to remain constant is attenuated by its being a human endeavour, as fault-ridden and time-bound as the young man is at this moment, and as the objects of poetry must have been in earlier days as well. The question of "whether we are mended" is a particularly pointed one given the two chronologies, Christian and classical time, because it superimposes Genesis onto the Ecclesiastes quotation that there is "nothing new under the sun." The pointed answer to the question of "whether we are mended" is no, we are still flawed. That answer results directly from the assumption of humanity's original sin and the injunction to reproduce (sonnet 1) that follows the initial corruption. The central Christian event of God's mercy and Christ's conception without sin (not to mention Mary's) stands as the sole possibility for relief from an endless cycle of successive descent from flawed sources. Sonnet 59 reconfirms the human corrupted state, where the young man's image cannot be perfect but must exist in a material form, "Since mind at first in character was done" (59.8). Beauty's transference to "character," that is, from a seemingly Platonic immaterial to a material form, implies imperfection. "Character" here calls us back to physical form: not that of the young man, but that of the book, so that this line is a subtle recognition that in his own age of mechanical reproduction, the poet's flawed copying of beauty via poetry, and the flawed copying of mental offspring in print, really are part of a larger pattern examined above, wherein all humans make faults.

At stake in this and other sonnets is no less than the relationship between sex, poetics, and identity, between successive versions of a human being and successive versions of the poems representing that human being. Sonnets 105 and 59 demonstrate how disorderly poetic reproduction can be, even as it strives for perfect copies. Significantly, sonnets 127–54, the so-called dark lady sonnets, do not dwell on sexual reproduction except to reject it. Kim Hall, Valerie Traub, and Margreta de Grazia have shown just how troubled Shakespeare's treatment of the dark lady is, particularly in terms of the human reproduction continually encouraged for the young man, but virtually unmentioned for the dark lady.[60] While they hardly mention offspring, these sonnets continually worry the issue of copulation, that is, of combining elements together, with the result of a new, hybrid being. If the sonnets do not strive for narrative cohesion, and in fact disrupt narrative succession as well as human and poetic succession, sonnets 127–54 provide the most startling instances of non-normative copulation, both sexual and poetic.

In what follows, I argue that the miscellaneous nature of these sonnets should encourage a different reading practice, one which is motivated by Shakespeare's treatment of copulation, *and* by the printed form of this book. If Shakespeare's speaker finds sexuality and coupling vexing and dangerous, we as readers should notice and pursue the effects of coupling together sonnets which are often treated as eminently separable.[61] This is a medium-close reading, because it expands the boundaries of single sonnets. But it also pays close attention to the medium of Shakespeare's sonnets, the 1609 quarto, which is itself often taken to be a printing that haphazardly sets sonnets against one another, particularly in this last section.

Thus, reexamining the juxtaposition of these sonnets is both thematically and materially motivated by the 1609 quarto. As we have already seen, John Benson is willing to create new poetic units with his aggregations of multiple sonnets. These combinations can be seen as copulations of sonnets, and they further the work of Shakespeare's poetics of desire, reproduction, and copying with a difference. They are also possible only at a medium-close level, which allows for readings beyond the close-reading level of the single poem, unmoored from any surrounding text.

Before proceeding with these readings, it is necessary to say a bit about Shakespeare's "copulatives." While many of the dark lady sonnets are concerned with sexual contact, there is no denying Fineman's assessment that they also engage with language, and particularly with the potential duplicity of truth statements.[62] Thus, Shakespeare's use of the word "is" occurs extraordinarily self-consciously, and achieves a range of textual effects, including simple declarative sentences of truth or identity, metaphoric statements of comparison, and paradoxical statements in which truth and falsehood both cohere. As is clear from Shakespeare's use of both "copulative" and "copulation," and from other sources of the period, including Latin grammars, these are terms that carried the full weight of grammatical relations, sexual relations, and existential or ontological statements.[63] In other words, statements using the verb "to be" had a range of purposes, at the core of which was the yoking together of terms in order to create hybrid identity.

Shakespeare's continuous play with these statements demonstrates a concern with the status of verbal linkage, of coupling terms together using "is." These include the famous "Shall I compare thee to a summer's day? / Thou art more lovely and more temperate" (18.1–2), and "Love is not love … O no, it is an ever-fixèd mark … It is the star to every wand'ring bark" (116.2, 5, 7). In addition to these, we find self-conscious poetic copulatives in "If hairs be wires, black wires grow on her head" (130.4), and "But wherefore says she not she is unjust? / And wherefore say not I that I am old?" (138.9–10). One of the best examples of Shakespeare's conscious examination of the copulative act of poetic comparison is sonnet 21, in which the speaker differentiates his style from that of another poet, who "heav'n itself for ornament doth use, / And every fair with his fair doth rehearse – / Making a couplement of proud compare / With sun and moon, with earth and sea's rich gems" (21.3–6).[64] Two statements at the extreme edge of these grammatical, metaphorical, and sexual couplings are the stark, and triply meaningful statement "Desire is death" (147.8), and sonnet 129, the first twelve lines of which are a double copulative, "Th'expense of spirit in a waste of shame / Is lust in action, and till action lust / Is perjured, murd'rous, bloody, full of blame …" (129.1–3). The bleakly final "Desire is death" should be read against the most familiar instance of desire in the sonnets, "From fairest creatures we desire increase." This version of desire is the one usually attached to the sonnets. It is a desire which leads to copulation, copies, *copia*, and comparisons, promising that desire is not death, but life eternal. But other sonnets resist or deny this end of desire, and we might ask what is to be gained by coupling, rather than dividing, these seemingly opposed results of desire.

The best place to begin is the supposed rift between sonnets 1–126 and 127–54. Shakespeare's willingness to explore and ruminate on copulative action means that we should examine this supposed division more closely. Sonnet 127 is generally considered the first of the dark lady sonnets, while sonnet 126 is sometimes called an "envoy" to the previous 125 sonnets because of its anomalous 12-line form, because it is the last to refer definitively to a male addressee, and because it was printed with two sets of parentheses for its last two, perhaps absent lines (see figure 5.3).[65] Nature enters both poems at the beginning of the second quatrain, and in both there is an unnatural intervention in the progression of human objects through time. In 126, Nature shields the addressee from aging, although the speaker eventually admits that this exemption cannot hold for long: "She may detaine, but not still keepe her tresure! / Her *Audite*, (though delayd) answer'd must be, / And her *Quietus* is to render thee" (*Shake-speares Sonnets* 1609, sig. H3r).[66] In 127, the unnatural action is human, and it involves perverting nature's unadorned beauty.

Far from opening a rift, the empty parentheses of sonnet 126 invite completion, comparison, and couplement. Time as *edax rerum* threatens in many other sonnets; poetry and human reproduction, though inherently flawed processes, provide a modicum of reassurance. This reassurance is often rendered in the bravura of the final couplet. Sonnet 126 admits that sequence, here in the form of aging, is inescapable; Nature cannot actually "time disgrace, and wretched mynuit kill" (*Shake-speares Sonnets* 1609, sig. H3r).[67] If the couplet is wanting from 126, as the compositor's empty parentheses imply, Nature herself may provide the coupling connection that is otherwise missing. If so, then the conservational task initially assigned to her is a red herring. She begins, in this poem and the larger book of Shakespeare's sonnets, by seeming to conserve the young man against Time's ravages. She is the "sovereign mistress over wrack" (126.5), but the poem ends with a negative: she cannot "keep," but instead must "render" (126.10, 12). This switch, from preservation to mutation, allows for a striking connection between 126 and 127, poems which are usually thought to be divided. Nature's presence unites them, and raises the expectation of change rather than stasis.

Sonnet 127 couples the failed, static reproduction of 126 to a new, dynamic *poiesis*, one which involves darkness and foulness in the form of slander, shame, borrowing, and false esteem. Fineman, Hall, de Grazia, and many other commentators have highlighted the darkness and dangers in the dark lady sonnets versus the fairness and idealism of the young man sonnets.[68] In sonnets 126 and

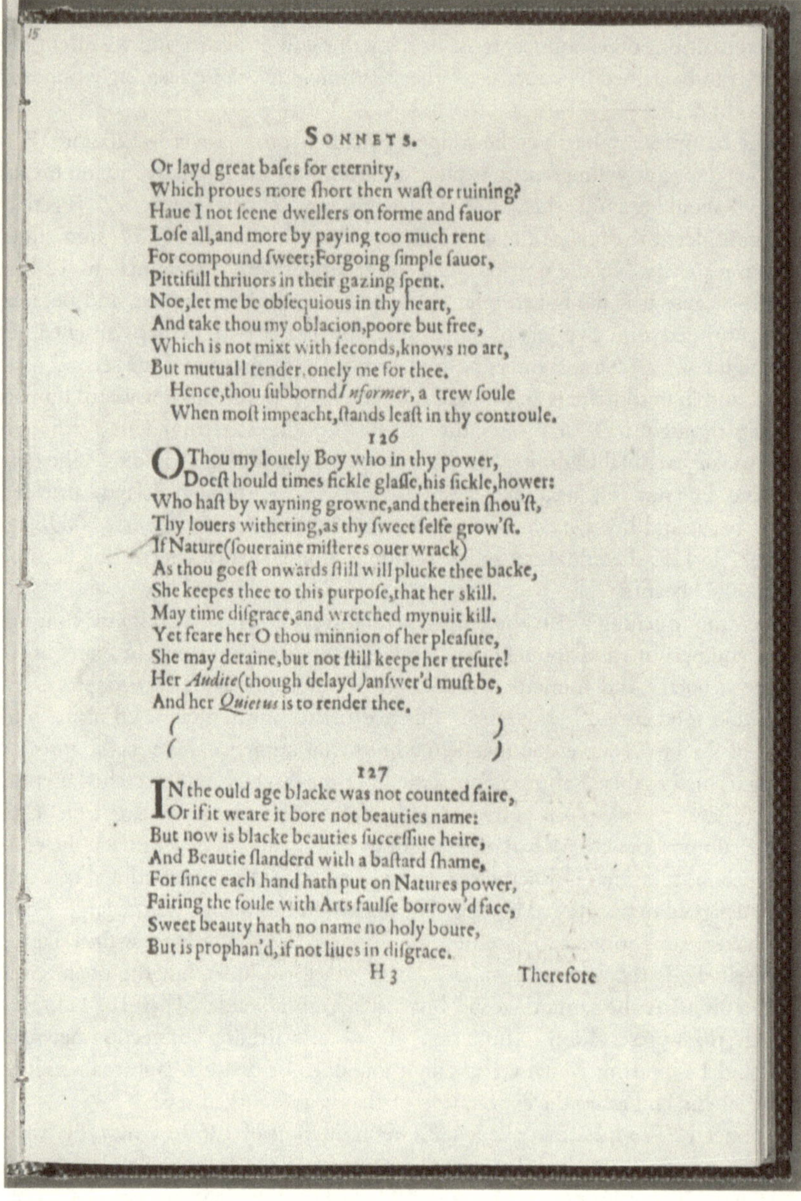

SONNETS.

Or layd great baſes for eternity,
Which proues more ſhort then waſt or ruining?
Haue I not ſeene dwellers on forme and fauor
Loſe all,and more by paying too much rent
For compound ſweet;Forgoing ſimple ſauor,
Pittifull thriuors in their gazing ſpent.
Noe,let me be obſequious in thy heart,
And take thou my oblacion,poore but free,
Which is not mixt with ſeconds,knows no art,
But mutuall render,onely me for thee.
Hence,thou ſubbornd *Informer*, a trew ſoule
When moſt impeacht,ſtands leaſt in thy controule.

126

O Thou my louely Boy who in thy power,
Doeſt hould times fickle glaſſe,his fickle,hower:
Who haſt by wayning growne,and therein ſhou'ſt,
Thy louers withering,as thy ſweet ſelfe grow'ſt.
If Nature(ſoueraine miſteres ouer wrack)
As thou goeſt onwards ſtill will plucke thee backe,
She keepes thee to this purpoſe,that her ſkill.
May time diſgrace,and wretched mynuit kill.
Yet feare her O thou minnion of her pleaſure,
She may detaine,but not ſtill keepe her treſure!
Her *Audite*(though delayd)anſwer'd muſt be,
And her *Quietus* is to render thee.
( )
( )

127

IN the ould age blacke was not counted faire,
Or if it weare it bore not beauties name:
But now is blacke beauties ſucceſſiue heire,
And Beautie ſlanderd with a baſtard ſhame,
For ſince each hand hath put on Natures power,
Fairing the foule with Arts faulſe borrow'd face,
Sweet beauty hath no name no holy boure,
But is prophan'd,if not liues in diſgrace.
H3 Therefore

Figure 5.3 *Shake-speares Sonnets* (1609), sig. H3r. This item is reproduced by permission of The Huntington Library, San Marino, California

127, Nature renders beauty, and mutates the lovely boy, but Nature and beauty are themselves rendered and mutated also. As we have already seen, the printed book of *Shake-speares Sonnets* is constructed so as to highlight the procreation sonnets to the young man: they occur first, and are arguably the most thematically constricted of any of the possible mini-sequences. But it is also true that sonnet 127 may have been composed before 126, and so may not revise, but precede it. The order of the book is at issue here. Among our many options are reading the sonnets straight through from 1 to 154, searching for a compositional order, or even, as we have already seen, in John Benson's edition, discarding order altogether. Standard reading practices foreclose the multiple temporalities of these two sonnets. Instead of sequentially, we might read them coextensively with, and as mutually constituting, one another. Their relationship could be described not in terms of sequence so much as coition.

This sort of sonnet copulation is an assertion that together, sonnets say differently, and say more, than apart. I take juxtaposition to be a key component of this kind of readerly copulation. That is, we can read sonnets nearby one another, or actively put sonnets next to one another as Benson does. Juxtaposition is key to this kind of medium-close reading because physical proximity matters, and it has an important analog in copulative statements, which yoke ideas together. Sonnet 127's traditional Petrarchan turning point bears the copulative statement "Therefore my mistress' eyes are raven black" (127.9). At the very least, the word "therefore" calls a shadow of doubt on the ensuing statement. Are they really black? Is this another reference to cosmetics? Or has the poet made them black? Critics have not spent much time on this conjunctive adverb, and tend to assert that whatever implications it may have, there is no question that the mistress' eyes really are black, or dark, in one way or another.[69] But "therefore" calls attention to copulative *poiesis*: it is a self-conscious statement about how to re-render beauty. The result may well be offspring that is "slandered with a bastard shame" (127.4), and that the speaker labels disturbingly dark and foul.[70] However, this metapoetic statement does belong with others in the sonnets, including some of the most famous: Sonnet 18, "Shall I compare thee to a summer's day"; Sonnet 116, "If this be error and upon me proved, / I never writ, nor no man ever loved"; sonnet 101, "Make answer, muse, wilt thou not haply say, / Truth needs no colour with his colour fixed," and sonnet 130, "My mistress' eyes are nothing like the sun." All call attention to the process of poetic copulation, of re-rendering beauty by textual manipulation and recombination.

Coincidentally, the word "therefore" is accented by the 1609 quarto edition, because the page ends just before this line, and "therefore" is printed as the catchword at the bottom of page H3r, and then appears again in the first line of H3v. The opening H3v–H4r also coincidentally accents the copulatives "Therefore my

Misteresse eyes are Rauen blacke," in the topmost line of the left-hand page with "My Mistres eyes are nothing like the Sunne" (sonnet 130) in the topmost line of the right-hand page. (See figure 5.4, showing this opening.) As Marcy North has shown, the continuous printing of sonnets is somewhat of a rarity during the sonnet vogue of the 1590s and early 1600s, and may indicate that the text was treated as a miscellaneous collection rather than a coherent sequence.[71] If so, the juxtaposition arising from this particular page arrangement is strikingly appropriate. Both poems arrive at a metapoetic statement through a seemingly simple declaration about the eyes of the beloved. In sonnet 127, "therefore" could signal a conscious decision on the part of the poet, either to celebrate the fact that his love object's features are now consonant with current fashion, or even to recreate those features, to remold them to this fashion. Conversely, the "therefore" copulative statement might be defending the poet's right to plain speech: her eyes really are dark, while others are "slandering creation" by falsely imitating this natural darkness. Both statements are in play; one primarily involves the state and nature of beauty in the present moment, while the other involves the poetic reproduction of beauty into words, and into future times.

This pattern has implications for sonnet 130, "My mistress' eyes are nothing like the sun," which has been taken to be a "winsome trifle" that has "no aim but to be funny."[72] The basis of this humour is the recognition that to literalize metaphorical statements like "My love's eyes are brighter than the sun" or "My love is a storm-tossed ship" is to render them ridiculous, monstrous, or disgusting.[73] But seen alongside 127 and other sonnets, 130 demonstrates Shakespeare's wider concern with the truthfulness of the copulative, declarative statements which define this love relationship. These are more readily apparent when similar statements are juxtaposed with one another: "Therefore my mistress's eyes are raven black" alongside "My mistress's eyes are nothing like the sun." Together, these statements constitute a more robust inquiry into the decision poetically to express identity through statements that function with the potential of both truths and artful lies.

Widening our purview to the opening H3v–H4r solidifies this sense because the six sonnets represented there (two only in part; see figure 5.4) range widely in their poetic, copulative statements. For example, sonnets 128 and 131 revise, undermine, or contrast the anti-Petrarchan, simple-speaking humour of 130. They do so with the same easily artful, playful metaphors which the speaker derides elsewhere: in 128 the lover's playing on the virginals *is*, and is not, a more lascivious and sexualized action than straightforward music-making. But sonnets 131 and 132 use the more traditionally poeticized terms of cruelty, tyranny, and mercy. Sonnets 130 and 131, joined together, cancel each other out, or work against one another because the speaker asserts plain, declarative speaking in the one, and flourishes the power to make false statements true in the other. As Shakespeare's sonnets increase in number, their copulative statements, especially the simplest statements of the form "Thou art ___" or "I am ___" join to each other and form another, hybrid identity which extends, broadens, and even contradicts the copulatives in any sonnet by itself. The opening H3v–H4r simply presents this pattern at a single glance. Reading "Your eyes are raven black" together with "Your eyes are nothing like the sun" together with "You are tyrannous" together with "Your eyes are merciful" means facing an inescapably multiple identity. The proliferation of these copulatives, once we begin reading them together, undermines the claims of continuity and identity seen throughout 1–126. In these sonnets, error proliferates. Here, the proliferation of these copulatives continues to reverse any notion we may have had of a simple, stable form of "increase," whether poetic or sexual.

"Desire is death" is the finest and most succinct version of this connection between human sex and Shakespeare's copulatives, which take the form of true statements, false statements, and metaphorical statements that are neither true nor false (or are both). Elsewhere, though Shakespeare does not phrase it quite this way, desire is life: it is desire that leads to increase, prolonging fairest creatures (1.1). It is the desire for identity to exist through time that, the speaker claims in the (numerically) early sonnets, requires the young man to copy himself. Yet that copying action, as a copulative "is" statement, is death. It makes something new of its subject, so that *poiesis* means the death of the poetic subject, rather than its eternal life.

This kind of poetic death through fair copying should be seen as optimistic rather than bleak, however. While Joel Fineman emphasizes desire in the sonnets as "continuous erotic nostalgia," and poetry as a process in which every word "effectively presents to [the speaker] the loss of his ideal,"[74] a different style of reading the sonnets can reveal the other side of desire: its connection to gain, increase, *copia*, and copying. This connection is more readily available in a reading of the sonnets which treats them as miscellaneous rather than monolithic, and as peripatetic rather than progressive or narrative. Especially for sonnets 127–54, this miscellaneous, copulative, and copious reading strategy also attenuates the perception that the dark lady sonnets are uniformly darker, or more bitterly ironic than 1–126. Included in the page opening H3v–H4r is sonnet 129, "Th'expense of spirit in a waste of shame," famous for its bleak depiction of sexual desire and for its intensely misogynist final couplet: "All this the world well knows, yet none knows well, / To shun the heav'n that leads men to this hell" (129.14).[75] (Perhaps its bleakness and sexual explicitness are what caused a reader to strike lines through this sonnet in one early copy; see figure 5.4.) The first twelve lines of this sonnet are comprised of two copulative statements, accented by the position of the word "is" twice at the beginning of a line, by the reversal of "lust in action" from predicate to subject, and by the centrality of physical copulation to the entire poem:

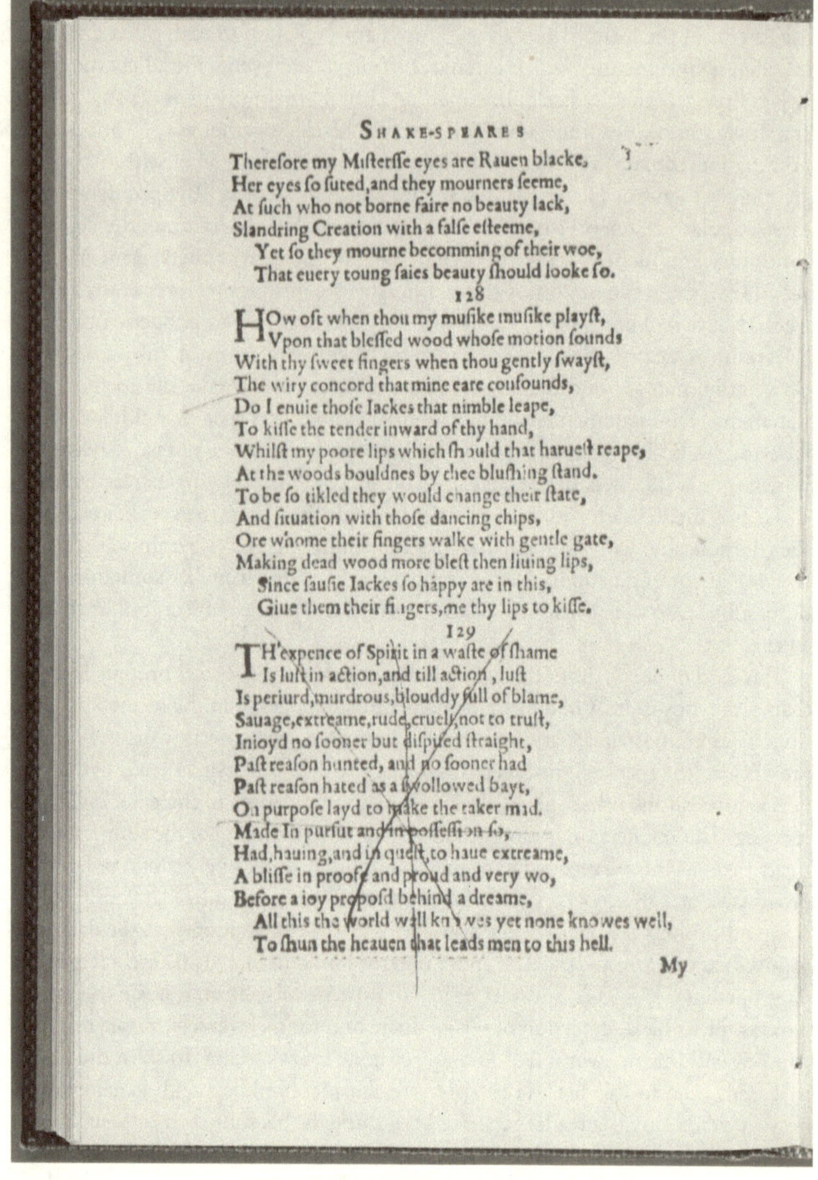

SHAKE-SPEARES

Thereſore my Miſterſſe eyes are Rauen blacke,
Her eyes ſo ſuted,and they mourners ſeeme,
At ſuch who not borne faire no beauty lack,
Slandring Creation with a falſe eſteeme,
  Yet ſo they mourne becomming of their woe,
  That euery toung ſaies beauty ſhould looke ſo.

128

HOw oft when thou my muſike muſike playſt,
Vpon that bleſſed wood whoſe motion ſounds
With thy ſweet fingers when thou gently ſwayſt,
The wiry concord that mine eare confounds,
Do I enuie thoſe Iackes that nimble leape,
To kiſſe the tender inward of thy hand,
Whilſt my poore lips which ſhould that harueſt reape,
At the woods bouldnes by thee bluſhing ſtand.
To be ſo tikled they would change their ſtate,
And ſituation with thoſe dancing chips,
Ore whome their fingers walke with gentle gate,
Making dead wood more bleſt then liuing lips,
  Since ſauſie Iackes ſo happy are in this,
  Giue them their fingers,me thy lips to kiſſe.

129

TH'expence of Spirit in a waſte of ſhame
Is luſt in action,and till action, luſt
Is periurd,murdrous,blouddy full of blame,
Sauage,extreame,rude,cruel,not to truſt,
Inioyd no ſooner but diſpiſed ſtraight,
Paſt reaſon hunted, and no ſooner had
Paſt reaſon hated as a ſwollowed bayt,
On purpoſe layd to make the taker mad.
Made In purſut and in poſſeſſion ſo,
Had,hauing,and in queſt,to haue extreame,
A bliſſe in proofe and proud and very wo,
Before a ioy propoſd behind a dreame,
  All this the world well knowes yet none knowes well,
  To ſhun the heauen that leads men to this hell.

My

Figure 5.4 *Shake-speares Sonnets* (1609); sigs H3v–H4r. This item is reproduced by permission of The Huntington Library, San Marino, California

SONNETS.

130

MY Miſtres eyes are nothing like the Sunne,
Currall is farre more red,then her lips red,
If ſnow be white,why then her breſts are dun:
If haires be wiers,black wiers grow on her head:
I haue ſeene Roſes damaskt,red and white,
But no ſuch Roſes ſee I in her cheekes,
And in ſome perfumes is there more delight,
Then in the breath that from my Miſtres reekes.
I loue to heare her ſpeake,yet well I know,
That Muſicke hath a farre more pleaſing ſound:
I graunt I neuer ſaw a goddeſſe goe,
My Miſtres when ſhee walkes treads on the ground.
And yet by heauen I thinke my loue as rare,
As any ſhe beli'd with falſe compare.

131

THou art as tiranous,ſo as thou art,
As thoſe whoſe beauties proudly make them cruell;
For well thou know'ſt to my deare doting hart
Thou art the faireſt and moſt precious Iewell.
Yet in good faith ſome ſay that thee behold,
Thy face hath not the power to make loue grone;
To ſay they erre,I dare not be ſo bold,
Although I ſweare it to my ſelfe alone.
And to be ſure that is not falſe I ſweare
A thouſand grones but thinking on thy face,
One on anothers necke do witneſſe beare
Thy blacke is faireſt in my iudgements place.
In nothing art thou blacke ſaue in thy deeds,
And thence this ſlaunder as I thinke proceeds.

132

THine eies I loue,and they as pittying me,
Knowing thy heart torment me with diſdaine,
Haue put on black,and louing mourners bee,
Looking with pretty ruth vpon my paine,

And

Figure 5.4 *Continued*

Th'expense of spirit in a waste of shame
Is lust in action, and till action lust
Is perjured, murd'rous, bloody, full of blame,
Savage, extreme, rude, cruel, not to trust ... (129.1–4)

The poem continues for eight more lines of apposition before the final couplet. Lust *is* many things, and lines 3–12 explode the term through serial comparison.[76] The poem's bleakness is not only its misogyny, but its connection of the terms of coupling, comparison, and *copia.* Not only "is" but other repetitions increase the sense of uncontrolled increase: the chiasmic "lust ... action ... action ... lust" (2), the doubled "Past reason hunted ... Past reason hated" (6–7), "mad / Made" (8–9), and four instances of the word "have," three of which occur in a single line. All of these reinforce a dark vision of copulation, but they also revise and repeat what we have seen already in the sonnets to the young man: that repetition and reproduction occur always with a difference, and so the central actions of sexual and grammatical copulation do not repeat; instead they reword, change, and increase.

"Th'expense of spirit" ought not to be read singly; its coiteration with the sonnets at the opening H3v–H4r provides one example of how sonnet juxtaposition and the thematics of poetic reproduction provoke a different reading strategy, one which reads medium-closely instead of isolating 129.[77] This sonnet is further linked to others, and to the poetics of copulation and reproduction, through its use of the word "hell," which, as has been widely noted, is early modern English slang for vagina. In sonnet 144.12 ("Two loves I have"), Shakespeare deploys the same pun: "I guess one angel in another's hell." Heaven and hell are also part of a wider treatment of reproduction and the afterlives of both people and texts, and the miscellaneity of Shakespeare's treatment of these terms recalls these sonnets of sexual betrayal into this larger meditation of identity and time. This coition is most apparent in a sonnet that receives very little critical attention, sonnet 145, "Those lips that love's own hand did make." It is usually taken to be unremarkable because of its simplicity. (Uncharacteristically, Booth's explication of this poem occupies less space than the poem itself.) Usually, critics call attention to its possible earliness in the Shakespearean oeuvre: Andrew Gurr, going on the potential pun between "hate away" and Hathaway, hypothesizes that this is Shakespeare's earliest poem.[78] It is also unique among the sonnets for its iambic tetrameter rhythm; like sonnet 126, its form differs slightly from the other sonnets. But this sonnet is also juxtaposed (at the opening of pages I2v–I3r) with sonnet 144, "Two loves I have of comfort and despair," and 146, "Poor soul, the center of my sinful earth" – each of which has inspired copious critical treatment. Sonnet 144's angelic and devilish lovers and sonnet 146's dialogue between body and soul together produce a much more complex analysis of identity than any of these poems would create singly, especially sonnet 145, with its more playful reference to the afterlife:

> I hate she altered with an end,
> That followed it as gentle day
> Doth follow night, who like a fiend
> From heav'n to hell is flown away.
>   I hate from hate away she threw,
>   And saved my life saying, not you. (145.9–14)

"Hell," in 144, signals not only the malevolence and malignance heaped abundantly on the dark lady in other sonnets, but also the poet's conception of monstrous femininity itself as emblematized in the hell-vagina pun. But here the term is used much more lightly, and combines several metaphorical comparisons: the female figure revises her statement "I hate" and this revision is like day following night, and also like a fiend fleeing heaven and returning to hell. Undoubtedly, despite this brief reference to infernal imagery, the tone of sonnet 145 is more relieved than condemnatory: the speaker, undergoing a traditional torture of courtly love, the displeasure of the mistress, is nevertheless saved by the sudden and merciful alteration of her sentence, which can be condensed into the negative in the last two syllables of the poem: "not you." Sonnet 145's reversal of the imagery of damnation in "Two loves I have of comfort and despair" has the potential to allay, or at least counter, the deep suspicions and disturbing wordplay in the phrase "I guess one angel in another's hell" (144.12).

But allaying and countering require ideas about succession and order: which sonnet is first, or which is more important. Andrew Gurr's conjecture about sonnet 145's primacy involves both the narrative and the composition of the sonnets. If his guess is correct, then there is a textual situation in which "a sonnet written to woo Mistress Hathaway by the eighteen-year-old poet survived in the author's possession through twenty-five years of travel and change, until it joined the hundred and twenty-six to the young man and the twenty or so to the dark lady in Thorpe's publication of 1609. Perhaps Shakespeare kept it for sentimental reasons."[79] This hypothetical *joining*, of course, might be an authorial, editorial, or interpretive action. But however we do it, joining sonnets 144–6 narratively would be quite difficult. The sonnets that directly follow 145 perhaps continue the developing theme of romantic life and death, but they in no way contribute to a comprehensible amatory narrative.[80] Rather, sonnet 146 patently resists such sequentiality because there is no reference whatsoever to the terms of other amorous poems, either the bitter irony of the dark lady sonnets or the lighter and more playfully hopeful poems also included in sonnets 127–54. Instead, the poem begins and ends with the speaker's address to his own soul, and thus participates in the tradition of medieval debates and dialogues between the body and the soul, and echoes Shakespeare's other considerations, chiefly in *Hamlet,* of the end of the body and eternal life of the soul. Sonnet 146 has inspired an ever-swirling vortex of critical statements and controversies. Its second line provides a textual crux, its uniqueness among the sonnets provides a potential site of authorial and sequential conjectures, and its vague but evocative terminology provides ample opportunity for intertextual connections to Aristotle, Plato, Paul, Psalms, Augustine, Spenser, Donne, and many others.[81] But the immediate intertexts, the adjoining sonnets, pull the reader both forward and backward, so that the soul's progress has no discernible direction in either time or space. Moving "backward" from sonnet 146 to 145 requires a reevaluation of the mercy and grace afforded by the statement that the addressee has "saved my life, saying 'not you'" (145.14). Petrarchan redemption and Christian redemption cannot so readily be juxtaposed, and their coition in these two sonnets creates a mutually challenging moment. Petrarchan redemption in 145 suddenly pales in comparison to eternal life and the death of death; but the stark, serious terms of eternal redemption in 146 fade in comparison to the physical imagery of 145's "those lips that love's own hand did make," of its image of mercy entering the lover's heart, and of day following night.

If we move "forward" from sonnet 146 to 147, we see that the body's presence cannot be so easily eschewed. The "fading mansion" or "sinful earth" of the body in sonnet 146 is languishing in sonnet 147: the central conceit is of love-sickness, "fever," "disease," and "ill." The triumphant final line of sonnet 146, "And death once dead, there's no more dying then," turns back on itself and becomes a more conventional, ever-suffering statement in which the lover is feverish and apt to die. If sonnets 145 and 146 challenge or undermine one another with Petrarchan and Christian redemption, sonnet 147 re-poses the threat of imminent, though metaphorical, death: "My love is as a fever." In sonnet 147 the speaker's desire, which seemed to have been relieved in 145 and perhaps completely conquered in 146, nevertheless recurs, and is equated both to death and to an endlessly insane search for expression:

My reason, the physician to my love,
Angry that his prescriptions are not kept,
Hath left me, and I desp'rate now approve
Desire is death, which physic did except.
Past cure I am, now reason is past care,

And, frantic mad with evermore unrest,
My thoughts and my discourse as mad-men's are,
At random from the truth vainly expressed … (147.5–12)

The search for systems of order, whether temporal, spatial, narrative, intellectual, or theological, is bound to break down as one reads across the sonnets. Such searches, pursued assiduously enough, produce conspiracy theories about the identity of the young man, or grand unified theories in which every sonnet fits neatly into an overarching narrative. But any desire for unity and coherence is bound both to frustrate and to be frustrated. Here, the problem of identity's coherence through time is couched in the direst possible terms: "Desire is death." What began as a harmless, artful metaphor, that love is fever, now reveals itself to be a much richer and more fundamental source of insanity, despair, and darkness. As a conventional poetic statement, "my love is as a fever" reproduces a recognizable Petrarchan metaphor. As the poem progresses, however, we find that "my love" in the first line both is, and is not, equivalent to "desire" in the eighth line. If the two are equivalent, then the speaker's love is a feverish sort of desire, and that desire is itself equated with death. More than this, Shakespeare's proliferation of "my love" throughout the sonnets concatenates this instance of the phrase with the others, perforce leading to a set of implied, copulative statements: this deathly desire *is* the young man and the dark lady, *is* the poet's love relationship with him, and with her, and *is* the textual product. This insane doubling, tripling, and multiplication is precisely what the speaker-poet says of the raving verse of sonnet 147, with its "thoughts and discourse" having been "expressed," or pressed out of, the singular truth.

Seen in this light, sonnet 147's final couplet seems to encapsulate not only a misogynistic accusation of feminine duplicity (this sense is undeniable and is itself repeated over multiple sonnets), but also the duplicity of a copulative expression of truth, when that truth comes from the mind of a desirous, mad man: "For I have sworn thee fair, and thought thee bright, / Who art as black as hell, as dark as night" (147.13–14). There is a range of potential intertextual coitions for this statement with others in the sonnets. Not least of these is the opposite, and equally certain banishment of hate from "heaven to hell" in sonnet 145, or the flat statement of duplicity "Two loves I have of comfort and despair" (144), which calls attention simultaneously to pairing and unpairing. But arguably the closest statement for textual coition and iteration is in sonnet 127's "Therefore my mistress' eyes are raven black." As discussed above, this line evinces the duplicity inherent in the feigning truths of poetic statements. It simultaneously reports, and creatively re-molds, the mistress. The close of sonnet 147, though a much darker copulative, still retains this basic poetic duplicity. In sonnet 127 we are likely first to be convinced of the simple, physical truth of dark eyes, and only gradually attuned to the potential feigning of this statement. In sonnet 147, the opposite is true: we are first alerted to the conventional hyperbole of the statement, its feigning poetic status, before gradually realizing that the statement is also meant as a more basic, physical, even unpoetical truth. The light, amusing, and feigning Petrarchan conceit of feverishness is not duplicated exactly but copied imperfectly, transformed into a paranoid commitment to this other truth. Shakespeare's fair copy of Petrarchan hyperbole renders a probing, problematic version of the copulative statement, one which says both true and false at the same time.

The 1609 quarto of *Shake-speares Sonnets* insists that an overall sequence, plot, or interpretation of the sonnets is bound to break down in the face of its miscellaneity and dark copulatives. Does the statement "Desire is death" exist as a rejoinder to the earlier procreation sonnets? Then it "happens" after them, though there is plenty to suggest that it was composed before. But we could also imagine the procreation sonnets as a kind of proffered solution to the conundrums of physicality, base desire, and betrayal found in this sonnet and in others: eschew these, and focus on higher, more idealistic forms of love and increase. Rather than the one following the other, or the other following the one, the sonnets require us to entertain simultaneously a love and desire that lead to increase and timeless identity, a poetic increase that conforms to human proneness to error, and a copulative desire which at its bleakest *is* death. Here in the same sonnet, as elsewhere in sonnets of dramatically altering tones, the light feigning lies of creative poetics coexist with the dark, difficult truths of human love and human time. To hold them both simultaneously is madness. Yet simultaneity is perhaps the best and only antidote to the dead end of sequence.

Coda:
The End of *Shake-speares Sonnets*

Chapter 5 claims, in part, that both Shakespeare and the printed mediums of his sonnets undermine sequentiality. They skew our sense of how works of art, and people, move through time, especially when they undergo mutation as a result of being reproduced in a new medium. Closing this study of Elizabethan lyric poetry by asking how *Shake-speares Sonnets* ends might, then, seem beside the point. However, in certain ways, this book can stand as an ending for the larger process I have been tracing. That process is the gradual incorporation of reproduction into English lyric poetry collections: as a theme, and as condition of production. Gascoigne, Sidney, Spenser, and Shakespeare all grapple with the immediate afterlives of their poetic collections even as those collections are being born. Their poetic speakers express anxiety, or bravado, or ambivalence, regarding the short-term fate of lyric expostulations. Yet these poetically expressed hopes and fears tend to match, or even presage, the actual short-term fates of these poets' lyric productions. For example, George Gascoigne's Master F.J. expresses concern about the "singularitie" of his letters, poems, and songs. This concern with singularity and multiplicity is borne out by the two substantially different early printed editions of his work, and by the way in which "Gascoigne's Lullaby" escapes its early printed context when John Payne Collier reinscribes it, centuries later, among other manuscript items. The lullaby already winkingly refers to the poem's existence beyond the life of its speaker, so that it is difficult to say whether Collier is copying the poem, or whether it is copying itself, through him.[1]

Spenser and Sidney, too, consider their reproductive poetic afterlives even during the first lives of their poems. Spenser's Colin Clout begins enmired in the dangers of solipsistic *poiesis*, and almost despite himself comes to a more community-based form of production. Sidney's lyrics are taken up and fostered by surrogate poetic agents, both in the fiction of the *Arcadia* and in the printed afterlives of this collection. Even Richard Tottel, whose monumental *Songes and Sonettes* opens this study, demonstrates the new potential for lyrics to be forwarded through time. His collection not only changes substantially in its first two printings, but it also registers the changes which he himself is willing to make to the poetry of Surrey, Wyatt, and others. He, just as much as the Elizabethan poets, paves the way for the poetic future which Horace and Ovid could only proclaim, the way towards a poetry that does indeed out-monumentalize the pyramids, or does advance the poet's "better part" or "indelible name" through the ages.[2] What for Horace and Ovid is a boast, for these textual agents is a practical concern: they usher poetic works through their first few iterations, and in doing so, sustain the earliest intimations of poetic immortality. But as each of the foregoing chapters shows, there is no such thing as a perfect copy of a poem, a book, or a person. Instead, the fairest copies are those that recognize, meditate on, and even celebrate their mutations.

For this reason, *Shake-speares Sonnets* ends this study. Shakespeare considers reproduction, textual and sexual, in the deepest and most sustained way of any of the authors, and his consideration differs not in kind, but in degree. Shakespeare's sonnets demonstrate just how vexed a relationship to reproduction lyric poetry can have, even as it makes good on certain promises of eternity, including the promise that the poems will be repeated in others' mouths, and seen by other eyes. With full recognition that each iteration of a poem is a mutation, Shakespeare's speaker nevertheless forges ahead into the poetic eternity of his textual love. That love, particularly its emphasis on fairness, is charged with Shakespeare's early modern anxieties of class, race, and dynastic succession.[3] But in later reproductions, those anxieties and resonances might be sheared away, mutated, denied, reiterated, or replaced. Their recovery, by literary and cultural historians, is an attempt to link meaning to Shakespeare's time and place, to uncover the connections which Shakespeare may have inserted into these poems. This is an admirable goal, which furthers our understanding of the sonnets. But it is not the only possible end (goal) for these poems.

Certainly, anyone who has heard Shakespeare's sonnet 116 ("Let me not to the marriage of true minds / Admit impediments") recited solemnly at a wedding can recognize the crossed ends of the poem as it exists in *Shake-speares Sonnets*, versus the poem as it is recited now, today. For the poem ends "If this be error, and upon me proved, / I never writ, nor no man ever loved." And while marriage between two men or two women has recently become legal in some places in the United States, I would wager that the vast majority of recitations of this poem occur, and have occurred, in heterosexual marriages. The poem ends, in the 1609 quarto context, with a slyly ambiguous reference to the young man, who appears nowhere in this poem, nor in any in the immediate vicinity (108 has "sweet boy"; 126 has "lovely boy"). The ending of 116 could ironically state "I never wrote anything, nor has any man ever loved," but it could also ironically state "I never wrote anything, nor have I ever loved any man." Whisking sonnet 116 out of the peculiarities and particularities of the 1609 quarto, and into the present situation, surely makes a mutation of the poem. Everything is changed: I, you, and occasion. Everything but the words. Yet those words, for most of the poem, are highly aphoristic and sententious in nature; they might well have been said by Polonius. In fact, their end (purpose) might simply be repetition, so that each mutated rendition of the poem actually brings us closer to its supposed constancies. The end of this sonnet is no end at all; its Shakespearean particularities are dissolved and reconstituted many times each year (mostly in June). Recitation brings the poem back from the dead into a new medium, us.

This mutation of Shakespeare's ends returns us to the question of how the book actually ends, and by extension, how all the books of poetry in this study end. *Shake-speares Sonnets* ends by not ending. First, there is no narrative conclusion, but rather the sudden intrusion of a new young man, Cupid. Second, the Cupid poem doubles itself: sonnet 153 and sonnet 154 tell substantially the same brief story, about a spring or well that becomes perpetually heated by the love-god's stolen, phallic "brand." Both make a brief reference to the speaker's own love for his mistress, and in both the speaker's love diseases him, and the malady is incurable even by the "seething bath" (153.7) or "healthful remedy" (154.11) of the love-infused water. These sonnets comprise a non-ending to this collection for several reasons. First, they are concerned with yet another reappraisal of sequence and identity through time, referring as they do to "a dateless lively heat" (153.6) and "heat perpetual" (154.10). Second, they reduplicate one another, creating two nearly identical poems which nevertheless are slightly different from themselves. They thus end the collection with an exemplary version of Shakespearean poetic increase: desire itself produces the poems, which are imperfect twins, doubled and mutated, fair copies of one another.

Except that they do not end the collection. *A Lover's Complaint* does, and as Kerrigan and others have noted, this poem comprises an integral part of the larger poetic book, with the relationship between parts being "mutually illuminating."[4] Even without the full examination which this work deserves, its immediate connection to the doubled end of the sonnets is apparent from the first line: "FRom off a hill whose concaue wombe reworded, / A plaintfull story from a sistring vale / My spirrits t'attend this doble voyce accorded …"[5] The doubling voice here doubles the doubled sonnets 153–4, and the figure of Echo is a fitting end to both the 1609 sonnets and to a study of textual reproduction with a difference. Echo, as we see both in Puttenham's treatise and in John Hollander's modern study, means both decay and augmentation. Echo herself is voice that has dwindled away, and therefore is perfect to use in moments of extreme loss: the voice goes out to the landscape, and encounters not the hearer it seeks, but only the echoing landscape. At the same time, the sound rebounds and comes back differently, so that there is an augmentation effect. Hollander puts it thus: "the central metaphoric use of our word, which ordinarily names an acoustical phenomenon in honor of the departed nymph, [means] an allusive resounding, a rebound across a gap not merely of many lines of text, but of many texts as well."[6]

After beginning with an echo, *A Lover's Complaint* ends with another kind of reduplication: the complaining lover, having been wronged, asserts that she would do it all over again, that all the falsities with which the male lover assailed her "Would yet againe betray the fore-betrayed, / And new peruert a reconciled Maide" (sig. L2v). *Shake-speares Sonnets* ends with one more variation on mutated copying. If the sonnets insist on the mutations and flaws inherent in any attempt at an identical copy, and if the printed editions and manuscripts and recitations of Shakespeare's sonnets demonstrate that the fairest copies are those that change and mutate, then *A Lover's Complaint* alerts us to the possibility that errors, at least, can be repeated. Amid all the crumbling assertions of constancy in the sonnets, this assertion, of constant inconstancy, offers a strange modicum of reassurance.

Despite the constant stream of adaptations and appropriations of his dramatic works, *Shake-speares Sonnets* have been treated far more statically. John Benson's edition of 1640 is a fair copy because it allows itself leeway to recombine sonnets, and even, as Tottel had done before him, to take liberties with Shakespeare's words. But for the next two hundred years, no editor-producer would allow himself such freedom. Benson's edition was reprinted throughout the eighteenth century, but "Malone's supplementary notes of 1780, published with the full edition of the works in 1790, conclusively ousted the 1640 *Poems* and instated the 1609 *Sonnets*."[7] Renewed attention to the 1609 quarto meant that editors could return to Shakespeare's poems, Shakespeare's sentiments, and in Malone's case, details of Shakespeare's own emotional life.[8] From this point forward, Shakespeare's sonnets, especially because there were no authoritative manuscript copies and few competing early printed editions, were a known and reproducible text. There were printing errors and textual cruxes in the 1609 quarto, but these could not stand in the way of the book of Shakespeare's sonnets being reproduced in a stable form.

However, this stability can and should be undermined in present and future reproductions of the sonnets. We have already seen how it is undermined when new people in new situations say "Let me not to the marriage of true minds admit impediments." But the most recent internet and hypertext editions of the sonnets employ the same critical habits, and loyalty to the 1609 quarto, that have been ingrained since the eighteenth century.[9] What Gascoigne, Sidney, Spenser, and Shakespeare call for is not the fantasy of perfect copying fidelity, but the kind of fair copies that are offspring, not clones, of their progenitors.

A now-defunct website, entitled *Linkerature*, at least demonstrated the possibility of a reproduction of the sonnets that creatively mutates them, by adding hypertextual links that expand the limits of each sonnet's meaning by offering associative connections, rather than commentary or Shakespeare-related materials. Performative sites like *Bardbox* (which as of September 2012 has ceased accepting new entries) also highlight appropriation and adaptation rather than strict fidelity.[10] These sites remind us that early modern poetry, despite three centuries of encrustation, is also undergoing medium changes in the form of the new reproducing, encoding, linking, and disseminating structures of internet technology; no less important are the new habits of internet culture, in which mash-ups and spin-offs appear almost as soon as their "originals" are born.[11] Early modern authors such as Sidney might not have been surprised by these; his *Arcadia* also was mashed up and spun off almost as soon as it was born. If these poetic works are to have no end, we ought to get behind the kind of reproduction with which I began, Chidiock Tichborne's Lament. As an example, we might consider a reproduction of this lyric poem, in the form of an eight-minute lounge-style jazz-rock hybrid.[12] It is unrecognizable as Tichborne's plangent expostulation of regret over the brevity of his life. Yet it deals justly, and beautifully, with its source. It is as fair a copy as we can desire.

Notes

Introduction

1 Hirsch, "The Works of Chidiock Tichborne (text)," 309–10.

2 Ibid., 305–6.

3 One count is thirty-seven different extant manuscript versions. See May and Ringler, *Elizabethan Poetry*, item 15464. For additional items, see Peter Beal, *Catalogue of English Literary Manuscripts* (accessed in online beta version, 4 February 2012).

4 Tichborne et al., *Verses of Prayse and Ioye Written Vpon Her Maiesties Preseruation.*

5 As of 2007, a voice recording of this poem, with a new stanza added at the end, could be found at Van Cleef, "Chidiock Tichborne's Lament," 2007. It is one of many now-defunct web sites, which is fitting, considering the subject matter of the poem. In 1973, Ben Sidran's "Now I Live (and Now My Life is Done)" was recorded on his record *Puttin' In Time on Planet Earth* on the Blue Thumb Records label. See Coda, n. 12. I thank Molly Murray for revealing this song to me.

6 See Fraser, *The Court of Venus.*

7 Rollins, *Tottel's Miscellany (1557–1587)*, 2:3–36.

8 See Marotti, *Manuscript, Print, and the English Renaissance Lyric*, 212–19. Marotti sees Tottel's editorial actions, especially his titles, as the "recoding of social verse as primarily *literary* texts in the print medium" (218; his emphasis). Wendy Wall argues that Tottel created a "prototype" for later printed miscellanies, but emphasizes his engagement with both manuscript social transactions and the authorization of print: "While *Tottels*'s appearance in print reveals its departure from the conventions of manuscript culture, it re-presents that culture through its organization of poetic material" (*The Imprint of Gender*, 26).

9 For examples, see Eckhardt, *Manuscript Verse Collectors*; and Beadle and Burrow, *Manuscript Miscellanies c. 1450–1700.*

10 Brooks, *The Well Wrought Urn*, x.

11 An influential example of this reading practice is Moretti, *Atlas of the European Novel, 1800–1900.*

12 Arthur Marotti groups many of these phenomena under the larger rubric of "social textuality." See chapter 3 of *English Renaissance Lyric.* See also his treatment specifically of sonnets handwritten on bifolia: "Shakespeare's Sonnets as Literary Property," 147. As will become clear in later chapters, my method of medium-close reading is indebted to Marotti's comprehensive work documenting and describing the systems of manuscript and print, and the printed and handwritten exemplars of poets, printers, and compilers. My readings, I hope, extend his and others' work by searching for cognizance on the part of these agents regarding their productive and reproductive strategies.

13 *Imprint of Gender*, 74–89. Wall is primarily concerned with the ways in which Daniel and Drayton gradually become more powerfully inscribed as authorial names in subsequent editions of their poetic collections. However, both poets also are steeped in Neoplatonic and Petrarchan modes of idealization of the love-object, so that they, like Shakespeare, consider reproduction in a number of ways in their poetic collections. Daniel, along with other English poets in this period, conceptualizes his art as an ongoing material process involving mutating copies, both in manuscript and print.

14 See de Grazia, "The Scandal of Shakespeare's Sonnets"; Hall, "'These Bastard Signs of Fair.'"

15 Scarry, *On Beauty and Being Just.* Scarry focuses on the draw of beauty, so that copying is only one part of a larger ethical treatment of beautiful objects that also includes care and preservation. As will become apparent in chapter 4, Sidney and other writers both depict and enact this sort of careful reproduction of poetry.

16 Ioppolo, *Dramatists and Their Manuscripts*, 78–9.

17 Bowers, *On Editing Shakespeare*, 13–15.

18 Greg, "The Rationale of Copy-Text," 21.

19 Bowers, "Textual Criticism," 33–7; Tanselle, "Textual Scholarship," 45–6.

20 Tanselle, "Textual Scholarship," 41.

21 McKenzie, *Bibliography and the Sociology of Texts*; McGann, *The Textual Condition.* See also Shillingsburg, *Scholarly Editing in the Computer Age,* esp. chap. 2, "Forms," and chap. 3, "Intention."

22 Marcus, *Unediting the Renaissance.*

23 Kastan, *Shakespeare and the Book*, 3.

24 Ibid., 119.

25 Greetham, *Textual Transgressions*, chap. 5.

26 Greg, "The Rationale of Copy-Text," 22. Nevertheless, Greg's influence regarding the primacy of copy-text, and his principles for establishing it, can be seen in critical studies of how early modern manuscripts relate to each other in terms of genealogical lines, chronology, and authority. See, for example, Harrier, *The Canon of Sir Thomas Wyatt's Poetry*; Skretkowicz, "Textual Criticism and the 1593 'Complete' *Arcadia*"; Woudhuysen, *Sir Philip Sidney and the Circulation of Manuscripts, 1558–1640.*

27 McGann, *Textual Condition*, 72–83.

28 In an edited collection of manuscript poetry, P.J. Croft confronts this issue: "Any text in the author's handwriting, in fact, possesses a validity of its own, while experience soon teaches that there can be no simple and all-embracing definition of the 'ideal' text." *Autograph Poetry in the English Language*, 1:xx.

29 The text provides the story and impresa and other accompanying textual devices. Titled *The Tale of Hemetes the Heremyte*, the presentation copy is British Library Royal MS 18 A.XLVIII.

30 McCoy, "Gascoigne's 'Poëmata Castrata'"; Wall, *Imprint of Gender*, 128–38. (The image is reproduced on the cover of this book.)

31 Gabriel Heaton argues that its author is Robert Garrett; see "The Queen and the Hermit." Others assume the author is Sir Henry Lee; see, for example, Austen, *Gascoigne*, 134–50. Austen argues elsewhere that this and other self-portraits of George Gascoigne show him manoeuvering for patronage by creating a variety of personae and self-portraits to match them. Austen, "Self-Portraits and Self-Presentation in the Work of George Gascoigne," par. 3.

32 See Anderson, "'A True Copie'"; Austen, *Gascoigne*, 50.

33 Bowers, "Today's Shakespeare Texts, and Tomorrow's," 59.

34 Moss, *Printed Commonplace-books*, especially chap. 7, 192–204.

35 Quoted in Havens, *Commonplace Books*, 14.

36 Whigham and Rebhorn, *The Art of English Poesy / by George Puttenham*, 93–4. Imitation is, of course, a key term in rhetorical treatises, and its application to poetic theory is apparent in Puttenham, Sidney, and others. Jonathan Bate notes the distinction between *imitatio / aemulatio* and *paradigma*, the imitation of prior examples: Bate, *Shakespeare and Ovid*, 83–7. On *imitatio*, see Russell, *The Orator's Education / Quintilian*, 4:323–37 (book 10 ch. 2). These sections include Quintilian's claim that imitation is not enough, and that creative use of prior authorities is better than slavish imitation.

37 Kerrigan, *The Sonnets; and, A Lover's Complaint / William Shakespeare*, 28.

38 Stewart and Wolfe, *Letterwriting in Renaissance England*. See also Jardine, "Reading and the Technology of Textual Affect." Alan Stewart extends Jardine's reading of letters in *King Lear* to a claim that Shakespeare's representation of letters on stage is distinctly un-Erasmian; see *Shakespeare's Letters*, esp. 12–16.

39 Moss, *Commonplace-books*, chap. 3.

40 For examples of these studies, see Roberts, *Reading Shakespeare's Poems in Early Modern England*; Woudhuysen, *Sidney and Circulation of Manuscripts*; Brayman Hackel, *Reading Material in Early Modern England*; Marotti, *English Renaissance Lyric*; Beal, *In Praise of Scribes*; Sherman, "Toward a History of the Manicule"; Eckhardt, *Manuscript Verse Collectors*; North, "Amateur Compilers, Scribal Labour."

41 Stephen Orgel, "Marginal Maternity," 288.

42 Daniel claims, in *Delia* (1592), that he never meant his poetry to be copied and disseminated, that he was "forced to publish that which I neuer ment," and that he and

his work have been "thrust out into the worlde." See Daniel, *Delia*, sig. A2r–v. This claim is quite common among Elizabethan poets, and in Daniel's case involves some truth: his verse had been published in 1591, along with Philip Sidney's *Astrophel and Stella*, almost certainly without Daniel's knowledge or supervision. Like other poets, Daniel claims that his work has been both unwittingly and unwillingly reproduced. Yet Daniel's involvement in multiple later editions of *Delia* show that he is also willing to participate in the continued reproduction of his work. Regarding Daniel's and other poets' professed reservations about appearing in print, the classic study, and a rejoinder to it, are Saunders, "The Stigma of Print"; May, "Tudor Aristocrats and the 'Stigma of Print.'"

43 See especially n. 9 to chap. 4; Sidney carefully composes his model of poetic reproduction from Platonic and Aristotelian models.

44 Ficino, *Commentary on Plato's Symposium on Love*, 40–1.

45 Berger, *Revisionary Play*, 230–1.

46 Ulreich, "'The Poets Only Deliver,'" 137.

47 Steven May supplants Saunders's "stigma of print" with a "stigma of poetry." Poets, in other words, are not denouncing printed publication so much as the frivolity of writing non-sacred poetry. (See note 42 above.)

48 Maus, "A Womb of His Own."

49 Rösslin, *When Midwifery Became the Male Physician's Province*, 2.

50 Ibid., 4–5.

51 Reynalde's edition was not based on the original German but instead on the Latin translation *De Partu Hominis* and Vesalius's *De Fabrica* and *Epitome*, from which the anatomical illustrations were drawn; see Rösslin, *The Birth of Mankind / by Thomas Reynalde, Physician, 1560*, xvi–xx.

52 Hobby, "'Secrets of the Female Sex,'" 202.

53 See de Grazia, "Imprints: Shakespeare, Gutenberg, and Descartes," 52; Guy-Bray, *Against Reproduction*, 8; MacFaul, *Poetry and Paternity in Renaissance England*.

54 Guy-Bray, however, sees his work as potentially *corrective* of the tendency to reproduce heterosexuality during critiques of reproductive metaphors, to elide, in other words, non-heterosexual reproduction and to ignore Renaissance texts in which human copies are either not the most readily available or the most important analogy to textual making.

55 Brooks, *Printing and Parenting in Early Modern England*, 3–18.

56 Ibid., 18.

57 Eisenstein, *The Printing Revolution in Early Modern Europe*, 46–101.

58 Dawkins, *The Selfish Gene*, 24–35. Longevity, fecundity, and copying-fidelity are the three properties of what Dawkins calls the "practical unit of natural selection" (35).

59 Ibid., 189–201.

60 Ibid., 322.

1. The "vnquiet state" of the Lover: Richard Tottel's Lyric and Legal Reproductions

1 Sara Lippincott, quoted in McPhee, "Personal History – Checkpoints," 59.

2 McKitterick, *Print, Manuscript and the Search for Order*, chap. 4, "A House of Errors."

3 On untimeliness, see Harris, *Untimely Matter in the Time of Shakespeare.*

4 Arber, *English Reprints*, vol. 6.

5 Collier, *Illustrations of Early English Poetry*; Davison, *Davison's Poetical Rhapsody*, 32; Warton, *History of English Poetry*, 3: 69.

6 Wentworth, *The Miscellanie*; Ravenscroft, *Pammelia, Musicks Miscellanie*; Jordan, *Piety, and Poesy Contracted.*

7 This point is also made by Wendy Wall, who compares the title *Tottel's Miscellany* to the *Norton Anthology* and argues that this kind of titling is a "vestige" of Renaissance deemphasis of authorial organization in favor of "commercial authority." See *Imprint of Gender*, 97.

8 Wall emphasizes the importance of both medieval manuscript practices and coterie manuscript practices in allowing the reader / writer to make the text one's own. See ibid., 102–9. Marotti emphasizes the "recontextualizing process" of bringing manuscript verse into print, and Tottel's and other editors' active roles in this process; see *English Renaissance Lyric*, 217–19.

9 Information on specific printing dates is from Arber, *A Transcript of the Registers of the Company of Stationers of London*, vols 1 and 5.

10 England and Wales, *A Colleccion of All the Statutes (from the Begynning of Magna Carta …)* (1557). (Parenthetical signature page references are to this edition except where noted.)

11 Quoted in Byrom, "Richard Tottell – His Life and Work," 203.

12 Graham, "The Rastells and the Printed English Law Book of the Renaissance."

13 Henderson, "Legal Literature and the Impact of Printing"; Henderson explains: "The practicing lawyer in the English central courts of the 15th and 16th centuries needed access to three kinds of written material: statutes, form books, and collections of case law" (288).

14 The form and function of the year books, including whether they were primarily used by students or practitioners, is a matter of some debate. See Ives, "The Purpose and Making of the Later Year Books"; Simpson, "The Source and Function of the Later Year Books"; Allen, *Law in the Making*, 190–207; John Hamilton Baker, *The Common Law Tradition*, 136–64.

15 Cromartie, *The Constitutionalist Revolution*, 17.

16 Ibid., esp. 100–3; Graham, "The Book That 'Made' the Common Law."

17 See, for example, Deppman, Ferrer, and Groden, *Genetic Criticism.*

18 England and Wales, *The Great Boke of Statutes.*

19 England and Wales, *Great Boke of Statutes*, 1542, sig. Fiiiv.

20 J.D. Mackie summarizes this statute's peculiarities as follows: "It was in effect a request to the king to grant the attainder approved by parliament, and that by royal letters patent; it laid down the doctrine that any unchaste woman marrying a king of England without declaration of her unchastity should be guilty of high treason." In *The Earlier Tudors*, 419.

21 John Hamilton Baker, *An Introduction to English Legal History*, 528.

22 England and Wales, *A Colleccion of All the Statutes* (1559), sig. Oiiiv.

23 Nicholas Grimald and John Harington are among the candidates; see Rollins, *Tottel's Miscellany*, 85–93; Byrom, "The Case for Nicholas Grimald as Editor of *Tottel's Miscellany*." Rollins's more conservative claim is that in the absence of positive evidence, we should consider Tottel the "guiding spirit, or editor" of the collection (93).

24 Both Marotti and Wall comment on the double use of authorial names and rank in English printed verse miscellanies: they accent rank and name in order to sell or authorize the texts, even as they emphasize a new phase of the lyric, one which frees poetry from original occasions to new social and literary uses. See Marotti, *English Renaissance Lyric*, 215–19; Wall, *Imprint of Gender*, 23–30 and 95–109.

25 Howard, *Songes and Sonettes* sig. A1v. (Parenthetical signatures are to this edition unless otherwise noted.)

26 Pomeroy, *The Elizabethan Miscellanies*, 31–52.

27 Ibid., 51.

28 Tichborne et al., *Verses of Prayse and Ioye*, sig. Aiiir. See introduction, pp. 3–4.

29 Hughey, *The Arundel Harington Manuscript of Tudor Poetry*, 1:58. Richard Harrier states that the Arundel Harington manuscript "is the only surviving manuscript directly descended from *E*[gerton] and likely to have served as the basis for the edited copy from which *T*[*ottel's Miscellany*] was printed." Harrier, *Wyatt's Poetry*, 20.

30 Marquis, *Richard Tottel's Songes and Sonettes*, xxii–xxvi. See also Rollins, *Tottel's Miscellany*, 2:12–20.

31 Regarding the truncation of Grimald's name and poetic contributions, see Pomeroy, *Elizabethan Miscellanies*, 44. A fuller, though perhaps overstated, argument about these truncations is Marquis, "Politics and Print."

32 Marquis, *Songes and Sonettes: Elizabethan Version*, xxxiv–xxxvi, and lviii–lxii.

33 See Byrom, "Tottel's Miscellany, 1717–1817."

34 This image bears a striking resemblance to what is called "A Roman Portrait" of Surrey in Sessions, *Poet Earl of Surrey*, 286–7.

35 Howard, *Certain Bokes Of Virgiles Aeneis*. *EEBO* presents two versions of this book (STC 24798), only one of which presents the portrait of Surrey. The image has not been added to the Bodleian library's copy (UMI reel 513:07), only to the British Library's copy (UMI reel 944:08). The tipping in of the Surrey portrait in *Songes*

and Sonettes was confirmed by Stephen Tabor, Huntington Library Curator of Early Printed Books, via email, 15 February 2006. The tipping in of the portrait in *Certain Bokes of Virgiles Aeneis* was confirmed by Malcolm Marjoram, British Library, via email, 16 February 2006.

36 *Songes and Sonettes*, 1557 Q2, sig. Z1r. On this poem in MS Harleian 78, there ascribed to Sir Antonie Sentlenger, see Rollins, *Tottel's Miscellany*, 2:318.

37 Proctor, *The Historie of Wyates Rebellion.*

38 Howard, *An Excellent Epitaffe of Sir Thomas Wyat.*

39 Leland, *Naeniae in Mortem Thomæ Viati Equitis Incomparabilis.*

40 Tromly, "Surrey's Fidelity to Wyatt in 'Wyatt Resteth Here,'" 377. See also Heale, *Wyatt, Surrey, and Early Tudor Poetry*, 19–23; Pérez Fernández, "'Wyatt Resteth Here': Surrey's Republican Elegy."

41 Sessions, *Poet Earl of Surrey*, 258.

42 *Songes and Sonettes*, 1557 Q2, sigs Diiiiv–Eir.

43 See Daalder, "Wyatt and Tottel."

44 My reading of names in *Songes and Sonettes* thus cleaves to similar arguments in Wall, *Imprint of Gender*, 97–9. Quite the opposite view is to be found in Marquis, *Songes and Sonettes: Elizabethan Version*, lxi – lxii: "In the Mid-Tudor period, the advantage of publishing a compilation of poems by other people was that once the poems were arranged, the lyric voices would speak for themselves, leaving virtually no trace of editorial presence, and thus little room for recrimination." This is a curious claim, given the high visibility of Tottel's editorial presence. In Peter Shillingsburg's terms, Marquis's editorial project has a historical orientation, since he reproduces a certain printing of *Songes and Sonettes*. But it is a historically oriented reproduction of Tottel's own *aesthetically* oriented reproduction of mid-Tudor poetry. See Shillingsburg, *Editing in the Computer Age*, 15–27. Marquis himself emphasizes the aesthetic significance of editorial changes throughout his edition, particularly in his arguments about arrangement. Regarding the Q3 changes, for example, Marquis states that "though Q3's editor respected the readings of Q1, he was motivated less by a need to restore that text than by a desire to continue the initiative, evident from the beginning of the project, to provide a consistent tone to individual poems and a uniform iambic measure to the verses as a whole, that is, to create a text more accessible to the reader" (lxi).

45 Curll, *The Praise of Geraldine (a Florentine Lady).* On the Geraldine story, see Rollins, *Tottel's Miscellany*, 2:71–5.

46 Marotti, *English Renaissance Lyric*, 219.

47 For a vivid account of the circumstances of Surrey's imprisonment in Winsdor castle in 1537, see Sessions, *Poet Earl of Surrey*, 128 ff.

48 Daalder, "Wyatt and Tottel," 5. See also Rollins, *Tottel's Miscellany*, 2:94–7; Kamholtz, "Thomas Wyatt's Poetry."

49 Shillingsburg, *Editing in the Computer Age*, 18–19. See n. 44 in this chapter.

50 Fraser, *Court of Venus*, 36–56. Fraser's appraisal is that the first edition was printed by Thomas Gybson as *The Court of Venus* sometime between 1535–9. The second edition, published as *A Boke of Balettes*, was printed by William Copland sometime between 1547–9. There may be another version around the time of *Songes and Sonettes*, but the third extant edition was printed by Thomas Marshe in the 1560s.

51 Fraser, *Court of Venus*, 114. For the manuscript variations, see Harrier, *Wyatt's Poetry*, 157–8.

52 Sherman, "Manicule."

53 John Hall, *The Couurte of Vertu*, sigs B5v–B6r.

54 Ibid., sigs M2v–M3r.

55 Ibid.

2. "Nedelesse Singularitie": George Gascoigne's Strategies for Preserving Lyric Delight

1 Gascoigne, *A Hundreth Sundrie Flowres*. Except where noted, quotations are from the first two editions, with signature numbers in parentheses: *HSF* is the 1573, and *The Posies* the 1575 edition.

2 The term "textual intercourse" comes from Masten, who focuses on authorial collaboration in drama; Gascoigne misleads the reader towards a collaborative model, and playfully reveals authorial singularity instead.

3 See Bradner, "The First English Novel"; Adams, "Gascoigne's 'Master F. J.' as Original Fiction."

4 See also Pigman, *A Hundreth Sundrie Flowres*. Pigman uses his own numbering for the poems called "Devises," and his edition uses two fonts, roman and italic, to approximate the original's use of three: black letter, roman, and italic. The visual effect of the three typefaces does influence the overall poetic effect. See, e.g., figure 2.1. On the national valences of typefaces, see Galbraith, "'English' Black-Letter Type." The second edition of the collection is George Gascoigne, *The Posies of George Gascoigne Esquire*. The "corrections" include, among others, a revamped *F.J.* that passes it off as an Italian romance, the categorization of *all* items as either "Flowres," "Weedes," or "Herbes," and the addition of some new material, with very few cuts. See Pigman, *HSF / Gascoigne*, l–lxv. Regarding the implications of creating one edition from two distinct printings, see Pigman, "Editing Revised Texts."

5 See Weiss, "Shared Printing." Weiss's month-by-month account of the printing of *HSF*'s sections allows him to conclude that *all* paratextual material was most likely written by Gascoigne, rather than by "G.T.," "H.W.," or the printer; that Gascoigne did not oversee printing; and that "Gascoigne intended that 'The Adventures of Master F.J.' appear first in the book," 98–9. While not all critics agree about whether the dates provided in *HSF* are fictional, and whether Gascoigne read proof (see Pigman,

HSF / Gascoigne, lvii–lvii), most accept that F.J. and G.T. are fictions rather than historical persons remaining semi-anonymous in the text.

6 Pigman, *HSF / Gascoigne*, 5.

7 Clegg, *Press Censorship in Elizabethan England*, chap. 5. Clegg argues that slander or offence to members of the court was the probable reason for censorship, rather than lascivious or lewd material.

8 See, respectively, Hughes, "Gascoigne's Poses"; Parrish, "The Multiple Perspectives of Gascoigne's 'The Adventures of Master F. J.'"; Schott, "The Narrative Stance in 'The Adventures of Master F.J.'"

9 "Posies," despite the traditional and often-employed homonym poesy-posy in the singular, usually refer to epigrams or mottoes rather than full poems, even short ones. See Whigham and Rebhorn, *The Art of English Poesy / by George Puttenham*, Book 1, chap. 30. This chapter, entitled, "Of short epigrams called posies," attests to their occasional quality: they were "sent usually for New Year's gifts or to be printed or put upon their banqueting dishes of sugarplate, or of marchpane ... and were made for the nonce" (146).

10 On anonymity, see North, *The Anonymous Renaissance*, esp. 68–9. On the "stigma of print" and a subsequent challenge to this terminology, see Saunders, "Stigma"; May, "Tudor Aristocrats." See also n. 42 to the introduction, above.

11 See introduction, pp. 11–12.

12 Helgerson, *The Elizabethan Prodigals*; McCoy, "Gascoigne's 'Poëmata Castrata.'"

13 McCoy, "Gascoigne's 'Poëmata Castrata,'" 30, 32.

14 Ibid., 32; Stewart, "Gelding Gascoigne," 161, notes that the phrase "*Poëmata castrata*" does not appear in Beza's writing. He also shows that unlike Gascoigne, Beza was not interested in the "continued publication" of his earlier poetry, since Beza's cuts were actually substantial excisions of earlier material (148).

15 Wall, *Imprint of Gender*, 127–40, 243–50.

16 Cicero, *De Oratore* 2.28.121 and 2.29.129, my emphasis. The first passage sets up "winning over," "instructing," and "stirring of men's minds" as three goals of oratory. The second passage connects each of these three goals to a style: winning over requires "gentleness of style," instructing requires "acuteness," and stirring minds requires a style "of energy." See Sutton, *Cicero, De Oratore*, 285, 291. One crux when it comes to applying these definitions to poetry is the problem of the verbs *movere*, in its sense of persuasion and of inciting emotional response, and later *concitare*, which is translated as "to excite." Neither has direct connections to the concept of causing pleasure, and here the separation between writing poetry and writing speeches is more clear. But Horace formulates a dual rather than triple characterization of poetry, usually summed up by "dulce et utile." The entire sentence reads, "He has won every vote who has blended profit and pleasure, at once delighting and instructing the reader." Here "instructing" is not from "docere" but from "monere," which includes the

senses of warning and admonishment. See Fairclough, *Horace: Satires, Epistles and Ars Poetica*, 478–9.

17 For a brief survey of the phrase in the context of Elizabethan English treatises, see Smith, *Elizabethan Critical Essays*, 1: xxv–xxvii. An immediate precursor of Gascoigne, Thomas Wilson, reproduces the standard Ciceronian triad in his *Arte of Rhetorique* (1553): "Three things are required of an orator: 1. To teach 2. To delight 3. And to persuade." In describing delight, Wilson directs readers to "cheer ... guests, and to make them take pleasure with hearing of things wittily devised and pleasantly set forth." Quoted in Vickers, *English Renaissance Literary Criticism*, 77. See also Smyth, "*Profit and Delight.*" In his discussion of the "declared purpose" of these miscellanies, the phrase "profit and delight" is all but absent, signalling a change in this time period to the goal of being "alluring conveyors of social status" (27).

18 Here I follow Pigman, *HSF / Gascoigne*, liv–lix, who judges that Gascoigne probably meant the miscellany to open with *The Adventures of Master F.J.* rather than with *Supposes* and *Jocasta.*

19 Pope also notices the conflicting interests of G.T. and H.W. in "The Printing of 'This Written Book.'" He claims that G.T. remains firmly in the mindset of manuscript circulation, while H.W. allies himself with the practices of print culture, 46–7.

20 Heale, *Autobiography and Authorship in Renaissance Verse*, 39.

21 There is another incident in which F.J.'s poetry reaches a wider audience than F.J. wishes. The poem "Beautie shut up thy shop," which contains some lines insulting courtiers' sartorial habits, was "by negligence of his Mistresse dispersed into sundry hands, and so at last to the reading of a Courtier," sig. Fiiv. For an examination of the complicated circulation of letters in *F.J.*, in which several letters also find their way into the wrong hands, or are written by the wrong hands, see Stewart, "Gelding Gascoigne," passim.

22 Here, there are three typefaces in the original printing: the poems are in black letter, the initial description is in a roman font, and the text beginning "The Dame," as with most of the titles or non-narrative text preceding poems in "The Devises," is in italic.

23 Kneidel, "Reforming George Gascoigne."

24 Nathan, "Gascoigne's 'Lullabie.'" Nathan's analysis highlights "the complex of feelings implied: fondness, indulgence, tenderness, irony, and a sense of duty" (68).

25 For a detailed description of the manuscript and an argument on Collier's hand in it, see Dawson, "John Payne Collier's Great Forgery."

26 Ibid., 12.

27 See Pigman, *HSF / Gascoigne*, 630. The probable source of comparison is Wyatt's translation of Petrarch in Tottel's *Songes and Sonettes.*

28 This crux term is discussed in ibid., 664. The possibilities include both "pregnant" and "worthless" in the sense of "skeleton-like" (*OED*, B3). In line 7, Gascoigne "wold faine hit the barren," which makes it seem as though a "barren" deer is desirable prey

but a "carren" one is not. Pigman rejects various editors' resolution that "carren" means pregnant, because of the context: the deer is not pregnant, but lactating. This explanation still begs the original question of why the speaker would want to hit a deer that is "barren," if not in contrast to a pregnant one.

29 See, for example, Austen, *Gascoigne*, 84–98. Austen argues that Gascoigne's revisions were "apparently designed to allow Gascoigne to sidestep the poor reputation of the material and reissue almost all of it" (87). Both Austen and Clegg point out the difficulty of claiming that there are substantive revisions as a result of either censorship or censure of the first edition; see Clegg, *Press Censorship in Elizabethan England*, esp. 112–19.

30 These publications and dedicatees are detailed in Pigman, *HSF / Gascoigne*, xxxix–xl.

31 On the garden metaphor, see Staub, "Dissembling His Art: 'Gascoigne's Gardnings.'"

3. Solitude, Poetic Community, and Lyric Recording in Spenser's *Shepheardes Calender* and *Colin Clovts Come home againe*

1 Bryskett, *A Discovrse of Civill Life*, sigs E1v–E2v. The translation includes Giraldi's "Tre diologhi della vita civile" as well as material from Guazzo, *La Civil Conversazione* and Piccolomini, *Della Institutione morale*. On this and the Sidney-Spenser-Bryskett connections, see Bryskett, *A Discourse of Civill Life*, ed. Thomas E. Wright, vii–xvii. Bryskett was a key figure in the Sidney-Spenser circle; he accompanied Sidney on his tour of the continent, and Spenser assisted him in his position as clerk of the Council of Munster from about 1584 to 1589. They may have known each other as early as 1577.

2 See Spiller, *Science, Reading, and Renaissance Literature*, chap. 2; MacFaul, *Poetry and Paternity*, 108–23.

3 The hypotheses are wide-ranging. Earlier searches for the person behind the initials lead to Edward Kirke as the leading candidate. These have given way to a rough consensus that Gabriel Harvey, or Harvey and Spenser, most likely wrote the glosses. On the possibility of a range of sound-based and grammatical puns on these initials, including "eke," "ecce," and many others; see Carroll, "The Meaning of 'E.K.'"

4 See Galbraith, "English Type."

5 Helgerson, *Self-crowned Laureates*.

6 North argues that Spenser's calculated anonymity in *The Shepheardes Calendar* functioned dually to allow patrons to express approval (by preserving his secrets) and to prevent everyone else from judging on the basis of anything but the poetry's quality (by withholding information about Spenser's own quality, or rank). See *Anonymous Renaissance*, 101–3. Wendy Wall sees Spenser as first using anonymity and the textual glosses and other features of *The Shepheardes Calender* as a way of first displaying a coded signature before later taking full, authorial credit for the work, once he turns to the masculinized poetry of *The Faerie Queene*. See *Imprint of Gender*, 233–43.

7 See Hamilton, *The Spenser Encyclopedia.* Louis Montrose claims that "Colin is not the image of a man in history but the image of a poet in literary history." "'The Perfecte Paterne of a Poete,'" 38.

8 Spenser, *The Shepheardes Calender*, 1579. Parenthetical signature numbers are to this edition.

9 Alpers, *What Is Pastoral?* 81.

10 See Moore, "Colin Breaks His Pipe"; Luborsky, "Illustrations to *Shepheardes Calender.*"

11 Wall, *Imprint of Gender*, 240–1.

12 Luborsky, "Illustrations to *Shepheardes Calender*," 10.

13 Luborsky presents evidence that the woodcuts are of uneven quality, and that their simplicity and allusiveness to other texts would have made them seem "quaint" to contemporary readers (ibid., 16).

14 On stringed instruments and the harmony of state, see Hollander, *The Untuning of the Sky*, 46–51. Hollander emphasizes the influence of Alciato's emblematic use of the lute as an image of *Foedera*, or political concord. David Lee Miller calls for an explicit connection between the lute or the harp and the "imperial staff of office," also by referencing Alciato, but with special emphasis on images of concord and discord between Ireland and England and between France and England. See Miller, "The Earl of Cork's Lute," 154–6. Both authors concentrate on the connection between stringed instruments and concord, without considering the bagpipe. *April*'s musical consort is made up of the Muses and the Graces, according to Davis, "Allusive Resonance in the Woodcut to Spenser's 'Aprill.'" As Davis notes, there are too few figures to accommodate the full complement of Graces and Muses; he identifies three Graces to Elizabeth's right, and seven Muses to her left.

15 For close attention to the images of instruments in the *Calender*, see Cain, *Praise in The Faerie Queene*, 24–8. Cain astutely identifies the instruments in these woodcuts, focusing on the cornett's role of "salute and convocation" in *April*, but he understates the relationship between images of music-making and Spenser's text. He does not mention, for example, the conflict between *April*'s image (in which Colin plays) and the text (in which Hobbinoll sings his song and afterward Thenot judges Colin to be talented, but foolish).

16 Heninger, "The Typographical Layout of Spenser's *Shepheardes Calender.*" Heninger also argues that "in the later stages of its composition a decision was made to recast *The Shepheardes Calender* as a reprise of Sannazaro's *Arcadia* in order to flatter Sidney, announce allegiance to him, and secure his good offices" (42), and that this decision was undertaken by none other than E.K., whom Heninger takes to be Gabriel Harvey.

17 Book 1, lines 878–87 of Nims, *Ovid's Metamorphoses.* Also see the note on Ovid in Hamilton, *Spenser Encyclopedia*, 527. For a history of the literary representations of the figure of Pan, see Merivale, *Pan, the Goat-god.*

18 Sannazaro, *Arcadia & Piscatorial Eclogues*, 103–5.

19 See the images reproduced by Heninger, "Typographical Layout," 52–71.

20 Critics differ about who offers the pipes to whom, about what the gesture of the figure on the right means, and perhaps most importantly, about which figure is Cuddie, and which is Piers. For some differing opinions, see Lane, *Shepheards Devises*, 166; McCabe, *Edmund Spenser*, 559; Luborsky, "Illustrations to *Shepheardes Calender*," 36.

21 Florio, *A Worlde of Wordes*, sig. Qq2r.

22 Ibid., sig. H1v.

23 See Battaglia, *Grande Dizionario Della Lingua Italiana*, 1051–2; Devoto, Oli, and Magini, *Nuovo Vocabolario Illustrato Della Lingua Italiana*, 1567. Among the associations noted are: of being a relentless boor or dullard, of being a deceptive person or liar, of engaging in chit-chat, of emitting banging little farts, and of loudly playing the instrument "tutto il santo giorno."

24 Piepho notes that "the bagpipe is unknown in ancient pastoral." *Adulescentia: The Eclogues of Mantuan*, 106.

25 See Sommer, *The Kalender of Shepherdes.*

26 The woodcuts of the early editions are catalogued in Hodnett, *English Woodcuts, 1480–1535*, image #1511. For descriptions of the woodcuts in the later editions, see Luborsky and Ingram, *A Guide to English Illustrated Books, 1536–1603.* Luborsky discusses the provenance and development of the images from the original *Compost et kalendrier* printed in Paris in 1493, 673–4, and shows that this woodcut was in Powell's 1556 and 1559 editions, East's edition c. 1570, and three later editions (2:52).

27 For the importance of Mantuan in sixteenth-century educational contexts, see Cullen, *Spenser, Marvell, and Renaissance Pastoral*, 2–3. Cullen's division between Mantuanesque and Arcadian pastoral is influential, but has been seen as oversimplifying a more complex, dialectic representation of the idyllic and fallen worlds, especially in Spenser's poetry. See, for example, Berger, *Revisionary Play*, 284.

28 See Piepho, *Mantuan's Eclogues*, 31–7.

29 The "lengthy and deeply learned instruction given by the Master Shepherd" is noted by Cooper, *Pastoral*, 78.

30 Piepho, *Mantuan's Eclogues*, 4–11.

31 Brant, *Stultifera Nauis*. There are no extant English copies of the *Ship* between 1517 and 1570, when it was published by John Cawood. On the early publication history of Barclay's eclogues, see White, *The Eclogues of Alexander Barclay*, lvi–lx.

32 Several commentators have noted that Barclay's eclogues, three of which are free translations of Pope Pius II's *Miseriae Curialium* and two of which are translations of Mantuan's eclogues, seem to have had no direct impact on Spenser's eclogues. For an example, see White, *The Eclogues of Barclay*, lxi–lxii n. However, in the same passage, White argues that "It is hardly possible that Spenser was ignorant of Barclay's poems," and Lynn Staley Johnson cites Barclay as one of several influences on Spenser's

moralizing passages: see Johnson, *The Shepheardes Calender: An Introduction*, 61, 63, 72. Another likely source of images were the printed, illustrated editions of Chaucer, popular throughout the late-fifteenth and sixteenth centuries, which show the Miller holding a shawm or tabor pipe rather than the bagpipe called for by the text. See Carlson, "The Woodcut Illustrations in Early Printed Editions of Chaucer's Canterbury Tales," 73–119; Luborsky and Ingram, *A Guide to English Illustrated Books, 1536–1603* (1: 276–8).

33 Also emphasizing vertical composition, Luborsky compares the *January* image to that of the emblem for Sloth in *The Cristall Glasse* (1569); see Luborsky, "Illustrations to *Shepheardes Calender*," 28.

34 This myth is treated in detail by Winternitz, *Musical Instruments and Their Symbolism in Western Art*, 150–64. Winternitz calls the Apollo / Marsyas story "deeply tragic," while the other story, with Pan playing against Apollo, is comedic, since it involves Midas's punishment – ass's ears – for judging Pan's music to be better. He also makes reference to the deeply layered differences between "the serene and silvery sound of plucked gut strings and the bleating shrill, guttural, exciting sound of a reed pipe ... the realm of inhibition, of reason, of measure ... as opposed to the realm of blind passion: in short, the antagonism between Apollo and Dionysus" (152). Finally, Winternitz states that he has found only three examples of the Apollo / Marsyas story in which Marsyas plays the bagpipes (154); one of these is *Ovidio Metamorphoseos Volgare*, published in Venice, 1501 (158). He does not list the image in *The Ship of Fools*. But from his discussion, it seems clear that the images in *The Ship of Fools* combine elements of the two stories: the fool figure prefers the debased sounds of the bagpipe, as Midas did, and he also receives the punishment for *hubris* that Marsyas suffered.

35 Not all contemporary portrayals of bagpipes are uniformly negative. An alternative view can be found in Thomas Whythorne, a professional musician and publisher of the first volume of English madrigals. See Osborn, *The Autobiography of Thomas Whythorne*. In his fascinating autobiography, Whythorne tells a tale involving bagpipes, in which a French king is captivated by their sound (241). On the next page, however, the sound of bagpipes is sufficient to drive away a pack of hungry wolves.

36 Sannazaro, *Arcadia & Piscatorial Eclogues*, 151.

37 Ibid., 15–19.

38 Frank Kermode's truism, "The first condition of Pastoral is that it is an urban product," belies his claim that the contemplative life is most often placed above the active in traditional hierarchies. See *English Pastoral Poetry, from the Beginnings to Marvell*, 14–17.

39 See, for example, Montrose, "Perfecte Paterne"; Patterson, "Reopening the Green Cabinet," 115–44. On archbishop Grindal in the *Calender*, see Lane, *Shepheards Devises*, esp. 60–1.

40 The terms and practice of secrecy are explored by Rambuss, *Spenser's Secret Career*.

41 The central moment of Augustine's conversion includes a moment in which Augustine moves away from his companion Alypius because "solitude seemed to me more appropriate for the business of weeping." See *Confessions*, 152.

42 Book 14 chap. 2 of Boccaccio's *De genealogia deorum* is "Poets Prefer Lonely Haunts as Favorable to Contemplation," quoted in Nash, *Arcadia & Piscatorial Eclogues*, 17.

43 Petrarca, *The Life of Solitude*, 157.

44 Sidney, *The Countess of Pembroke's Arcadia (The Old Arcadia)*, ed. Jean Robertson, xv–xix.

45 See Stewart, *Philip Sidney*. Stewart says of Sidney's literary endeavours, "far from being part of a courtly *areopagus*, Philip was writing most of his important verse far away from the bustle of the court" (224). As will be discussed in the next chapter, it is no longer the assumption that Sidney was "banished" from court for his letter to Elizabeth regarding her potential marriage to the French duke, yet there is also no denying his time at Wilton. In a treatment of Sidney and politics, Blair Worden asserts that he almost certainly wrote the letter to Elizabeth at the risk of his career, but "It was poverty that kept him from court ... in 1580, when he retreated to Wilton house and wrote the *Arcadia*." See *The Sound of Virtue*, 43. In these and other accounts, critics and biographers accentuate the difference between the busyness, intrigue, and corrupting influences of court life versus the peacefulness and productive potential of such retreats.

46 This episode is in the so-called Old Arcadia. I examine the thorny textual issues surrounding this work in chapter 4. Quotation from Duncan-Jones, *The Countess of Pembroke's Arcadia*, 15.

47 Stewart, *Philip Sidney*, 148.

48 See, for example, Baynes, *Solitarinesse*, 54–6, which describes the solitary and the busy man as they emerge from their houses in the morning. This passage is taken more or less directly from *De vita solitaria* 1.2.2.

49 Weiss, "Watermark Evidence and Inference."

50 Galbraith, "English Type." Galbraith shows that the printer Hugh Singleton was probably not in a financial position to commission the woodcuts to the *Calender*, nor was he likely to have possessed the Greek type scattered throughout the work. He suggests that Spenser collaborated with Singleton and Harvey in the design of the book, and that the Earl of Leicester may also have been involved.

51 *OED* "recreative" adj.1 and adj.2.

52 The former is from Berger, *Revisionary Play*, 223–33. The latter, from Montrose, "Perfecte Paterne," 38.

53 The *OED* ("record" v.1) includes senses of "record" that are linked to memory and reflection; to the heart; to recitation, practise, and rote learning; and to songbirds and song-singing in general. As will become clear, Spenser makes full use of this wide range of associations.

54 Montrose, "Perfecte Paterne," 42.

55 Sidney's formulation hyperbolically sets poets' creations above those of nature: "Nature neuer set forth the earth in so rich tapistry, as diuers Poets haue done, neither with plesant riuers, fruitful trees, sweet smelling flowers: nor whatsoeuer els may make the too much loued earth more louely. Her world is brasen, the Poets only deliuer a golden." See *The Defence of Poesie*, sig. C1v.

56 Still, the ominous results of poor judgment are never quite extinguished, especially as they recur in the figure of Cuddie. Here, Willye compares Cuddie's judgment of beauty to that of "The shepheard of *Ida*, that iudged beauties Queene" (sig. I.ir). E.K. names that shepherd, Paris, but without reminding us of the disastrous consequences of his judgment, nor that he had been bribed in this judgment of beauty with the promise of beauty, Helen of Troy. *August*'s woodcut contains this small detail: a woman extending her hand, in which a fruit is visible. This could be just an apple – late August is harvest time – but it also recalls Ate's apple of discord and Eve's fruit of the Christian fall.

57 John Hollander traces the many potential meanings of the Echo myth, and calls the sestina "a most resounding form" because it enables the poet to change the meanings of the repeated words so that each iteration augments the overall sense of the words. See *The Figure of Echo*, 34–43.

58 See Cullen, *Renaissance Pastoral*, 108–11. He also accents Willye's playful, undermining verses, but he assesses the sestina as simply another example of the "waste and failure surrounding Colin" (111). See also Montrose, "Perfecte Paterne," 43–4.

59 The novelty of the poem extends to its printed context as well: it is the only poem which E.K. does not gloss. This fact has led to speculation that it was a late addition to the *Calender*, and perhaps that deliberate juxtaposition with the roundelay was intended, whether by Spenser, Harvey, Singleton, or some other agent is not known. Heninger, "Typographical Layout," 42. My emphasis on Colin's dependency on his poetic community for lyric reproduction differs somewhat from Wendy Wall's appraisal of *August*; she takes Colin as the implicit, though absent, winner of the poetic striving. This episode thus helps to consolidate and emphasize his laureate authorship. See *Imprint of Gender*, 237.

60 See Hollander, *Echo*, 43. Hollander mistakenly calls the sestina "Cuddie's," but this mistake reveals Spenser's focus on poetic reproduction. Once the poem has been repeated and reproduced in a new context, its authorship changes as well.

61 The fruits of Spenser's labours support this mixed view. On the one hand, books I–III of *The Faerie Queene* had been published in 1590 to great success: he was granted a £50 per year pension in 1591. But in the same year, Burghley had attempted to call in the newly published *Complaints*, probably because of passages from *Mother Hubberds Tale* which he deemed offensive. See Maley, *A Spenser Chronology*, 56–7.

62 See, for example, Lethbridge, "Spenser's Last Days." Lethbridge conjectures a very specific moment of composition for the *Two Cantos of Mutabilitie* (after 15 October 1598), but also argues that far from exhibiting disillusionment with the world, Spenser's later poetry evinces "an always present realization that some virtues will never be wholly successfully achieved in the world at large" (334). McCabe, "'Little Booke: Thy Selfe Present,'" renounces earlier historicist readings that exclude everything but the political and religious references in the *Calender*, but he also draws attention to the Alençon affair, the be-handing of Stubbes, and Archbishop Grindal's fall amid the prophesying debate. For an opposing view, see Cheney, *Spenser's Famous Flight*, 151. Cheney concentrates on love lyrics in Spenser's later career, and his view of the career path is essentially hopeful: love lyric as regeneration after epic exhaustion.

63 Hamilton, Yamashita, and Suzuki, *Spenser: The Faerie Qveene*.

64 Greenblatt reads the destruction of the Bower of Bliss as a classic moment of self-fashioning; Quilligan reads the boar's imprisonment as envisioning rampant male sexuality brought under control by female power. Greenblatt, *Renaissance Self-fashioning*; Quilligan, "The Gender of the Reader."

65 James Nohrnberg calls the episode "valedictory;" in "Acidale" in *The Spenser Encyclopedia*, 4–6.

66 Spenser, *Colin Clovts Come home againe. By Ed. Spencer* (1595). Parenthetical signature numbers are to this edition.

67 McCabe, *Shorter Poems*, 649. Elsewhere, McCabe says that the poem concentrates upon "themes of lost potential and wasted opportunity." See McCabe, "Edmund Spenser, Poet of Exile," 94.

68 Hadfield, *Spenser's Irish Experience*, 35, 129.

69 See note 6 of this chapter.

70 Halfway through the volume printed in 1595, the end of *Colin Clovts* is juxtaposed with the beginning of *Astrophel*. Both works have their own separate title pages, but they are printed as a single object by William Ponsonby, who printed all of Spenser's poetry throughout the 1590s. *Astrophel* occupies sigs E3r–K4r, and is almost exactly as long as *Colin Clovts* (A1r–E2v). *Astrophel* begins in the middle of gathering E of the volume, which makes it unlikely to have been sold as a separate unit, unlike the separate sections of the *Complaints*; see Weiss, "Watermark Evidence in Spenser's Complaints," 131–2. On Ponsonby's 1590s printings of Spenser and Sidney, see Brennan, "William Ponsonby"; Brink, "William Ponsonby's Rival Publisher."

71 On Spenser's version of the elegy as a "gesture of comfort" in the tradition of Chaucer's *Book of the Duchess*, see Kay, *Melodious Tears*, 51–7. Kay argues that *Astrophel* enacts a progression from Bion's lament of Adonis, Ovid's version in the *Metamorphoses*, and Spenser's immediate model, Ronsard's *L'Adonis* (1563), by infusing both Christian eternity and a more hopeful transformation of the lovers "into a single flower."

72 Pigman, *Grief and English Renaissance Elegy*, 57–9.

73 For details on the attributions, see Rollins, *The Phoenix Nest, 1593*, 115–31.

74 On these lines, see Sacks, *The English Elegy*, 52: "This is clearly an assured bid for inclusion in the company of poets." To this, I would add that that company is quite specific in this case, far more so than in the *Shepheardes Calender*.

75 See Tromly, "Lodowick Bryskett's Elegies on Sidney in Spenser's *Astrophel* Volume." Tromly suggests that Spenser conceived of *Astrophel* and masterminded its production, and that Bryskett composed *A pastorall Aeglogue* after having read Spenser's *Astrophel*; see esp. p. 386.

76 Sidney Herbert, *Selected Works of Mary Sidney Herbert*, ed. Hannay, Kinnamon, and Brennan, 136–9; McCabe, *Shorter Poems*, 661–3. Hannay's position is considerably more nuanced, however. In two studies, she argues that Mary Sidney Herbert likely collaborated with Lodowick Bryskett and Spenser, and that her undisputed poetry also bears stylistic similarities to Spenser's, making her a "Spenserian" poet and rendering the attribution question more complex. See Hannay, *Philip's Phoenix*, and "The Countess of Pembroke as a Spenserian Poet."

77 See Clarke, "'In Sort as She It Sung.'" Clarke calls for a reexamination of authorship, but in asserting that Spenser appropriates and controls the voice of Mary Sidney Herbert, she instead reinscribes Spenser as an authority-wielding *auctor*, and ignores signals of a more collaborative and exchange-based authorship system which the paratextual material, other poems, and fictional depictions of poetic reproduction via "rehearsing" provide. Dennis Kay also overestimates Spenser's role as author, director, and laureate of the volume when he argues that "Spenser in effect invented the vernacular funeral anthology, and the Countess of Pembroke became the first Spenserian poet." See *Melodious Tears*, 61.

78 Tromly, "Bryskett's Elegies," 386.

79 Spenser, *Colin Clovts Come Home Againe* (1611). In the same year, Lownes printed a folio edition of *The Faerie Qveene* followed by Spenser's other poetic works. Unlike the Jonson and Shakespeare folios, the 1611 folio Spenser is not a monumental edition, but a malleable, mutable, and "no-frills" collection of Spenser's works, according Galbraith, "Spenser's First Folio."

80 Hannay argues that Spenser's poem, the poem beginning "Ay me to whom shall I may case complaine" (now usually called "The Doleful Lay of Clorinda," and the poem titled "*The mourning* Muse *of* Thestylis" were all "deliberately dovetailed" with one another: See her *Selected Works of Mary Sidney Herbert*, 137. Mary Ellen Lamb argues nearly the opposite: that "probably various authors wrote their elegies individually before Spenser gathered them together in *Astrophel*." See her *Gender and Authorship in the Sidney Circle*, 63. Theodore Steinberg, examining the imagery of flowers, argues Spenser's poem and the "Doleful Lay" (but not the "Mourning Muse") form an "obvious unit" because of their imagistic counterpoint. See his "Spenser, Sidney, and the Myth of Astrophel."

81 Spenser expresses regret at not yet composing poetry for Sidney as early as 1591, when he dedicates *The Ruines of Time* to Mary Sidney Herbert. In this dedication, he apologizes for allowing Philip Sidney's name to "sleep in silence and forgetfulnesse." See his *Complaints Containing Sundrie Small Poemes of the Worlds Vanitie*, sig. A3v. His ongoing collaboration with the poets printed in *Astrophel* is unlikely. Though Spenser had worked closely with Ponsonby on the printing of the *Complaints* and *Daphnaida* in 1591, he was back at Kilcolman by 27 December 1591, and *Colin Clovts / Astrophel* was not published until 1595. This time-line has been established by Weiss, "Watermark Evidence in Spenser's Complaints."

4. Lyric Surrogacy: Reproducing the "I" in Sidney's *Arcadia*

1 See Fraunce, *The Arcadian Rhetorike.* This work combs Sidney's *Arcadia* for rhetorical devices, and sets Sidney alongside other great authors. See also Whigham and Rebhorn, *Art of English Poesy*, 29, 310. Two other recent studies on Abraham Fraunce's early reproduction of Sidney's work, in both manuscript and printed contexts, are May, "Marlowe, Spenser, Sidney and-Abraham Fraunce?" and Martin, "Made Plaine by Examples."

2 Surrogacy and a state of childish helplessness, as Tom MacFaul has shown, are also central to *The Four Foster Children of Desire* and to *Astrophel and Stella.* He claims that Sidney manipulates tropes of childishness and dependent, immature states; see *Poetry and Paternity*, chap. 3. Katherine Duncan-Jones emphasizes Sidney's actual poetic immaturity, short life, and regrets; see "Philip Sidney's Toys." Their emphasis is thus on Sidneian surrogacy from the author's perspective; mine is on the surrogacy of taking up and fostering his poetic works, on the immediate afterlife of trifling, needy poems.

3 Sidney, *Defence*, sig. G2r.

4 Rösslin and Raynalde, *The Byrth of Mankynde,* sigs Eviiiv–Fir. See also Rösslin, *Birth of Mankind*, xxi.

5 The notion of male and female sperm goes back at least as far as Hippocrates, *The Seed*, § 5–8. Aristotle is most commonly thought of as having a one-seed model, and arguing that males supply form and females matter, but according to A.L. Peck, this is a misunderstanding of Aristotle's larger theory of generation. For him, "it is clear that fundamentally the contributions of both parents in generation are identical," and Aristotle echoes Hippocrates's ideas on male and female semen; see Peck, *Aristotle. Generation of Animals*, § 721b–2b. See also §729a 11 and Peck's introduction, p. xiv.

6 Spiller, *Science, Reading, and Renaissance Literature*, chap. 2, esp. 67–9.

7 For one treatment of this metaphor, see Rose, *Authors and Owners*, 38.

8 Montaigne, *The Complete Essays of Montaigne*, 291.

9 Ulreich, "Sidney's Conception of Mimesis," 142.

10 Sidney, *Defence*, sig. F2r. See also Mack, *Sidney's Poetics*, 110.

11 Warkentin, "Patrons and Profiteers"; Marotti, *English Renaissance Lyric*, esp. 228–38. See also Mentz, "Selling Sidney"; Hannay, "The Countess of Pembroke's Agency in Print and Scribal Culture."

12 Alexander, *Writing after Sidney*, xxviii.

13 Vincent Casaregola calls this trend the "*Arcadia* Project." See "Unstable Elements."

14 Alan Stewart argues that "the birth of *The Arcadia* was implicitly likened to the birth of Mary's son," born in summer, 1580, when Philip likely finished the Old *Arcadia*. See *Philip Sidney*, 226.

15 On J.W. Saunders's influential term "the stigma of print," see the introduction, notes 42 and 47. Modifying Saunders's conclusions are May, "Tudor Aristocrats"; and Krevans, "Print and the Tudor Poets." Sidney's exclusively manuscript production process and his "preference for manuscript publication" are discussed in Woudhuysen, *Sidney and Circulation of Manuscripts*, 210–13.

16 A common metaphor; see MacFaul, *Poetry and Paternity*, 7–10. MacFaul here emphasizes the prospect that poems, "considered as children, take on a life of their own, and find their own way in the world like sons" (10); my own emphasis is on how fostering agents care for, and in the process, change poems.

17 See Crawford, *Marvelous Protestantism.*

18 Sidney, *The Covntesse of Pembrokes Arcadia* (1590), sig. A3v.

19 Katharine Eisaman Maus, *Inwardness and Theater in the English Renaissance*, 187–8. Maus notes Philip Sidney's playful tone and Mary Sidney's role as patron / *pater*. Wendy Wall astutely observes that "Sidney's evocation of thwarted infanticide is recast as a kind of Caesarian posthumous birthing performed by Mary Sidney and the publisher. See Wall, *Imprint of Gender*, 156. My examination of "lyric surrogacy" is indebted to Maus's and Wall's analysis of Mary Sidney's and Hugh Sanford's editorial actions, and the metaphors of birth and parentage. But I would extend these readings to the fictive, poetic situations of reproduction that occur in the *Arcadia* and its adaptations. Doing so reveals the extent to which Sanford's images of surrogacy and care of the text during its rebirth are already present in images of textual reproduction in the *Arcadia.*

20 William A. Ringler, *The Poems of Sir Philip Sidney*, 525–31.

21 Hannay, "Pembroke's Agency," 30.

22 Woudhuysen, *Sidney and the Circulation of Manuscripts*, 224–32.

23 Ibid., 228. Rowe, "The Countess of Pembroke's Editorship of the *Arcadia*," establishes that Mary Sidney did not make alterations or corrections to the text of the *Arcadia*, but instead that the editorial procedures of the 1590 text were called into question under her auspices.

24 Hannay, "Pembroke's Agency," 17, states that "Philip Sidney began the *Psalmes* and Pembroke completed them." See also Alexander, *Writing after Sidney*, 89–105.

25 Joel Davis, "Multiple *Arcadias* and the Literary Quarrel between Fulke Greville and the Countess of Pembroke." The pastoral location and elements of the *Arcadia* are present in both editions, but accented in the earlier, "Old Arcadia" which supplies books 4–5, missing from the 1590 edition. Sidney's pastoral elements connect the work to Wilton, where he wrote the work in retirement from court, and where his text was more closely connected to his sister, if Sidney's dedication to Mary can be taken at face value.

26 Sidney, *The Covntesse of Pembrokes Arcadia* (1593), sig. ¶4r.

27 Ibid., sig. ¶4v.

28 Alexander, *Writing after Sidney*, 87, also notices the prevalence of paternal and maternal images in these letters. He variously describes her role as "adoptive mother," "godparent," and "mother, midwife, and foster parent."

29 Alpers, *Pastoral*, 81.

30 Sidney, *Arcadia, 1590*, sig. Z8v.

31 The pronoun "she" should be used advisedly. The disguised "Cleophila" in the Old *Arcadia* is renamed "Zelmane" in the New. In both cases, neither the masculine nor the feminine pronoun is sufficient, and that is the point. Studies exploring the desire that Philoclea feels for the disguised Cleophila, called an "uncouth love, which nature hateth most" in the initial prophecy, include Crawford, "Sidney's Sapphics"; Bates, *Masculinity, Gender and Identity in the English Renaissance Lyric*, 89–135.

32 See Prendergast, "Philoclea Parsed." Prendergast focuses perhaps too narrowly on Pyrocles's narcissism, without paying sufficient attention to the overwhelming impression that such self-absorption is only part of the proceedings, and not the most important part.

33 See Bates, *Masculinity*, 122–30. Bates notices Sidney's adoption of the metre of French poets such as Marot, and also comments perceptively on the blazon's simultaneous fragmenting and totalizing of the body being described, which I argue is amplified in projects attempting to complete or perfect Sidney's own literary corpus. Bates finds that the reproduction of this poem in manuscript miscellanies renders it "no longer part of an integrated whole but a detached and free-floating textual 'part' as discrete and isolable as the female 'parts' it blazons" (124).

34 Ringler, *Poems of Sidney*, 410.

35 Skretkowicz, "'A More Lively Monument.'"

36 Dickenson, *Arisbas*, sig. G1r.

37 Sidney, *Arcadia, 1593*, sig. Ccir.

38 Basilius's goal is thus primarily praise, rather than lamentation. On the rhetorical underpinnings of Renaissance elegies, see Pigman, *Renaissance Elegy*, esp. 40–51.

39 For additional information, see Ringler, *Poems of Sidney*, 493. Ringler, 370–83, suggests that Mary Sidney might have written the poem as a way to complete the blank, and discusses his hypothesis for the transmission of the New *Arcadia* from

manuscript to print. An exhaustive set of descriptions and connections of the Old *Arcadia* manuscripts can be found at Woudhuysen, *Sidney and Circulation of Manuscripts*, 299–355. But Woudhuysen spends little time on the Cambridge manuscript of the New *Arcadia*. See also Skretkowicz, *The Countess of Pembroke's Arcadia*, lv–lvi.

40 Pigman, *Renaissance Elegy*, 57–67; Kay, *Melodious Tears*, 67–78.

41 Baker-Smith, "'Great Expectation': Sidney's Death and the Poets," 90. Other essays in this collection provide a view of both collective and individual textual actions that arose following Sidney's death.

42 See Kalas, *Frame, Glass, Verse*, 1–105. Kalas makes reference to blank almanacs, emblem books with blanks, and the *album amicorum* as contemporary examples of texts in which blank spaces, often framed, were printed with the intention of later completion in manuscript.

43 See Fleming, *Graffiti*. Fleming describes "I was here" as "the graffito's most simple and paradigmatic instance" (72).

44 Quarles, *Argalus and Parthenia*.

45 Other names written into this copy are "Anna Levys" or "Lewys" (264v), "Mr. Bellinger," and "Etheldred Bellinger Her Booke" (348v). I would like, but cannot prove, Elizabeth Bastard to be the daughter of Thomas Bastard (1565–1618), who was one of the contributors to a memorial volume to Sidney: John Lloyd, *Peplvs. Illvstrissimi Viri D. Philippi Sidnaei*.

46 Brayman Hackel, *Reading Material*, 159–60.

5. "All Men Make Faults": Begetting Error in *Shake-speares Sonnets*

1 Rothenberg, "Ensuring the Longevity of Digital Information." The version of this article consulted is an expanded version of the above, revised 22 February 1999; http://www.kb.nl/hrd/dd/dd_links_en_publicaties/publicaties/dig-info-paper.rothenberg.pdf, consulted 2-17-2010.

2 Except where noted, all quotations of Shakespeare's sonnets are from Stephen Booth, ed., *Shakespeare's Sonnets*. This edition reprints the 1609 quarto alongside his edited version; I quote Booth's edited version. The first edition, which I refer to frequently (and in a few cases reproduce in facsimile), is *Shake-speares Sonnets. Neuer Before Imprinted* (At London: By G. Eld for T.[homas] T.[horpe] and are to be solde by William Aspley, 1609).

3 The argument between complexity and simplicity in sonnet sequences is a long-standing one, going as far back as the early readership and copying of the sonnets, and more recently in arguments that revel in the complexities of the sonnets. For the latter, see especially the commentary in Booth and in Fineman, *Shakespeare's Perjured Eye*. But as Sasha Roberts has shown in *Reading Shakespeare's Poems*, this reading style

bears little resemblance to how early modern readers approached Shakespeare's poetry, especially in their tendency to extract *sententiae* from poetry, even from erotic works like *Venus and Adonis*. John Benson, in the preface to his 1640 edition of Shakespeare's poetry, calls Shakespeare's language "Seren, cleere and eligantly plaine … no intricate or cloudy stuffe to puzzell intellect, but perfect eloquence." *Poems: VVritten by Wil. Shake-speare. Gent*, sig. *2v.

4 Both recent and classic critiques overemphasize exact or perfect copying in the sonnets, especially when it comes to their ability to preserve the young man. Cleanth Brooks claims that Shakespeare and other poets "evidently thought that they were able to transcend the limitations of their own generation," and then quotes sonnet 65's "miracle … [t]hat in black ink my love may still shine bright" as evidence. Brooks, *Well-Wrought Urn*, xi. Aaron Kunin interrogates what he calls Shakespeare's "preservation fantasy," but throughout the essay he assumes that poetry can and does preserve something without changing it, and he focuses only on the procreation sonnets. See "Shakespeare's Preservation Fantasy."

5 There is more controversy about this assertion than there used to be. Colin Burrow cites Sidney Lee's (1904) invective against the printer Thomas Thorpe as unscrupulous, but also cites Katherine Duncan-Jones (1983) as saying the opposite. See Burrow, "Editing the Sonnets"; Duncan-Jones, "Was the 1609 *Shake-speares Sonnets* Really Unauthorized?" A balanced treatment of the issue is Marotti, "Literary Property."

6 Not least of these editors is George Steevens, who "thought that the sonnets were an abomination." Quoted in Burrow, "Editing the Sonnets," 151.

7 See Stallybrass, "Editing as Cultural Formation."

8 Rollins, *A New Variorum Edition of Shakespeare*, 2:18–28, finds extreme fault with Benson. Bennett, "Benson's Alleged Piracy of *Shakespeares Sonnets* and of Some of Jonson's Works," is the first of the modern studies to examine Benson's textual actions outside of an author-centred model of textual production and publication. She concludes that "[Benson's] *Poems* of 1640 is not a pirated edition of *Shake-speares Sonnets* but an edition to rescue them from oblivion, as it did" (248).

9 Kerrigan, *Sonnets and A Lover's Complaint*.

10 See especially North, "The Sonnets and Book History."

11 Wilson, *Shakespeare's Sugared Sonnets*, 146–67.

12 See Brooks, *Printing and Parenting*, 35, 110. See also Burrow, *William Shakespeare: The Complete Sonnets and Poems*, 402. Burrow notes the connection between "copy" and *copia*, which "gives an organic strength to the mechanical process of reproduction."

13 In asserting the essential connection between biological and textual reproductive mutation, my reading differs somewhat from that of MacFaul, *Poetry and Paternity*, chap. 5. MacFaul asserts that the relationship is complicated, but that Shakespeare

believes in, and works towards the permanence, posterity, and perfection of poetic representations over that of biological offspring.

14 The goal of the perfect version may, however, be off the mark. John Pitcher suggests instead that Daniel, in his revisions, seems to be "trying to pierce and vent the stability of the text, rather than perfect it." See "Benefiting from the Book," 74.

15 Shakespeare, *The Passionate Pilgrime. By W. Shakespeare.*

16 The oft-cited lines by Thomas Heywood, appended to Heywood's *An Apologie for Actors* in 1612, assert that Shakespeare was "much offended" with Jaggard for printing under Shakespeare's name poems which were in fact by Heywood and had been printed in *Troia Britannica* (1609); quoted in Rollins, *New Variorum Sonnets*, 533–8. Burrow, *Complete Sonnets and Poems*, 77–9 recommends caution when jumping to the conclusion that Shakespeare was irate over the unauthorized printing of poems in his name or that Jaggard was simply unscrupulous and piratical in his printing methods. Marotti likewise shows that Jaggard does not deserve the label "pirate," since "printing the Shakespeare poems and mixing them with the verse of other writers was quite legitimate." But he calls Jaggard's Shakespearean authorship ascription "another issue." "Literary Property," 153–4.

17 *Sonnets*, 477. Marotti favours the theory of memorial reconstruction for sonnets 138 and 144; see "Literary Property," 151–2. Taylor, "Some Manuscripts of Shakespeare's Sonnets," argues that manuscript witnesses of sonnet 2 demonstrate a likelihood that the sonnet was revised between composition and printing in the 1609 Quarto, while sonnets 6, 106, and 128 probably circulated as individual poems. Duncan-Jones instead contends that these changes are much more likely to have arisen through the normal variations involved in manuscript circulation, copying, and modification, and proffers the possibilities of "copying inattentively" or failure to learn the poem exactly by heart for manuscript versions of sonnet 2. See her edition, *Shakespeare's Sonnets*, 453–6.

18 *Sonnets*, 479–80.

19 Perhaps the best introduction to, and critique of, these terms is McGann, *A Critique of Modern Textual Criticism*. He demonstrates their introduction by Pollard, Greg, McKerrow, Bowers, Tanselle, and the other exponents of the New Bibliography, 23–36, and 39: "The theory of final intentions aims to provide a rule for the choice of a text under circumstances where several apparently fully authoritative texts exist." However, it does not generally account for collaborative publication or the actions of other professionals involved in the publication project (42–3).

20 See McGann, *The Textual Condition*; Love, *The Culture and Commerce of Texts*; Kastan, *Shakespeare and the Book*; de Grazia, *Shakespeare Verbatim*.

21 See especially Marcus, *Unediting the Renaissance*; McLeod, "UnEditing Shakespeare." The preponderance of the word "unediting" in article titles indicates that this textual

critical development is not limited to early modern studies, but rather is linked to the growing availability of digital copies of all kinds of literary texts. See introduction, p. 11.

22 Marotti, "Literary Property," 165. (His emphasis.)

23 Grafton, "'Discitur Ut Agatur'"; Fred Schurink, "Manuscript Commonplace Books, Literature, and Reading in Early Modern England." See also Brayman Hackel, *Reading Material.*

24 *Sonnets*, 189–90.

25 Ibid., 176 (my emphasis). The thy / their error is "an easy printer's error" that occurs fourteen times in the sequence. Duncan-Jones, *Shakespeare's Sonnets*, 35, gives instead "Excusing these sins more than these sins are:" and conjectures that the compositor read "theis" as "their." Rollins, *New Variorum Sonnets*, 1:100–1 shows that many combinations of "their," "thy," and "thee" have been attempted. Most of these attempt to get at the basic sense that the addressee's faults are being extenuated, and that this extenuation serves to corrupt the speaker.

26 Horace provides the classic statement on poetic endurance, in which the poet has raised a monument more durable than bronze. Neither poet quite says that his poetry will outlast the pyramids. Shakespeare's formulation is "The pyramids built up with newer might / To me are nothing novel, nothing strange" (123.2–3). Horace's is that his verses are "higher than the regal site of the pyramids" (regalique situ pyramidum altius); see Horace, *Q. Horati Flacci Opera*, book 3, ode 30. Another influential statement on poetic immortality comes from Ovid, *Metamorphoses* 15.875–6, where Ovid boasts of the survival of his "better part" and "indelible name." For Shakespeare, of course, it is always "you" or "your name" that the speaker claims will survive. Gordon Braden sees Shakespeare's version of this name-based survival as "the lover's affirmation of a transcendent dependence on the beloved" which mutates Ovid's authorial boast; "Ovid, Petrarch, and Shakespeare's Sonnets," 97. For a provocative, though hyperbolic, examination of what is preserved and how in the sonnets, see Kunin, "Shakespeare's Preservation Fantasy."

27 See introduction, pp. 12–14.

28 See Moss, *Commonplace-books*, esp. chs. 6 and 7.

29 Marotti, "Literary Property," 147–8.

30 Stallybrass et al., "Hamlet's Tables and the Technologies of Writing in Renaissance England."

31 Booth, *Sonnets*, 412, points out the potential heart / art pun and calls this poem "rhetorically suicidal" since it undermines its initial assertion. I do not agree that "line 10 has made it clear that the speaker is talking about a blank notebook which he himself was expected to fill" (413). The rest of the sonnet emphasizes writing's relationship to memory to such a degree that this line's prosaic sense must be something like, "I do not need to keep track of your love in such a crude way as cutting notches into a stick."

32 Lesser and Stallybrass, "The First Literary *Hamlet* and the Commonplacing of Professional Plays." Importantly for my study of Shakespeare's poetry, Lesser and Stallybrass connect the emergent trend of literary commonplacing in printed texts to John Bodenham, a printer of the verse collection *Belvedere*, and Nicholas Ling, printer of *Englands Parnassus*, also a collection of verse quotations.

33 Lesser and Stallybrass cite five printed playbooks in which in-line commonplace markers occur, three of which are by Jonson. They hypothesize that this particular commonplace marker suggests "somewhat more strongly the author's hand" (ibid., 401–2).

34 All quotations of *Hamlet* are from Furness, *A New Variorum Edition of Shakespeare: Hamlet*. Parenthetical line numbers are to this edition.

35 These and other questions are tracked by ibid., vols 3–4:107–8.

36 Sonnet 69, which contains one well-known crux ("ſolye" in 69.14, usually modernized as "soil"), and two other words that are usually emended ("end" to "due," 69.3, and "Their" to "Thy," 69.5). The printed versions of sonnets 67 and 124 (which also allude to reproduction, bastardy, and the potential for poetry to outlast other monuments) have been called "monstrosities" that contain "almost as many perversions of his [Shakespeare's] meaning in each as there are lines." Howard Staunton, quoted in Rollins, *New Variorum Sonnets*, 1:177. For example, 67.6's "dead seeing" has sometimes been emended to "dead seeming," and the phrase "proud of many" (67.12) to "prov'd" or "'priv'd" or "poore" (ibid). Booth observes that "no satisfactory explanation has been offered for" the phrase "proud of many." The four possibilities he offers all demonstrate the importance of increase, reproduction, and creation to the sense of this phrase and this sonnet; *Sonnets*, 251. On "seeing" versus "seeming," see Burrow, *Complete Sonnets and Poems*, 516.

37 Marotti, "Literary Property," 158–63; Burrow, *Complete Sonnets and Poems*, 93–4; Bennett, "Benson's Alleged Piracy"; Baker, "Cavalier Shakespeare."

38 Smyth, *Profit and Delight*. Smyth's descriptions of these miscellanies reinforce the idea that they were valued for use in social situations.

39 "Literary Property," 164.

40 If Benson did try to get rid of male pronouns in favour of female ones, he did so haphazardly and rather unsuccessfully. The issue has been examined by de Grazia, "The Scandal of Shakespeare's Sonnets." See also Burrow, *Complete Sonnets and Poems*, 93–4.

41 These are described exhaustively for studies between the eighteenth century and 1944 by Rollins, *New Variorum Sonnets*, 2:133–277. See also Burrow, *Complete Sonnets and Poems*, 98–103.

42 Rollins, *New Variorum Sonnets*, 2:74–116.

43 Stirling, *The Shakespeare Sonnet Order*.

44 More recent criticism tends to side with the hypothesis that Shakespeare authorized the printing of the sonnets, and perhaps oversaw their arrangement as well. See especially Duncan-Jones, "1609 Sonnets Unauthorized"; Marotti, "Literary Property." René Graziani makes the argument that Shakespeare arranged some of the sonnets according to numerological associations. If, as he argues, sonnets 12 and 60 refer to the minutes and hours of clocks, and sonnet 126 to the number of the so-called grand climacteric, then at least some of the sonnets are carefully crafted to match number and theme. I would point out, however, that this kind of organizational tendency 1) need not have been effected by Shakespeare and 2) does not facilitate an overall narrative. Quite the opposite: it isolates individual sonnet-moments and obscures any sense of a story-based structure. See "The Numbering of Shakespeare's Sonnets: 12, 60, and 126."

45 See Hieatt, Hieatt, and Prescott, "When Did Shakespeare Write *Sonnets* 1609?"; Jackson, "Vocabulary and Chronology." Both analyses employ a methodology that relies on the incidence of rare Shakespearean words. Hieatt et al. conclude that Shakespeare's sonnets underwent "composition at widely varying times" (85). Jackson extends this examination, and agrees that the "Zone 4" sonnets, the so-called dark lady sonnets 127–54, were composed early in Shakespeare's career, while "the majority, if not all, of the last twenty-odd of the sonnets to the Friend were written in the seventeenth century" (75).

46 *Between Men*, 35.

47 "The Sonnets: Sequence, Sexuality, and Shakespeare's Two Loves," 295.

48 Fineman, *Perjured Eye*, 171.

49 Burrow, *Complete Sonnets and Poems*, 134, also notices the potential contradiction, and more circumspectly suggests that Fineman's study and de Grazia's "The Scandal of Shakespeare's Sonnets" should be "slightly re-tuned."

50 See Marotti, "Literary Property," 147; North, "Book History," 210–11.

51 See Dubrow, "'Incertainties Now Crown Themselves Assur'd.'" Valerie Traub challenges the validity of Dubrow's claims by concentrating on the sonnets' depiction of the "two genders as incommensurable opposites," and on the production of misogyny itself as an "ideological effect" of Shakespeare's deployment of discourses of sodomy to describe heterosexual union and heteroeroticism. See Traub, "Sex Without Issue." As will become clear, my reading of copulatives in the sonnets is indebted to both of these studies.

52 Wendy Wall argues for an "evolution" in printings of *Astrophel and Stella*, from a more miscellaneous text in 1591 to a more ordered text by 1598. Printed numerals and even page numbers "heightened the linear nature of the reading experience." *Imprint of Gender*, 70–1. As I argue below, *Shake-speares Sonnets* resists this linear experience both thematically and formally.

53 For example, Peter Herman argues that Shakespeare's references to usury are entirely inappropriate to the initial, procreation sonnets, and create a failed economy of love and procreation, in "What's the Use?"

54 See, for example, Burrow, *Complete Sonnets and Poems*, 133. See also Fineman, *Perjured Eye*, 140–4.

55 In addition to its playful allusion to the trinitarian mystery of three aspects conjoined in one overall being, this triad has been seen as a Platonic statement that "the good, the beautiful, and the true are but different phases of one reality." J.S. Harrison, *Platonism in English Poetry*, 128, quoted in Rollins, *New Variorum Sonnets*, 1: 159.

56 Sonnet 1's "commitment to profusion" is remarked on by critics including Vendler, *The Art of Shakespeare's Sonnets*, 47–8; Booth, *Sonnets*, 135. The phrase is Vendler's, but demonstrating multiple syntactic and associative meanings is Booth's primary critical action. With this in mind, we should note the perhaps accidental difference of "beauties *Rose*" in Q and "beauty's rose" in most modern editions. Whether we call it accidental or substantive, the potential confusion between the possessive and plural forms of "beauty" makes it possible that there are multiple vehicles for beauty, and even multiple versions of this seemingly Platonic ideal category. The potential ambiguity of "beauties *Rose*" provides for just the kind of confusion between singularity and multiplicity that Shakespeare makes more obvious in sonnet 59 and elsewhere. See also de Grazia, "Revolution in *Shake-speares Sonnets*." De Grazia reproduces this spelling even as she notes that "In order for 'beauties *Rose*' to survive it must be reproduced as faithfully as possible: a mimesis closer to mechanical duplication than artful imitation" (65).

57 See Montaigne, "Of the affection of fathers for their children," in Frame's edition, *The Complete Essays of Montaigne*, 278–93; Plato, *Timaeus*; Sidney's *Defense of Poesy* and *The Countesse of Pembroke's Arcadia*; and many other sources on parenting texts. These are discussed at greater length in chapter 4.

58 "Revolution in *Shake-speares Sonnets*." However, de Grazia perhaps overemphasizes "revolution" as denoting constancy in the first 126 sonnets; Shakespeare does not so straightforwardly show that "The poet's poetics, as well as his subject and his love for his subject, will triumph over change by remaining selfsame" (66). Rather, assertions of selfsameness are undermined by doubting perfection, demonstrating physical change, and exposing textual flaws.

59 *The Art of Shakespeare's Sonnets*, 282.

60 de Grazia, "The Scandal of Shakespeare's Sonnets"; Hall, "Literary Whiteness in Shakespeare's Sonnets"; Traub, "Sex Without Issue."

61 On how clusters of sonnets might go together, see Stirling, *Sonnet Order*, passim, esp. 16–23. Stirling judiciously avoids the claim of an overarching narrative, but retains the principle of narrative coherence in short clusters of sonnets. According to Stirling, this principle is Shakespeare's. Stirling thus rearranges sonnets that violate his sense of

coherence and order. His willingness actively to read and rearrange the sonnets qualifies him, to my mind, as a creator of a "fair copy" of *Shake-speares Sonnets* because he reproduces them with a difference. The trouble is that he claims to have found the single, *right* order, rather than one among many; this certainty leads to many claims such as "No poet capable of writing 129 would have placed it in the context of 128 and 130" (24), a statement that clearly overemphasizes thematic coherence and chronological narrative at the expense of miscellaneity, contrast, and juxtaposition, all of which are equally possible arrangement strategies.

62 See *Perjured Eye*, esp. 174–86, and 279–96.

63 The availability to Shakespeare of the terms "copulation" as sexual coupling (with the implied possibility of offspring) and "copulative" as a grammatical linking term is crucial to my understanding of Shakespeare's poetics of identity. Sexual "copulation" occurs in both *Lear* and *As You Like It.* "Copulative" as a grammatical term occurs in Latin grammars of the period (*OED* "copulative," A1a, and *OED* "copulation," 1a and 2). In *As You Like It*, Touchstone uses the term facetiously in connection with the swearing and physical combination involved in marriage. The crucial process by which identity and existence are conjured through the use of copulative statements is the subject of "The Supplement of Copula," a section of Jacques Derrida, *Margins of Philosophy*, esp. 196–205. An acknowledgment of the constituent role of copulative statements in expressions of identity is precisely what Derrida claims to be missing from not only Aristotelian ontology but also twentieth-century comparative linguistic studies, especially those claiming there are some languages which lack the verb "to be." Heidegger's analysis of this grammatical structure also reveals the central relationship between saying that something "is" and its ontological status as a being. See *An Introduction to Metaphysics*, 52–74. I do not mean to claim that Shakespeare anticipates post-structuralism or Heideggerian metaphysics. Instead, Shakespeare's repeated manipulation of copulative "is" statements reveals his interest in pushing the limits of such statements so that the apparent truth-value of the speaker's statements is at odds with the grammatical construction. That construction is constitutive of identity, according to Heidegger and other metaphysical philosophers.

64 For a full examination of the complex couplings in these lines, see Booth, *Sonnets*, 165–8. To Booth's observation that pairing is inherent in comparison, so that Q's "coopelment" implies linguistic coupling, I would add that this sonnet ought to be coupled thematically and syntactically with sonnet 130 ("My mistress' eyes are nothing like the sun"). Coupling these metapoetic statements about plain speaking reveals how closely they echo one another, despite their "distance" from one another (separated by 110 sonnets): "And then believe me, my love is as fair / As any mother's child" (21.9–10); "And yet by heav'n I think my love as rare / As any she belied with false compare" (130.13–14). The *OED* notes early modern instances of "couplement"

that invoke the senses of matrimony, love, and poetry (definitions 1, 2a, 2b), and cites Shakespeare in this instance and in *Love's Labours Lost.*

65 The two sets of parentheses have been interpreted in myriad ways; many of these involve a combination of finality and indeterminacy. See Duncan-Jones, *Shakespeare's Sonnets*, note to p. 366.

66 Here, the 1609 quarto's italics are both visually and thematically important to the sense of these lines: Nature presides over the legal processes activated by "*Audite*" and "*Quietus*," even as she renders the addressee into a new form. "Quietus" is used elsewhere only in *Hamlet*, where Q1 and F, but not Q2, italicize it.

67 *Pace* Burrow, *Complete Sonnets and Poems*, 633, regarding the emendation of "minutes" for Q's "mynuit"; this emendation restricts a number of available puns or secondary meanings, as well as the minute / minion sound-play of lines 8–9; see Booth, *Sonnets*, 433.

68 Hall and de Grazia focus on the connection of fairness and darkness to socioeconomic, dynastic, and racial reproduction and anxieties over purity; see "Literary Whiteness in Shakespeare's Sonnets," esp. 78; "The Scandal of Shakespeare's Sonnets," passim. Among many discussions, Fineman sees praise of, and sex with, the dark lady as "the undoing of that which she attracts" and as "the perversion of … idealization"; *Perjured Eye*, 58.

69 This statement's interpretive crux does receive attention from Duncan-Jones, *Shakespeare's Sonnets*, note 9 to p. 127. In her view, the line suggests either that the speaker has deliberately chosen a dark-eyed lover because the new fashion demands it, or that she herself has chosen this colour of eye-shadow. Booth does not gloss this word, while Burrow maintains that "because of beauty's profanation (by the abuse of cosmetics) [the eyes of the mistress] are black in mourning." *Complete Sonnets and Poems*, 634. Vendler, *The Art of Shakespeare's Sonnets*, 540–1 suggests that the speaker is defending an "aesthetically anomalous choice."

70 For Hall, we ignore the racial and colonial connotations of blackness here, and in other sonnets, at the risk of fueling white hegemony; "Literary Whiteness in Shakespeare's Sonnets," 81.

71 "Book History," 207–11. North also remarks that printing single sonnets on individual pages *also* renders them potentially miscellaneous and unsequential. See also Wall, *Imprint of Gender*, 70–1. Page breaks and continuous printing are the subject of Hutchison, "Breaking the Book Known as Q." This essay raises the question of what and how line and page breaks might mean, but offers no specific answers, either hermeneutic or material, partly because of its narrow focus on sonnet sequences instead of printed poetry collections.

72 Booth, *Sonnets*, 452–4. Examples of fulsome hyperbolic mistress-praise are found in Constable's *Diana* and Lynche's *Diella*; see Burrow, *Complete Sonnets and Poems*, 640. Sonnet 130 seems to echo Thomas Watson's "Harke you that list to heare what sainte

I serve" (VII of *Hekatompathia*), according to Heylin, *So Long as Men Can Breathe*, 36.

73 For a famous image of Petrarchan metaphors grotesquely literalized, in which a female figure has miniature suns for eyes, coral for lips, and globoid breasts, see *The Extravagant Shepherd*, 1654; the image is reproduced in Booth, *Sonnets*, 453.

74 *Perjured Eye*, 24.

75 See Traub, "Sex without Issue," 442–3.

76 Booth and Vendler emphasize the aphoristic, philosophical, or homiletic diction and tone of the sonnet, Booth by citing related proverbs (see *Sonnets*, 441) and Vendler by contrasting timeless aphoristic statements with the lived experience of lust (see *The Art of Shakespeare's Sonnets*, 550–4). A L. Rowse suggests that the poem "is a literary exercise" and "is, in a sense, in inverted commas." See *Shakespeare's Sonnets*, 268.

77 The height of isolative, single-poem readings of this sonnet is Jakobson and Jones, *Shakespeare's Verbal Art in Th'expence of Spirit*. Sonnet 129 is the subject of at least fifteen articles since the 1970s.

78 "Shakespeare's First Poem: Sonnet 145."

79 Ibid., 226.

80 Earlier critics often notice that sonnet 145 has a very different tone from 144 and 146, and seeking an overall narrative, conjecture that this poem is out of sequence, though still Shakespearean. Some earlier critics felt confident that sonnet 145 is "spurious;" see Rollins, *New Variorum Sonnets*, 1: 372–3.

81 See the critical summary in ibid., 1: 374–8. See also Booth, *Sonnets*, 501–17. Sisson, quoted there, calls 146.2 "the prize crux of the Sonnets" (503). Booth chooses to make his most comprehensive methodological statement in the course of his commentary on sonnet 146. In the peroration to this statement, Booth explains his choice to gloss in a "pluralistically-committed way" (508), by making reference to both John Benson's evaluation of the sonnets as "seren, cleere and eligantly plaine" and to the ambiguities, contradictions, and "complexities modern critics see" (516). Because of his overwhelming emphasis on the single poem as the unit of scrutiny, I would argue that Booth's methods are persistently New Critical and formalist, as Kerrigan argues of twentieth-century critics from Robert Graves and Laura Riding to Helen Vendler, in "Shakespeare's Poems," 74. Burrow suggests that along with 144.6 and 145 as an early sonnet, the error in 146.2 might suggest "illegible or partially revised copy"; see *Complete Sonnets and Poems*, 672.

Coda: The End of *Shake-speares Sonnets*

1 J. P. Collier is in this view the host of a textual virus. One memorable formulation of this relationship is "a scholar is a library's way of reproducing itself. " See Dennett, *Darwin's Dangerous Idea*, 346.

2 See n. 26 to chapter 5 on claims of the durability of poetry.

3 See chapter 5, particularly n. 60 and n. 68.

4 Kerrigan, *Sonnets and A Lover's Complaint*, 14. See also Burrow, *Complete Sonnets and Poems*, 140.

5 *Shake-speares Sonnets*, 1609, sig. K1v.

6 Hollander, *Echo*, 61. Puttenham refers to Echo in his entry for *epanalepsis*, but he is referring to a word both beginning and ending a line. See Whigham and Rebhorn, *Art of English Poesy*, 284. Sidney's echo poem "Faire Rocks, goodly rivers" in *Arcadia*'s second eclogues perhaps sets the standard, though it does have contemporaries and precursors. See Ringler, *Poems of Sidney*, 402.

7 de Grazia, *Verbatim*, 173.

8 Ibid., 152–63. For another, differently inflected account of eighteenth-century editorial development, see McKerrow, "The Treatment of Shakespeare's Text by His Earlier Editors, 1709–1768."

9 For a typical example, see Larsen, "Essays on Shakespeare's Sonnets."

10 "Linkerature: Classical Literature 'Annotated' with Links."

11 Of the many treatments considering literary theory and the hypertextual environment, George P. Landow's remains an excellent introduction. See *Hypertext.* The technological, historical, and social dimensions of editing poetry in the electronic medium are explored by Fraistat and Jones, "The Poem and the Network." But in the introduction to this work, Thomas Tanselle reminds us of the continuity between mediums, returning us to an issue I have been examining throughout this book: "The philosophical conundrum as to where a text resides is exactly the same as it always was"(6).

12 Sidran, *Now I Live*. See introduction, pp. 3–4. Published too late for me to examine for this book, a fascinating example of editorial and poetic license taken with Shakespeare's sonnets is a book of poems edited by Sharmila Cohen and Paul Legault, *Translating and Rewriting Shakespeare*. They commissioned poets to write "English to English" translations and adaptations of Shakespeare's sonnets, in fulfilment of a familiar directive, that "Shakespeare's sonnets live on" (i–ii).

Works Cited

Primary Works

Baynes, Roger. *The Praise of Solitarinesse, Set down in the Form of a Dialogue, Wherein Is Conteyned, a Discourse Philosophical, of the Lyfe Actiue, and Contemplatiue*. Imprinted at London: By Francis Coldocke and Henry Bynneman, 1577.

Brant, Sebastian. *Stultifera Nauis Qua Omnium Mortalium Narratur Stultitia, Admodum Vtilis & Necessaria Ab Omnibus Ad Suam Salutem Perlegenda, è Latino Sermone in Nostrum Vulgarem Versa, & Iam Diligenter Impressa. An. Do. 1570. = The Ship of Fooles, Wherin Is Shewed the Folly of All States, with Diuers Other Workes Adioyned Vnto the Same, Very Profitable and Fruitfull for All Men. Translated Out of Latin into Englishe by Alexander Barclay Priest*. [Imprinted at London: In Paules Churchyarde by Iohn Cavvood Printer to the Queenes Maiestie], 1570.

Bryskett, Lodowick. *A Discovrse of Civill Life: Containing the Ethike Part of Morall Philosophie. Fit for the Instructing of a Gentleman in the Course of a Vertuous Life*. London: Printed [by R. Field] for Edvvard Blovnt, 1606.

Curll, Henry, ed. *The Praise of Geraldine (a Florentine Lady.) Being, the Celebrated Love Poems Of the Right Honourable Henry Howard, Earl of Surrey, and Knight of the Most Noble Order of the Garter ; Who Was Beheaded by King Henry VIII, in the Year 1546, Also the Poetical Recreations Of Sir Thomas Wyate, Called The Delight of the Muses*. London: Printed for Henry Curll in Clement's-Inn-Passage, 1728.

Daniel, Samuel. *Delia. Containing Certaine Sonnets: With the Complaynt of Rosamond.* At London: Printed by J.C. for S. Watersonne, 1592.

Dickenson, John. *Arisbas, Euphues Amidst His Slumbers: Or Cupids Iourney to Hell. Decyphering A Myrror of Constancie, a Touch-stone of Tried Affection, Begun in Chaste Desires, Ended in Choise Delights: And Emblasoning Beauties Glorie, Adorned by Natures Bountie. VVith The Triumph Of Trve Loue, in the Foyle of False Fortune*. Imprinted at London: By Thomas Creede, for Thomas Woodcocke, and are to be sold at his shop in Paules Church-yard, 1594.

England and Wales. *A Colleccion of All the Statutes (from the Begynning of Magna Carta Vnto the Yere of Our Lorde, 1557) Which Were Before That Yere Imprinted. And Furst a Pistle, Necessary to Be Redde by Them That Shall Vse This Booke.* [Imprinted at London in Fletestrete within Temple Barre, at the signe of the hande & starre by Richard Tottyll], 1557.

– *A Colleccion of All the Statutes (from the Begynning of Magna Carta Vnto the Yere of Our Lorde, 1557) Whiche Were Before That Yere Imprinted. VVhereunto Be Addyd the Colleccion of the Statutes, Made in the Fourth and Fift Yeres of the Reignes of Kyng Philip and Quene Mary, and Also the Statutes Made in the Fyrst Yere of the Raigne of Our Souerayne Lady Quene Elizabeth. And Furst a Pistle, Necessary to Be Redde by Them That Shall Vse This Booke.* [Imprinted at London in Fletestrete within Temple Barre, at the signe of the hande & starre: by Richard Tottyll], 1559.

– *The Great Boke of Statutes Conteynyng All the Statutes Made in the Parlyamentes from the Begynnynge of the Fyrst Yere of the Raigne of Kynge Edwarde the Thyrde Tyll the Begynnyng of the. xxxiiii. Yere of the Most Gracyous Raigne of Our Soueraigne Lorde Kyng Henry the .viii.* [Imprynted at London: By VVyllyam Meddelton cum priuilegio Regali], 1542.

Florio, John. *A Worlde of Wordes, Or Most Copious, and Exact Dictionarie in Italian and English, Collected by Iohn Florio.* Printed at London: By Arnold Hatfield for Edw. Blount, 1598.

Fraunce, Abraham. *The Arcadian Rhetorike: Or The Praecepts of Rhetorike Made Plaine by Examples Greeke, Latin, English, Italian, French, Spanish, Out of Homers Ilias, and Odissea, Virgils Aeglogs, [...] and Aeneis, Sir Philip Sydnieis Arcadia, Songs and Sonets [...].* At London: Printed by Thomas Orwin, 1588.

Gascoigne, George. *A Hundreth Sundrie Flowres Bounde Vp in One Small Poesie. Gathered Partely (by Translation) in the Fyne Outlandish Gardins of Euripides, Ouid, Petrarke, Ariosto, and Others: And Partly by Inuention, Out of Our Owne Fruitefull Orchardes in Englande: Yelding Sundrie Svveete Sauours of Tragical, Comical, and Morall Discourses, Bothe Pleasaunt and Profitable to the Well Smellyng Noses of Learned Readers.* At London: Imprinted [by Henrie Bynneman] for Richarde Smith, [1573].

– *The Posies of George Gascoigne Esquire. Corrected, Perfected, and Augmented by the Authour.* Imprinted at London: By H. Bynneman for Richard Smith, 1575.

Hall, John. [*The Couurte of Vertu Contaynynge Many Holy or Spretuall Songes Sonettes Psalmes Ballettes Shorte Sentences as Well of Holy Scriptures as Others &c.*]. [Imprinted at London: In fleete streete nighe unto S. Dunstanes churche: by Thomas Marshe, 1565.]

Henry Howard, Earl of Surrey. *An Excellent Epitaffe of Syr Thomas Wyat, With Two Other Compendious Dytties, Wherein Are Touchyd, and Set Furth the State of Mannes Lyfe.* [Imprynted at London: by John Herforde for Roberte Toye, 1542.]

– *Certain Bokes Of Virgiles Aeneis Turned* into *English Meter by the Right Honorable Lorde, Henry Earle of Surrey.* [Imprinted at London in flete strete within Temple barre, at the sygne of the hand and starre, by Richard Tottell], 1557.

– *Songes and Sonettes, Written by the Right Honorable Lorde Henry Haward Late Earle of Surrey, and Other.* [Imprinted at London in flete strete within Temple barre, at the sygne of the hand & starre, by Richard Tottell], 1557.

Jordan, Thomas. *Piety, and Poesy. Contracted, in a Poetick Miscellanie of Sacred Poems.* London: printed by Rob: Wood, [1643].

Leland, John. *Naeniae in Mortem Thomæ Viati Equitis Incomparabilis. Ioanne Lelando Antiqvario. Avtore.* [Londini: Ad signum ænei Serpentis], 1542.

Lloyd, John. *Peplvs. Illvstrissimi Viri D. Philippi Sidnaei Svpremis Honoribus Dicatvs.* Oxonii: Excudebat Iosephus Barnesius, 1587.

Proctor, John. *The Historie of Wyates Rebellion, with the Order and Maner of Resisting the Same, Wherunto in the Ende Is Added an Earnest Conference with the Degenerate and Sedicious Rebelles for the Serche of the Cause of Their Daily Disorder.* [Imprynted at London by Robert Caly within the precincte of the late dissolued house of the grey friers, nowe connected to an Hospitall, called Christes Hospital], 1554.

Quarles, Francis. *Argalvs and Parthenia.* London: Printed for Iohn Marriott in St. Dunstons Church:yard fleetstreet, 1629.

Ravenscroft, Thomas. *Pammelia. Mvsicks Miscellanie. Or, Mixed Varietie of Pleasant Roundelayes, and Delightfull Catches, of 3. 4. 5. 6. 7. 8. 9. 10. Parts in One. None so Ordinarie as Musicall, None so Musical, as Not to All, Very Pleasing and Acceptable.* London: Printed by [John Windet for] William Barley, for R. B[onian] and H. W[alley] and are to be sold at the Spread Eagle at the great north doore of Paules, 1609.

Rösslin, Eucharius, and Thomas Raynalde. *The Byrth of Mankynde, Otherwyse Named the Womans Booke. Newly Set Furth, Corrected and Augmented. Whose Contentes Ye Maye Rede in the Table of the Booke, and Most Playnly in the Prologue. By Thomas Raynold Phisition.* [Imprynted at London: By Tho. Ray.], 1545.

Shakespeare, William. *Poems: VVritten by Wil. Shake-speare. Gent.* Printed at London: By Tho. Cotes, and are to be sold by Iohn Benson, dwelling in St. Dunstans Church-yard, 1640.

– *Shake-speares Sonnets. Neuer Before Imprinted.* At London: By G. Eld for T.[homas] T.[horpe] and are to be solde by William Aspley, 1609.

– *The Passionate Pilgrime. By W. Shakespeare.* At London: Printed [by T. Judson] for W. Iaggard, and are to be sold by W. Leake, at the Greyhound in Paules Churchyard, 1599.

Sidney, Philip. *The Covntesse of Pembrokes Arcadia, Written By Sir Philippe Sidnei.* London: Printed by Iohn Windet for William Ponsonbie, 1590.

– *The Covntesse of Pembrokes Arcadia. Written by Sir Philip Sidney Knight. Now Since The First Edition Augmented and Ended.* London: Printed [by John Windet] for William Ponsonbie, 1593.

– *The Defence of Poesie. By Sir Phillip Sidney, Knight.* London: Printed for VVilliam Ponsonby, 1595.

Spenser, Edmund. *Colin Clovts Come Home Againe. By Ed. Spencer.* London: Printed [by T.C.] for VVilliam Ponsonbie, 1595.

– *Colin Clovts Come Home Againe. By Edm. Spencer.* At London: Printed by H.L. for Mathew Lownes, [1611].

– *Complaints. Containing Sundrie Small Poemes of the Worlds Vanitie. VVhereof the Next Page Maketh Mention. By Ed. Sp.* London: Imprinted for VVilliam Ponsonbie, dwelling in Paules Churchyard at the signe of the Bishops head, 1591.

– *The Shepheardes Calender Conteyning Tvvelue AEglogues Proportionable to the Twelue Monethes. Entitled To The Noble And Vertvous Gentleman Most Worthy of All Titles Both of Learning and Cheualrie M. Philip Sidney.* At London: Printed by Hugh Singleton, dwelling in Creede Lane neere vnto Ludgate at the signe of the gylden Tunne, and are there to be solde, 1579.

Tichborne, Chidiock, and T.K. [Thomas Kyd or Thomas Knell]. *Verses of Prayse and Ioye, Written Vpon Her Maiesties Preseruation. Whereunto Is Annexed Tychbornes Lamentation, Written in the Towre with His Owne Hand, and an Aunswere to the Same.* London: Printed by Iohn Wolfe, 1586.

[Wentworth, Paul]. *The Miscellanie, Or, A Registrie, and Methodicall Directorie of Orizons. Exhibiting A Presentment of the Soules Requestes in the High Court of the Heauenly Parliament: Prefaced with Meditations of a Three-fold Distinct Nature, Preparatiuely Instructing the Christian Soule.* Imprinted at London: [By William White and Thomas Creede] for I. Harison, dwelling at the signe of the golden Anchor in Paternoster row, 1615.

Secondary Works and Editions Published After 1750

Adams, Robert. "Gascoigne's 'Master F.J.' as Original Fiction." *PMLA* 73, no. 4 (1958): 315–26.

Alexander, Gavin. *Writing after Sidney: The Literary Response to Sir Philip Sidney, 1586–1640.* Oxford: Oxford University Press, 2006.

Allen, Carleton Kemp. *Law in the Making.* Oxford: Clarendon Press, 1964.

Alpers, Paul. *What Is Pastoral?* Chicago: University of Chicago Press, 1996.

Anderson, Susan. "'A True Copie': Gascoigne's Princely Pleasures and the Textual Representation of Courtly Performance." *Early Modern Literary Studies* 14, no. 1 (May 2008): 43 paragraphs.

Arber, Edward. *A Transcript of the Registers of the Company of Stationers of London: 1554–1640, A.D.* London, 1875.

– ed. *English Reprints. Tottel's Miscellany. Songes and Sonettes by Henry Howard, Earl of Surrey, Sir Thomas Wyatt, the Elder, Nicholas Grimald, and Uncertain Authors. First Edition of 5th June; Collated with the Second Edition of 31st July, 1557.* New York: AMS Press, 1966.

Augustine. Saint, Bishop of Hippo. *Confessions: Saint Augustine.* Trans. Henry Chadwick. Oxford: Oxford University Press, 1991.

Austen, Gillian. *George Gascoigne.* Woodbridge: D.S. Brewer, 2008.

– "Self-Portraits and Self-Presentation in the Work of George Gascoigne." *Early Modern Literary Studies* 14, no. 1 (2008): 34 paragraphs.

Baker, David. "Cavalier Shakespeare: The 1640 *Poems* of John Benson." *Studies in Philology* 95, no. 2 (May 1998): 152–73.

Baker, John Hamilton. *The Common Law Tradition: Lawyers, Books, and the Law.* London: Hambledon Press, 2000.

– *An Introduction to English Legal History*. London: Butterworths Lexis Nexis, 2002.

Baker-Smith, Dominic. "'Great Expectation': Sidney's Death and the Poets." In *Sir Philip Sidney: 1586 and the Creation of a Legend*, ed. Jan Van Dorsten, Dominic Baker-Smith, and Arthur F. Kinney, 83–103. Leiden: Published for the Sir Thomas Browne Institute [by] J.Brill/Leiden University Press, 1986.

Bate, Jonathan. *Shakespeare and Ovid.* Oxford: Clarendon Press, 1993.

Bates, Catherine. *Masculinity, Gender and Identity in the English Renaissance Lyric.* Cambridge: Cambridge University Press, 2007.

Battaglia, Salvatore. *Grande Dizionario Della Lingua Italiana.* Turin: Unione tipografico-editrice torinese, 1961.

Beadle, Richard, and Colin Burrow, eds. *Manuscript Miscellanies c. 1450–1700.* English Manuscript Studies 1100–1700, Vol. 16. Chicago: University of Chicago Press, 2011.

Beal, Peter. *In Praise of Scribes: Manuscripts and Their Makers in Seventeenth-century England.* Oxford: Clarendon Press, 1998.

Bennett, Josephine W. "Benson's Alleged Piracy of *Shakespeares Sonnets* and of Some of Jonson's Works." *Studies in Bibliography: Papers of the Bibliographical Society of the University of Virginia* 21 (1968): 235–48.

Berger, Harry. *Revisionary Play: Studies in the Spenserian Dynamics.* Berkeley: University of California Press, 1988.

Booth, Stephen, ed. *Shakespeare's Sonnets.* New Haven: Yale Nota Bene, 2000.

Bowers, Fredson. *On Editing Shakespeare.* Charlottesville, VA: University Press of Virginia, 1966.

– "Textual Criticism." In *The Aims and Methods of Scholarship in Modern Languages and Literatures*, ed. James Thorpe, 29–54. New York: Modern Language Association of America, 1970.

– "Today's Shakespeare Texts, and Tomorrow's." *Studies in Bibliography: Papers of the Bibliographical Society of the University of Virginia* 19 (1966): 39–65.

Braden, Gordon. "Ovid, Petrarch, and Shakespeare's Sonnets." In *Shakespeare's Ovid: The Metamorphoses in the Plays and Poems*, ed. A.B. Taylor, 96–112. Cambridge: Cambridge University Press, 2000.

Bradner, Leicester. "The First English Novel: A Study of George Gascoigne's *Adventures of Master F.J.*" *PMLA* 45, no. 2 (1930): 543–52.

Brayman Hackel, Heidi. *Reading Material in Early Modern England: Print, Gender, and Literacy.* Cambridge: Cambridge University Press, 2005.

Brennan, Michael G. "William Ponsonby: Elizabethan Stationer." *Analytical & Enumerative Bibliography* 7, no. 3 (1983): 91–110.

Brink, Jean R. "William Ponsonby's Rival Publisher." *Analytical & Enumerative Bibliography* 12, no. 3–4 (2001): 185–205.

Brooks, Cleanth. *The Well Wrought Urn: Studies in the Structure of Poetry*. New York: Harvest, 1956.

Brooks, Douglas A., ed. *Printing and Parenting in Early Modern England*. Aldershot, England: Ashgate, 2005.

Bryskett, Lodowick. *A Discourse of Civill Life*. Ed. Thomas E. Wright. Northridge, CA: San Fernando Valley State College, 1970.

Burrow, Colin. "Editing the Sonnets." In *A Companion to Shakespeare's Sonnets*, ed. Michael Carl Schoenfeldt, 145–62. Malden, MA: Blackwell, 2007.

Burrow, Colin, ed. *William Shakespeare: The Complete Sonnets and Poems*. Oxford: Oxford University Press, 2002.

Byrom, H.J. "The Case for Nicholas Grimald as Editor of *Tottel's Miscellany*." *Modern Language Review* 27, no. 2 (1932): 125–43.

– "Richard Tottell – His Life and Work." *Library* ser. 4, vol. 8, no. 2 (1927): 199–232.

– "Tottel's Miscellany, 1717–1817." *Review of English Studies* 3, no. 9 (January 1927): 47–53.

Cain, Thomas H. *Praise in The Faerie Queene*. Lincoln: University of Nebraska Press, 1978.

Carlson, David R. "The Woodcut Illustrations in Early Printed Editions of Chaucer's Canterbury Tales." In *Chaucer Illustrated: Five Hundred Years of the Canterbury Tales in Pictures*, ed. William K. Finley and Joseph Rosenblum, 73–119. Newcastle, DE: Oak Knoll Press, 2003.

Carroll, D. Allen. "The Meaning of 'E.K.'" *Spenser Studies* 20 (2005): 169–81.

Casaregola, Vincent. "Unstable Elements: The Explosion of the 'Arcadia Project.'" In *Narrative Strategies in Early English Fiction*, ed. Wolfgang Görtschacher and Holger Klein, 147–65. Salzburg Studies in English Literature: Elizabethan & Renaissance, Vol. 118. Lewiston, NY: Mellen, 1995.

Cheney, Patrick. *Spenser's Famous Flight: A Renaissance Idea of a Literary Career*. Toronto: University of Toronto Press, 1993.

Clarke, Danielle. "'In Sort as She It Sung': Spenser's 'Doleful Lay' and the Construction of Female Authorship." *Criticism* 42, no. 4 (2000): 451–68.

Van Cleef, Jabez L. "Chidiock Tichborne's Lament," 2007. http://www.garageband.com/user/jabez/podcast/main.

Clegg, Cyndia Susan. *Press Censorship in Elizabethan England*. Cambridge: Cambridge University Press, 1997.

Cohen, Sharmila, and Paul Legault, eds. *The Sonnets: Translating and Rewriting Shakespeare*. Brooklyn: Telephone Books, 2012.

Collier, J.P. *Illustrations of Early English Poetry*. London: Privately printed, 1866.

Cooper, Helen. *Pastoral: Mediaeval into Renaissance*. Ipswich: Brewer, 1977.

Crawford, Julie. *Marvelous Protestantism: Monstrous Births in Post-Reformation England*. Baltimore: Johns Hopkins University Press, 2005.

– "Sidney's Sapphics and the Role of Interpretive Communities." *English Literary History* 69, no. 4 (2002): 979–1007.

Croft, P.J. *Autograph Poetry in the English Language: Facsimiles of Original Manuscripts from the Fourteenth to the Twentieth Century*. 2 vols. London: Cassell, 1973.

Cromartie, Alan. *The Constitutionalist Revolution: An Essay on the History of England, 1450–1642*. New York: Cambridge University Press, 2006.

Cullen, Patrick. *Spenser, Marvell, and Renaissance Pastoral*. Cambridge, MA: Harvard University Press, 1970.

Daalder, Joost. "Wyatt and Tottel: A Textual Comparison." *Southern Review: Literary and Interdisciplinary Essays* 5 (1972): 3–12.

Davis, Hugh. "Allusive Resonance in the Woodcut to Spenser's 'Aprill.'" *Renaissance Papers* (2000): 25–40.

Davis, Joel. "Multiple *Arcadias* and the Literary Quarrel between Fulke Greville and the Countess of Pembroke." *Studies in Philology* 101, no. 4 (2004): 401–30.

Davison, Francis. *Davison's Poetical Rhapsody, With a Preface, by Sir Egerton Brydges*. Kent: Printed at the private press of Lee Priory by Johnson and Warwick, 1814.

Dawkins, Richard. *The Selfish Gene*. Oxford: Oxford University Press, 1989.

Dawson, Giles E. "John Payne Collier's Great Forgery." *Studies in Bibliography: Papers of the Bibliographical Society of the University of Virginia* 24 (1971): 1–26.

Dennett, Daniel C. *Darwin's Dangerous Idea: Evolution and the Meanings of Life*. New York: Simon & Schuster, 1995.

Deppman, Jed, Daniel Ferrer, and Michael Groden, eds. *Genetic Criticism: Texts and Avant-textes*. Philadelphia: University of Pennsylvania Press, 2004.

Derrida, Jacques. *Margins of Philosophy*. Trans. Alan Bass. Chicago: University of Chicago Press, 1982.

Devoto, Giacomo, Gian Carlo Oli, and Lorenzo Magini. *Nuovo Vocabolario Illustrato Della Lingua Italiana*. Milan: Selezione dal Reader's Digest, 1987.

Dubrow, Heather. "'Incertainties Now Crown Themselves Assur'd': The Politics of Plotting Shakespeare's Sonnets." *Shakespeare Quarterly* 47, no. 3 (1996): 291–305.

Duncan-Jones, Katherine. *The Countess of Pembroke's Arcadia (The Old Arcadia)*. Oxford: Oxford University Press, 1994.

– "Philip Sidney's Toys." *Proceedings of the British Academy* 66 (1980): 161–78.

– ed. *Shakespeare's Sonnets*. England: Thomas Nelson and Sons, 1997.

– "Was the 1609 *Shake-speares Sonnets* Really Unauthorized?" *Review of English Studies: A Quarterly Journal of English Literature and the English Language* 34, no. 134 (May 1983): 151–71.

Eckhardt, Joshua. *Manuscript Verse Collectors and the Politics of Anti-courtly Love Poetry.* Oxford: Oxford University Press, 2009.

Eisenstein, Elizabeth L. *The Printing Revolution in Early Modern Europe.* Cambridge: Cambridge University Press, 2005.

Fairclough, H. Rushton, trans. *Horace: Satires, Epistles and Ars Poetica.* London: William Heinemann, 1955.

Ficino, Marsilio. *Commentary on Plato's Symposium on Love.* Trans. Sears Jayne. Dallas: Spring Publications, 1985.

Fineman, Joel. *Shakespeare's Perjured Eye: The Invention of Poetic Subjectivity in the Sonnets.* Berkeley: University of California Press, 1986.

Fleming, Juliet. *Graffiti and the Writing Arts of Early Modern England.* London: Reaktion, 2001.

Fraistat, Neil, and Steven Jones. "The Poem and the Network: Editing Poetry Electronically." In *Electronic Textual Editing,* ed. Lou Burnard, John Unsworth, and Katherine O'Brien O'Keeffe, 105–21. New York: Modern Language Association of America, 2006.

Fraser, Russell A., ed. *The Court of Venus.* Durham, NC: Duke University Press, 1955.

Furness, Howard, ed. *A New Variorum Edition of Shakespeare: Hamlet.* Vols 3–4. New York: Dover, 1963.

Galbraith, Steven K. "'English' Black-Letter Type and Spenser's *Shepheardes Calender.*" *Spenser Studies* 23 (2008): 13–40.

– "Spenser's First Folio: The Build-It-Yourself Edition." *Spenser Studies* 21 (2006): 21–49.

Grafton, Anthony. "'Discitur Ut Agatur': How Gabriel Harvey Read His Livy." In *Annotation and Its Texts,* ed. Stephen A. Barney, 108–29. New York: Oxford University Press, 1991.

Graham, Howard Jay. "The Book That 'Made' the Common Law: The First Printing of Fitzherbert's *La Graunde Abridgement,* 1514–1516." *Law Library Journal* 51 (1958): 100–16.

– "The Rastells and the Printed English Law Book of the Renaissance." *Law Library Journal* 47 (1954): 6–25.

De Grazia, Margreta. "Imprints: Shakespeare, Gutenberg, and Descartes." In *Printing and Parenting in Early Modern England,* ed. Douglas A. Brooks, 29–58. Aldershot, England: Ashgate, 2005.

– "Revolution in *Shake-speares Sonnets.*" In *A Companion to Shakespeare's Sonnets,* ed. Michael Carl Schoenfeldt, 57–69. Malden, MA: Blackwell, 2007.

– "The Scandal of Shakespeare's Sonnets." *Shakespeare Survey: An Annual Survey of Shakespeare Studies and Production* 46 (1993): 35–49.

– *Shakespeare Verbatim: The Reproduction of Authenticity and the 1790 Apparatus.* Oxford: Clarendon Press, 1991.

Graziani, René. "The Numbering of Shakespeare's Sonnets: 12, 60, and 126." *Shakespeare Quarterly* 35, no. 1 (spring 1984): 79–82.

Greenblatt, Stephen. *Renaissance Self-fashioning: From More to Shakespeare*. Chicago: University of Chicago Press, 1980.

Greetham, David. *Textual Transgressions: Essays toward the Construction of a Biobibliography*. New York: Garland, 1998.

Greg, W.W. "The Rationale of Copy-Text." *Studies in Bibliography: Papers of the Bibliographical Society of the University of Virginia* 3 (1950): 19–36.

Gurr, Andrew. "Shakespeare's First Poem: Sonnet 145." *Essays in Criticism* 21, no. 3 (1971): 221–6.

Guy-Bray, Stephen. *Against Reproduction: Where Renaissance Texts Come From*. Toronto: University of Toronto Press, 2009.

Hadfield, Andrew. *Spenser's Irish Experience: Wilde Fruit and Salvage Soyl*. Oxford: Clarendon Press, 1997.

Hall, Kim F. "'These Bastard Signs of Fair': Literary Whiteness in Shakespeare's Sonnets." In *Post-Colonial Shakespeares*, ed. Martin Orkin and Ania Loomba, 64–83. London: Routledge, 1998.

Hamilton, A.C., ed. *The Spenser Encyclopedia*. Toronto: University of Toronto Press, 1990.

Hamilton, A.C., Hiroshi Yamashita, and Toshiyuki Suzuki, eds. *Spenser: The Faerie Queene*. New York: Longman, 2001.

Hannay, Margaret P. "The Countess of Pembroke as a Spenserian Poet." In *Pilgrimage for Love: Essays in Early Modern Literature in Honor of Josephine A. Roberts*, ed. Sigrid King, 41–62. Tempe: Arizona Center for Medieval and Renaissance Studies, 1999.

– "The Countess of Pembroke's Agency in Print and Scribal Culture." In *Women's Writing and the Circulation of Ideas: Manuscript Publication in England, 1550–1800*, ed. George L. Justice and Nathan Tinker, 17–49. Cambridge: Cambridge University Press, 2002.

– *Philip's Phoenix: Mary Sidney, Countess of Pembroke*. New York: Oxford University Press, 1990.

Harrier, Richard C. *The Canon of Sir Thomas Wyatt's Poetry*. Cambridge, MA: Harvard University Press, 1975.

Harris, Jonathan Gil. *Untimely Matter in the Time of Shakespeare*. Philadelphia: University of Pennsylvania Press, 2009.

Havens, Earle. *Commonplace Books: A History of Manuscripts and Printed Books from Antiquity to the Twentieth Century*. New Haven, CT: Beinecke Rare Book and Manuscript Library, 2001.

Heale, Elizabeth. *Autobiography and Authorship in Renaissance Verse: Chronicles of the Self*. New York: Palgrave Macmillan, 2003.

– *Wyatt, Surrey, and Early Tudor Poetry*. London: Longman, 1998.

Heaton, Gabriel. "The Queen and the Hermit: The 'Tale of Hemetes' (1575)." In *Elizabeth I and the Culture of Writing*, ed. Peter Beal and Grace Ioppolo, 87–114. London: The British Library, 2007.

Heidegger, Martin. *An Introduction to Metaphysics*. Trans. Ralph Manheim. New Haven: Yale University Press, 1959.

Helgerson, Richard. *The Elizabethan Prodigals*. Berkeley: University of California Press, 1976.

– *Self-crowned Laureates: Spenser, Jonson, Milton, and the Literary System*. Berkeley: University of California Press, 1983.

Henderson, Edith G. "Legal Literature and the Impact of Printing on the English Legal Profession." *Law Library Review* 68 (1975): 288–93.

Heninger, S.K. "The Typographical Layout of Spenser's *Shepheardes Calender*." In *Word and Visual Imagination: Studies in the Interaction of English Literature and the Visual Arts*, ed. Karl Josef Höltgen, Peter M. Daly, and Wolfgang Lottes, 33–71. Nürnberg: Univ.-Bibliothek Erlangen, 1988.

Herman, Peter. "What's the Use? Or, the Problematic of Economy in Shakespeare's Procreation Sonnets." In *Shakespeare's Sonnets: Critical Essays*, ed. James Schiffer, 263–83. New York: Garland, 1999.

Heylin, Clinton. *So Long as Men Can Breathe: The Untold Story of Shakespeare's Sonnets*. Cambridge, MA: Da Capo Press, 2009.

Hieatt, A. Kent, Charles W. Hieatt, and Anne Lake Prescott. "When Did Shakespeare Write *Sonnets* 1609?" *Studies in Philology* 88, no. 1 (winter 1991): 69–109.

Hirsch, Richard S.M. "The Works of Chidiock Tichborne (text)." *English Literary Renaissance* 16, no. 2 (1986): 303–18.

Hobby, Elaine. "'Secrets of the Female Sex': Jane Sharp, the Reproductive Female Body, and Early Modern Midwifery Manuals." *Women's Writing* 8, no. 2 (2001): 201–12.

Hodnett, Edward. *English Woodcuts, 1480–1535*. Oxford: Oxford University Press, 1973.

Hollander, John. *The Figure of Echo: A Mode of Allusion in Milton and After*. Berkeley: University of California Press, 1981.

– *The Untuning of the Sky: Ideas of Music in English Poetry, 1500–1700*. Princeton: Princeton University Press, 1961.

Horace. *Q. Horati Flacci Opera*. Edited by Edvardvs C. Wickham. Oxford: Clarendon Press, 1986.

Hughes, Felicity A. "Gascoigne's Poses." *SEL: Studies in English Literature, 1500–1900* 37, no. 1 (1997): 1–19.

Hughey, Ruth Willard, ed. *The Arundel Harington Manuscript of Tudor Poetry*. Columbus, OH: Ohio State University Press, 1960.

Hutchison, Coleman. "Breaking the Book Known as Q." *PMLA* 121, no. 1 (January 2006): 33–66.

Ioppolo, Grace. *Dramatists and Their Manuscripts in the Age of Shakespeare, Jonson, Middleton and Heywood: Authorship, Authority and the Playhouse*. London: Routledge, 2006.

Ives, E.W. "The Purpose and Making of the Later Year Books." *Law Quarterly Review* 89 (1973): 64–86.

Jackson, MacDonald P. "Vocabulary and Chronology: The Case of Shakespeare's Sonnets." *Review of English Studies: A Quarterly Journal of English Literature and the English Language* 52, no. 205 (February 2001): 59–75.

Jakobson, Roman, and Lawrence G. Jones. *Shakespeare's Verbal Art in Th'expence of Spirit.* The Hague: Mouton, 1970.

Jardine, Lisa. "Reading and the Technology of Textual Affect: Erasmus's Familiar Letters and Shakespeare's *King Lear.*" In *The Practice and Representation of Reading in England*, ed. James Raven, Helen Small, and Naomi Tadmor, 77–101. Cambridge: Cambridge University Press, 1996.

Kalas, Rayna. *Frame, Glass, Verse: The Technology of Poetic Invention in the English Renaissance.* Ithaca, NY: Cornell University Press, 2007.

Kamholtz, Jonathan Z. "Thomas Wyatt's Poetry: The Politics of Love." *Criticism: A Quarterly for Literature and the Arts* 20 (1978): 349–65.

Kastan, David Scott. *Shakespeare and the Book.* Cambridge: Cambridge University Press, 2001.

Kay, Dennis. *Melodious Tears: The English Funeral Elegy from Spenser to Milton.* Oxford: Clarendon Press, 1990.

Kermode, Frank, ed. *English Pastoral Poetry, from the Beginnings to Marvell.* New York: Norton, 1972.

Kerrigan, John. "Shakespeare's Poems." In *The Cambridge Companion to Shakespeare*, ed. Margreta de Grazia and Stanley Wells, 65–81. Cambridge: Cambridge University Press, 2001.

– ed. *The Sonnets; and, A Lover's Complaint / William Shakespeare.* Harmondsworth: Viking, 1986.

Kneidel, Gregory. "Reforming George Gascoigne." *Exemplaria: A Journal of Theory in Medieval and Renaissance Studies* 10, no. 2 (fall 1998): 329–70.

Krevans, Nita. "Print and the Tudor Poets." In *Reconsidering the Renaissance: Papers from the Twenty-First Annual Conference*, ed. Mario Di Cesare, 301–13. Binghamton, NY: Medieval & Renaissance Texts & Studies, 1992.

Kunin, Aaron. "Shakespeare's Preservation Fantasy." *PMLA* 124, no. 1 (January 2009): 92–106.

Lamb, Mary Ellen. *Gender and Authorship in the Sidney Circle.* Madison: University of Wisconsin Press, 1990.

Landow, George P. *Hypertext: The Convergence of Contemporary Critical Theory and Technology.* Baltimore: Johns Hopkins University Press, 1992.

Lane, Robert. *Shepheards Devises: Edmund Spenser's Shepheardes Calender and the Institutions of Elizabethan Society.* Athens: University of Georgia Press, 1993.

Larsen, Kenneth J. "Essays on Shakespeare's Sonnets", n.d. http://www.williamshakespeare-sonnets.com/contents.

Lesser, Zachary, and Peter Stallybrass. "The First Literary *Hamlet* and the Commonplacing of Professional Plays." *Shakespeare Quarterly* 59, no. 4 (winter 2008): 371–420.

Lethbridge, J.B. "Spenser's Last Days: Ireland, Career, Mutability, Allegory." In *Edmund Spenser: New and Renewed Directions*, 302–36. Madison, NJ: Fairleigh Dickinson University Press, 2006.

"Linkerature: Classical Literature 'Annotated' with Links." *Linkerature*, 1 February, 2005. http://tsja.editthispage.com/linkerature/.

Love, Harold. *The Culture and Commerce of Texts: Scribal Publication in Seventeenth-Century England.* Amherst: University of Massachusetts Press, 1998.

Luborsky, Ruth Samson. "The Illustrations to *The Shepheardes Calender.*" *Spenser Studies: A Renaissance Poetry Annual* 2 (1981): 3–53.

Luborsky, Ruth Samson, and Elizabeth Morley Ingram. *A Guide to English Illustrated Books, 1536–1603.* Tempe, AZ: Medieval & Renaissance Texts & Studies, 1998.

MacFaul, Tom. *Poetry and Paternity in Renaissance England: Sidney, Shakespeare, Donne and Johnson.* Cambridge: Cambridge University Press, 2010.

Mack, Michael. *Sidney's Poetics: Imitating Creation.* Washington, DC: Catholic University of America Press, 2005.

Mackie, J.D. *The Earlier Tudors: 1485–1558.* Oxford: Clarendon Press, 1992.

Maley, Willy. *A Spenser Chronology.* Houndmills, Basingstoke, Hampshire: Macmillan, 1994.

Marcus, Leah S. *Unediting the Renaissance: Shakespeare, Marlowe, Milton.* New York: Routledge, 1996.

Marotti, Arthur F. *Manuscript, Print, and the English Renaissance Lyric.* Ithaca: Cornell University Press, 1995.

– "Shakespeare's Sonnets as Literary Property." In *Soliciting Interpretation: Literary Theory and Seventeenth-Century English Poetry*, ed. Elizabeth D. Harvey and Katharine Eisaman Maus, 143–73. Chicago: University of Chicago Press, 1990.

Marquis, Paul A. "Politics and Print: The Curious Revisions to *Tottel's Songes and Sonettes.*" *Studies in Philology* 97, no. 2 (2000): 145–64.

– ed. *Richard Tottel's Songes and Sonettes: The Elizabethan Version.* Tempe, AZ: Arizona Center for Medieval and Renaissance Studies, 2007.

Martin, Christopher. "Made Plaine by Examples: Parceling Philip Sidney in Abraham Fraunce's Arcadian Rhetorike." *Sidney Journal* 24, no. 2 (2006): 67–82.

Masten, Jeffrey. *Textual Intercourse: Collaboration, Authorship, and Sexualities in Renaissance Drama.* Cambridge: Cambridge University Press, 1997.

Maus, Katharine Eisaman. *Inwardness and Theater in the English Renaissance.* Chicago: University of Chicago Press, 1995.

– "A Womb of His Own: Male Renaissance Poets in the Female Body." In *Printing and Parenting in Early Modern England*, ed. Douglas A. Brooks, 89–108. Aldershot, England: Ashgate, 2005.

May, Steven W. "Marlowe, Spenser, Sidney and Abraham Fraunce?" *Review of English Studies* 62, no. 253 (February 2011): 30–63.

– "Tudor Aristocrats and the 'Stigma of Print.'" *Renaissance Papers* 10 (1980): 11–8.

May, Steven W., and William Ringler. *Elizabethan Poetry: A Bibliography and First-line Index of English Verse, 1559–1603.* 3 vols. London: Thoemmes Continuum, 2004.

McCabe, Richard A. "Edmund Spenser, Poet of Exile." *Proceedings of the British Academy* 80 (1993): 73–103.

– *Edmund Spenser: The Shorter Poems.* New York: Penguin Books, 1999.

– "'Little Booke: Thy Selfe Present': The Politics of Presentation in *The Shepheardes Calender.*" In *Presenting Poetry: Composition, Publication, Reception: Essays in Honour of Ian Jack,* ed. Howard Erskine-Hill and Richard A. McCabe, 15–40. Cambridge: Cambridge University Press, 1995.

McCoy, Richard C. "Gascoigne's 'Poëmata Castrata': The Wages of Courtly Success." *Criticism: A Quarterly for Literature and the Arts* 27, no. 1 (1985): 29–55.

McGann, Jerome J. *A Critique of Modern Textual Criticism.* Charlottesville, VA: University Press of Virginia, 1992.

– *The Textual Condition.* Princeton: Princeton University Press, 1991.

McKenzie, D.F. *Bibliography and the Sociology of Texts. The Panizzi Lectures.* London: British Library, 1986.

McKerrow, Ronald B. "The Treatment of Shakespeare's Text by His Earlier Editors, 1709–1768." In *Proceedings of the British Academy,* 19:89–122. London: British Academy, 1933.

McKitterick, David. *Print, Manuscript and the Search for Order, 1450–1830.* Cambridge: Cambridge University Press, 2003.

McLeod, Randall. "UnEditing Shakespeare." *SubStance* 33/4 (1982): 26–55.

McPhee, John. "Personal History – Checkpoints: Fact-checkers Do It a Tick at a Time." *The New Yorker,* 9 February 2009, 56–63.

Mentz, Steven. "Selling Sidney: William Ponsonby, Thomas Nashe, and the Boundaries of Elizabethan Print and Manuscript Cultures." *Text: An Interdisciplinary Annual of Textual Studies* 13 (2000): 151–74.

Merivale, Patricia. *Pan, the Goat-god, His Myth in Modern Times.* Cambridge: Harvard University Press, 1969.

Miller, David Lee. "The Earl of Cork's Lute." In *Spenser's Life and the Subject of Biography,* ed. Judith H. Anderson, Donald Cheney, and David A. Richardson, 146–71. Amherst: University of Massachusetts Press, 1996.

de Montaigne, Michel. *The Complete Essays of Montaigne.* Trans. Donald Frame. Stanford: Stanford University Press, 1979.

Montrose, Louis Adrian. "'The Perfecte Paterne of a Poete': The Poetics of Courtship in The Shepheardes Calender." *Texas Studies in Literature and Language: A Journal of the Humanities* 21 (1979): 34–67.

Moore, John W., Jr. "Colin Breaks His Pipe: A Reading of the 'January' Eclogue." *English Literary Renaissance* 5, no. 1 (1975): 3–24.

Moretti, Franco. *Atlas of the European Novel, 1800–1900.* London: Verso, 1998.

Moss, Ann. *Printed Commonplace-books and the Structuring of Renaissance Thought.* Oxford: Clarendon Press, 1996.

Nathan, Leonard. "Gascoigne's 'Lullabie' and Structures in the Tudor Lyric." In *The Rhetoric of Renaissance Poetry from Wyatt to Milton*, ed. Thomas O. Sloan and Raymond B. Waddington, 58–72. Berkeley: University of California Press, 1974.

Nims, John Frederick, ed. *Ovid's Metamorphoses. The Arthur Golding Translation, 1567.* Philadelphia: Paul Dry Books, 2000.

Nohrnberg, James. "Acidale." In *The Spenser Encyclopedia*, ed. A.C. Hamilton, 4–6. Toronto: University of Toronto Press, 1990.

North, Marcy L. "Amateur Compilers, Scribal Labour, and the Contents of Early Modern Poetic Miscellanies." *English Manuscript Studies 1100–1700* 16 (2011): 82–111.

– *The Anonymous Renaissance: Cultures of Discretion in Tudor-Stuart England.* Chicago: University of Chicago Press, 2003.

– "The Sonnets and Book History." In *A Companion to Shakespeare's Sonnets*, ed. Michael Carl Schoenfeldt, 204–21. Malden, MA: Blackwell, 2007.

Orgel, Stephen. "Marginal Maternity: Reading Lady Anne Clifford's *A Mirror for Magistrates.*" In *Printing and Parenting in Early Modern England*, ed. Douglas A. Brooks, 267–89. Aldershot, England: Ashgate, 2005.

Osborn, James Marshall, ed. *The Autobiography of Thomas Whythorne.* Oxford: Clarendon Press, 1961.

Parrish, Paul A. "The Multiple Perspectives of Gascoigne's 'The Adventures of Master F. J.'" *Studies in Short Fiction* 10 (1973): 75–84.

Patterson, Annabel. "Reopening the Green Cabinet: Clément Marot and Edmund Spenser." In *The Classical Heritage: Vergil*, ed. Craig Kallendorf, 115–44. New York: Garland, 1993.

Peck, A.L., trans. *Aristotle. Generation of Animals.* Cambridge, MA: Harvard University Press, 1963.

Pérez Fernández, José María. "'Wyatt Resteth Here': Surrey's Republican Elegy." *Renaissance Studies* 18, no. 2 (2004): 208–38.

Petrarca, Francesco. *The Life of Solitude.* Trans. Jacob Zeitlin. Urbana, IL: University of Illinois Press, 1924.

Piepho, Lee, trans. *Adulescentia: The Eclogues of Mantuan.* New York: Garland, 1989.

Pigman, G.W. "Editing Revised Texts: Gascoigne's *A Hundredth Sundrie Flowres* and *The Posies.*" In *New Ways of Looking at Old Texts*, II, ed. W. Speed Hill, 1–9. Tempe, AZ: MRTS, 1998.

– *Grief and English Renaissance Elegy.* Cambridge: Cambridge University Press, 1985.

– ed. *A Hundreth Sundrie Flowres / George Gascoigne.* Oxford: Clarendon Press, 2000.

Pitcher, John. "Benefiting from the Book: The Oxford Edition of Samuel Daniel." *Yearbook of English Studies* 29 (1999): 69–87.

Pomeroy, Elizabeth W. *The Elizabethan Miscellanies: Their Development and Conventions.* Berkeley: University of California Press, 1973.

Pope, John C. "The Printing of 'This Written Book': G.T. and H.W.'s Editorial Disputes in *The Adventures of Master F.J.*" In *Renaissance Papers* (2003): 45–53.

Prendergast, Maria. "Philoclea Parsed: Prose, Verse, and Femininity in Sidney's *Old Arcadia.*" In *Framing Elizabethan Fictions: Contemporary Approaches to Early Modern Narrative Prose*, ed. Constance C. Relihan, 99–116. Kent, OH: Kent State University Press, 1996.

Quilligan, Maureen. "The Gender of the Reader and the Problem of Sexuality." In *Critical Essays on Edmund Spenser*, ed. Mihoko Suzuki, 133–51. New York: G.K. Hall, 1996.

Rambuss, Richard. *Spenser's Secret Career.* Cambridge: Cambridge University Press, 1993.

Ringler, William A. *The Poems of Sir Philip Sidney.* Oxford: Clarendon Press, 1962.

Roberts, Sasha. *Reading Shakespeare's Poems in Early Modern England.* New York: Palgrave Macmillan, 2003.

Rollins, Hyder Edward. *Tottel's Miscellany (1557–1587).* Cambridge: Harvard University Press, 1965.

– ed. *A New Variorum Edition of Shakespeare: The Sonnets.* 2 vols. Philadelphia: J.B. Lippincott, 1944.

– ed. *The Phoenix Nest, 1593.* Cambridge, MA: Harvard University Press, 1969.

Rose, Mark. *Authors and Owners: The Invention of Copyright.* Cambridge, MA: Harvard University Press, 1993.

Rösslin, Eucharius. *The Birth of Mankind / by Thomas Reynalde, Physician, 1560.* Edited by Elaine Hobby. Farnham, England: Ashgate, 2009.

– *When Midwifery Became the Male Physician's Province: The Sixteenth Century Handbook The Rose Garden for Pregnant Women and Midwives, Newly Englished.* Trans. Wendy Arons. Jefferson, NC: McFarland & Company, 1994.

Rothenberg, Jeff. "Ensuring the Longevity of Digital Documents." *Scientific American* 272, no. 1 (January 1995): 42–7.

Rowe, Kenneth Thorpe. "The Countess of Pembroke's Editorship of the *Arcadia.*" *PMLA* 54, no. 1 (March 1939): 122–38.

Rowse, A.L. *Shakespeare's Sonnets: The Problems Solved.* New York: Harper & Row, 1973.

Russell, Donald, trans. *The Orator's Education / Quintilian.* Loeb Classical Library. Cambridge, MA: Harvard University Press, 2001.

Sacks, Peter M. *The English Elegy: Studies in the Genre from Spenser to Yeats.* Baltimore: Johns Hopkins Press, 1985.

Sannazaro, Jacopo. *Arcadia & Piscatorial Eclogues.* Trans. Ralph Nash. Detroit: Wayne State University Press, 1966.

Saunders, J.W. "The Stigma of Print: A Note on the Social Bases of Tudor Poetry." *Essays in Criticism* 1, no. 2 (1951): 139–64.

Scarry, Elaine. *On Beauty and Being Just*. Princeton: Princeton University Press, 1999.

Schott, Penelope Scambly. "The Narrative Stance in 'The Adventures of Master F.J.': Gascoigne as Critic of His Own Poems." *Renaissance Quarterly* 29, no. 3 (autumn 1976): 369–77.

Schurink, Fred. "Manuscript Commonplace Books, Literature, and Reading in Early Modern England." *Huntington Library Quarterly* 73, no. 3 (2010): 453–69.

Sedgwick, Eve Kosofsky. *Between Men: English Literature and Male Homosocial Desire*. New York: Columbia University Press, 1985.

Sessions, William A. *Henry Howard, the Poet Earl of Surrey: A Life*. Oxford: Oxford University Press, 1999.

Sherman, William. "Toward a History of the Manicule." In *Owners, Annotators and the Signs of Reading*, ed. Robin Myers, Michael Harris, and Giles Mandelbrote, 19–48. New Castle, DE: Oak Knoll Press, 2005.

Shillingsburg, Peter L. *Scholarly Editing in the Computer Age: Theory and Practice*. 3rd ed. Ann Arbor: University of Michigan Press, 1996.

Sidney, Philip. *The Countess of Pembroke's Arcadia (The Old Arcadia)*. Edited by Jean Robertson. Oxford: Clarendon Press, 1973.

Sidney Herbert, Mary. *Selected Works of Mary Sidney Herbert, Countess of Pembroke*. Edited by Margaret P. Hannay, Noel J. Kinnamon, and Michael G. Brennan. Tempe: Arizona Center for Medieval and Renaissance Studies, 2005.

Sidran, Ben. *Now I Live (And Now My Life Is Done)*. MP3. The Verve Music Group, 1973.

Simpson, A.W.B. "The Source and Function of the Later Year Books." *Law Quarterly Review* 87 (January 1971): 94–118.

Skretkowicz, Victor, ed. *The Countess of Pembroke's Arcadia: The New Arcadia*. Oxford: Clarendon Press, 1987.

– "'A More Lively Monument': Philisides in *Arcadia*." In *Sir Philip Sidney's Achievements*, ed. M.J.B. Allen, 194–200. New York: AMS Press, 1990.

– "Textual Criticism and the 1593 'Complete' *Arcadia*." *Sidney Journal* 18, no. 2 (winter 2000): 37–70.

Smith, G. Gregory. *Elizabethan Critical Essays*. London: Oxford University Press, 1950.

Smyth, Adam. *"Profit and Delight": Printed Miscellanies in England, 1640–1682*. Detroit: Wayne State University Press, 2004.

Sommer, H. Oskar, ed. *The Kalender of Shepherdes: The Edition of Paris 1503 in Photographic Facsimile, a Faithful Reprint of R. Pynson's Edition of London 1506*. 3 vols. London: Kegan Paul, Trench, Trubner & Co., 1892.

Spiller, Elizabeth. *Science, Reading, and Renaissance Literature: The Art of Making Knowledge, 1580–1670*. Cambridge: Cambridge University Press, 2004.

Staley Johnson, Lynn. *The Shepheardes Calender: An Introduction*. University Park: Pennsylvania State University Press, 1990.

Stallybrass, Peter. "Editing as Cultural Formation: The Sexing of Shakespeare's Sonnets." In *Shakespeare's Sonnets: Critical Essays*, ed. James Schiffer, 75–88. New York: Garland, 1999.

Stallybrass, Peter, Roger Chartier, J. Franklin Mowery, et al. "Hamlet's Tables and the Technologies of Writing in Renaissance England." *Shakespeare Quarterly* 55, no. 4 (winter 2004): 379–419.

Staub, Susan C. "Dissembling His Art: 'Gascoigne's Gardnings'." *Renaissance Studies* 25, no. 1 (February 2011): 95–110.

Steinberg, Theodore L. "Spenser, Sidney, and the Myth of Astrophel." *Spenser Studies* 11 (1994): 187–201.

Stewart, Alan. "Gelding Gascoigne." In *Prose Fiction and Early Modern Sexualities in England, 1570–1640*, ed. Constance C. Relihan and Goran V. Stanivukovic, 147–69. New York: Palgrave Macmillan, 2004.

– *Philip Sidney: A Double Life*. London: Chatto & Windus, 2000.

– *Shakespeare's Letters*. Oxford: Oxford University Press, 2008.

Stewart, Alan, and Heather Wolfe. *Letterwriting in Renaissance England*. Washington, DC: Folger Shakespeare Library, 2004.

Stirling, Brents. *The Shakespeare Sonnet Order: Poems and Groups*. Berkeley: University of California Press, 1968.

Sutton, E.W., trans. *Cicero, De Oratore*. 2 vols. Cambridge, MA: Harvard University Press, 1988.

Tanselle, Thomas. "Textual Scholarship." In *Introduction to Scholarship in Modern Languages and Literatures*, ed. Joseph Gibaldi, 29–52. New York: Modern Language Association of America, 1981.

Taylor, Gary. "Some Manuscripts of Shakespeare's Sonnets." *Bulletin of the John Rylands University Library of Manchester* 68, no. 1 (1985): 210–46.

Traub, Valerie. "Sex Without Issue: Sodomy, Reproduction, and Signification in Shakespeare's Sonnets." In *Shakespeare's Sonnets: Critical Essays*, ed. James Schiffer, 431–52. New York: Garland, 1999.

Traub, Valerie. "The Sonnets: Sequence, Sexuality, and Shakespeare's Two Loves." In *A Companion to Shakespeare's Works*. Vol. 4, *The Poems, Problem Comedies, Late Plays*, ed. by Richard Dutton and Jean E. Howard, 275–301. Oxford: Blackwell, 2005.

Tromly, Frederic B. "Lodowick Bryskett's Elegies on Sidney in Spenser's *Astrophel* Volume." *Review of English Studies: A Quarterly Journal of English Literature and the English Language* 37, no. 147 (August 1986): 384–8.

– "Surrey's Fidelity to Wyatt in 'Wyatt Resteth Here'." *Studies in Philology* 77 (1980): 376–87.

Ulreich, John C. "'The Poets Only Deliver': Sidney's Conception of Mimesis." In *Essential Articles for the Study of Sir Philip Sidney*, ed. Arthur F. Kinney, 135–54. Hamden, CT: Archon Books, 1986.

Vendler, Helen. *The Art of Shakespeare's Sonnets*. Cambridge, MA: Harvard University Press, 1997.

Vickers, Brian. *English Renaissance Literary Criticism*. Oxford: Clarendon Press, 1999.

Wall, Wendy. *The Imprint of Gender: Authorship and Publication in the English Renaissance.* Ithaca: Cornell University Press, 1993.

Warkentin, Germaine. "Patrons and Profiteers: Thomas Newman and the 'Violent Enlargement' of *Astrophil and Stella.*" *Book Collector* 34, no. 4 (1985): 461–87.

Warton, Thomas. *History of English Poetry in Four Volumes: A Facsimile of the 1774 Edition with a New Introduction by René Wellek.* New York: Johnson Reprint, 1968.

Weiss, Adrian. "Shared Printing, Printer's Copy, and the Text(s) of Gascoigne's *A Hundreth Sundrie Flowres.*" *Studies in Bibliography: Papers of the Bibliographical Society of the University of Virginia* 45 (1992): 71–104.

– "Watermark Evidence and Inference: New Style Dates of Edmund Spenser's Complaints and Daphnaida." *Studies in Bibliography: Papers of the Bibliographical Society of the University of Virginia* 52 (1999): 129–54.

Whigham, Frank, and Wayne A. Rebhorn, eds. *The Art of English Poesy / by George Puttenham.* Ithaca: Cornell University Press, 2007.

White, Beatrice, ed. *The Eclogues of Alexander Barclay: from the Original Edition by John Cawood.* London: Oxford University Press, 1960.

Wilson, Katharine M. *Shakespeare's Sugared Sonnets.* London: Allen & Unwin, 1974.

Winternitz, Emanuel. *Musical Instruments and Their Symbolism in Western Art: Studies in Musical Iconology.* New Haven: Yale University Press, 1979.

Worden, Blair. *The Sound of Virtue: Philip Sidney's Arcadia and Elizabethan Politics.* New Haven, CT: Yale University Press, 1996.

Woudhuysen, H.R. *Sir Philip Sidney and the Circulation of Manuscripts, 1558–1640.* Oxford: Clarendon Press, 1996.

Index

Page numbers in italics refer to illustrations

www.ingramcontent.com/pod-product-compliance
Lightning Source LLC
LaVergne TN
LVHW090157080826
844660LV00013B/840/J

* 9 7 8 1 4 4 2 6 4 7 1 8 3 *